To Dorothy Callison
a pleasure to stand with you
on the street corner.
—Sam Day
Long Beach
March 28, 1992

# CROSSING THE LINE

## From Editor to Activist to Inmate—
## A Writer's Journey

**SAMUEL H. DAY, JR.**

Fortkamp Publishing Company
Baltimore, Maryland

Book cover and design by Bonnie Urfer
Laser Typography by Maurice Thaler, I/O Consulting

Fortkamp Publishing Company
4811 Crowson Avenue
Baltimore, Maryland 21212

This limited edition of
*Crossing the Line* is published by
Fortkamp Publishing Company for
  Nukewatch
  P.O. Box 2658
  Madison, Wisconsin  53701

# Table of Contents

# Preface

This book began as a prison journal. Sentenced to six months for cutting my way into a nuclear missile launch site in Missouri, I wrote letters that were typed and distributed by my friends on the outside. First from a county jail near Kansas City, then from Leavenworth penitentiary and half a dozen other penal institutions, the letters chronicled my passage through the Federal prison system as an inmate who refused to cooperate with his captors.

My refusal to do prison labor brought banishment to the world of "disciplinary segregation," where I was locked in cages and taken in handcuffs from one place to another. But my noncooperation also gave me the time I needed to do my own work. From manuscripts sent through the mail, I edited a book written by other convicted antinuclear activists. When that was done, I turned to my own story.

The first few chapters of this book were written in a prison cell in Minnesota where I spent my last thirty days of solitary confinement. I wrote them in longhand on prison stationery and later supplemented them with excerpts from childhood letters that had been saved over the years by my mother.

The rest of the autobiography took almost a year to finish. It came, struggling, from stories preserved in scrapbooks and bound volumes of the dozen publications I have worked or written for in a journalism career spanning forty years.

In reprinting some of the writings over these four decades I give grateful acknowledgement to the *Washington Evening Star*; the *Grape Leaf* (43rd Infantry Division), published by the United States Army; the Associated Press; the *Lewiston* (Idaho) *Morning Tribune*; the *Salmon* (Idaho) *Recorder-Herald*; the *Intermountain Observer*; the *Bulletin of the Atomic Scientists*; *The Progressive; Isthmus,* and *Nuclear Times*. In most instances these publications are credited in the text; but in some cases, where the narative led itself to this treatment, I have reprinted some of my writings verbatim without specific attribution. Thanks also to Howard

Morland for permission to reprint excerpts from "The H-Bomb Secret," published in *The Progressive* of November 1979.

I am indebted to many people for help in preparing this work. They include Matthew Rothschild and Erwin Knoll of *The Progressive*, Bill Lueders and Marc Eisen of *Isthmus,* my Nukewatch colleagues Bonnie Urfer and Susan Nelson, Alice Dieter of the old *Intermountain Observer* staff, my sister Mayflower Day Brandt, and my wife Kathleen Day, all of whom provided valuable editorial criticism; Theo. Kramer and Linda Rocawich, who did the word-processing, and proofreader Diana Cook. All of them share in the credit, but I alone take the responsibility.

My gratitude to Ellen Elizabeth Barfield, Louise Barry, Jean Bernstein, Genevieve R. Bock, Nancy Bokich, George L. Crookham, Robert and Barbara DeWitt, Kay and Leo Drey, Lawrence D. Egbert, Carol and Ping Ferry, Roger Franklin, Francis Hole, Trudy Karlson, Larry and Lindy Lange, Eva Leo, Axel and Cecile Meyer, Adele O'Shaughnessy, Louis River III, Jackie Rivet River, Phillip Runkel, Max Samter, Ethel Sanjines, Frank H. Teagle, Jr., Carolyn Tyner, David Weber, and Max and Sylvia Wohl for financial assistance to Nukewatch to help meet the costs of publication.

—Samuel H. Day, Jr.
Madison, Wisconsin
September, 1990

# Introduction: The Right Ground

The first time I crossed the line was in Boise, Idaho, on a November afternoon in 1971. With nineteen companions, I formed a human chain across Capitol Boulevard, a main thoroughfare in the heart of the city. There were just enough of us to block the boulevard from curb to curb.

Walking into the street that day, into the middle of traffic, I felt alternately foolish and scared. Would my nerve fail at the last minute? Would I find myself all alone, dodging cars while motorists honked and spectators laughed? Would blood run on Capitol Boulevard, spilled as a consequence of my rash words? Would I be arrested, mugged, fingerprinted, jailed, given a police record?

When the first blockader reached the far curb we stopped and turned, facing the oncoming cars. The traffic came to a stop. Our supporters worked their way from car to car, explaining the delay, asking drivers to turn their lights on if they agreed with us.

We heard honks and yells. Then some lights came on, then more. In a short time officers arrived from the police station, just two blocks away. Slowly they moved up and down the line, taking our photographs. Would we be dragged or simply led away? I wondered when the arrests would begin.

Incredibly, there were no arrests. The police allowed us to continue blocking the boulevard for the remainder of our half-hour vigil, directing traffic into other streets. At exactly 3 o'clock, as a three-megaton nuclear blast went off on schedule in far-off Alaska, we trooped off Capitol Boulevard, walking on air, delighted with ourselves at having conducted Idaho's first nonviolent civil disobedience action in memory.

I was a forty-five-year-old journalist at the time, married and the father of three sons, editor of a weekly political newspaper, the *Intermountain Observer*, a radical and sometimes strident organ of social protest. We had been at the forefront of social protest in Idaho through the 1960s. On this occasion we were protesting the U.S. Atomic Energy Commission's plan to test an antiballistic missile nuclear warhead off the island of Amchitka in Alaska. It was a project that had stirred widespread opposition from environmentalists and peace activists but had just been given a final go-ahead by virtue of a five-to-four decision of the United States Supreme Court.

Throughout the nation there were protest rallies on the day of the test explosion. In Boise the protest took the form of a spontaneous blockade of traffic—a demonstration of outrage that I had proposed and led.

The fear, stress, and exhilaration of our stand on Capitol Boulevard forged a bond among us. We felt like survivors of an earthquake, a flood, a battle in which we had risked much and won. As newspaper people and political activists many of us already were part of a closely knit group. Three of us comprised the entire paid staff of the *Observer*. Others were VISTA volunteers in the war on poverty, environmentalists, veterans of the civil rights and antiwar movements. Most of us had standing in Idaho's liberal Democratic establishment. The Amchitka action, requiring a measure of physical courage and moral certitude surpassing the demands of conventional journalism and politics, gave us a heightened feeling of closeness with each other. It produced a euphoria that proved to be short-lived.

That night, at a social gathering of liberal Democrats, the attorney general of the state of Idaho, a close friend whose election I had helped engineer the previous fall, went into shock when we paused to watch the television news. There, in full view, were the protesters blocking a city street, with police standing by. The camera zoomed in on his wife, Betsy Park, breaking the law with the whole world watching, while the commentator made pointed reference to her husband, the state's chief legal officer.

Scarcely less shocked or pained was my own wife, Kathleen, who, like Tony Park and some other spouses of the demonstrators, had had no advance notice of the Amchitka action. The demonstration opened a breach between us on the matter of personal risk-taking as a form of social action.

But that was just the beginning of the fallout. A few days later the *Observer*'s advertising representative reported wholesale defections in the thin ranks of our business patrons along Main Street. I was surprised by the severity of the backlash.

Even more astonishing to me was the reaction of our principal advertiser, the local CBS radio and television station, KBOI-TV, which also happened to be our owner. When I paid my weekly call on the station's business manager to pick up her advertisement for the next issue, she explained, firmly but with some embarrassment, that there would be none. "It's a matter of principle," she said. "I just cannot condone that sort of thing."

A few days later I was called to the desk of KBOI news director Dick Eardley, a friend of many years and a popular Boise sportscaster who then served on the city council and was on his way to becoming mayor of the city. Eardley sat me down in the "goldfish bowl," a glassed-in library and conference room used for private conversations.

"Sam, I don't know how to tell you this," he began, half apologetically, "but we've decided to take you off the air." He went on to explain that I had crossed over into an area forbidden to professional journalists. He was sorry about it, and maybe he was mistaken, but that was the way it would have to be.

For leading a street demonstration against the testing of a nuclear bomb on an Alaskan island I had been judged no longer fit for writing, for reporting, for broadcasting at KBOI. How was this violation of journalistic neutrality different from a news director casting a city council vote for a multi-million-dollar downtown shopping mall? I saw no point in arguing the issue with Eardley because the difference was clear to both of us. The difference was in the style and purpose of our activism, not in activism itself. And the message in the goldfish bowl was equally clear: There was no room at KBOI for this kind of activism.

In the newsroom of Boise's most enlightened corporate media outlet, in the liberal business community, on the Democratic Party cocktail circuit, and in my own household I came up against the limits of tolerance in the weeks following my decision to stand in the street with others. I felt the pain of rejection and the gnawing fear of the loosening of career security. But the new ground onto which I had marched or stumbled or strayed felt right to me. I decided to stay there.

Less than a month after Amchitka, with other *Observer* staff members, I was escorted off a nearby Air Force base for helping to sell copies of a GI antiwar newspaper banned by the base commander. For months we had worked closely with dissident airmen to raise the issue of U.S. involvement in the Vietnam war. Our act of solidarity was to precipitate the *Observer*'s final break with KBOI.

In later years, following the demise of the *Intermountain Observer* in 1973 and a four-year stint as editor of the *Bulletin of the Atomic Scientists* in Chicago, I found myself in increasingly frequent confrontation with legally constituted authority. As managing editor of *The Progressive* magazine in Madison, Wisconsin, I came up against the full power of the United States as a defendant in the Federal Government's attempt to suppress an article about nuclear weapons secrecy.

As a journalist and political organizer seeking to raise nuclear weapons issues, I have been dragged from shopping malls, ejected from courthouse lobbies, led out of corporate boardrooms, ordered at gunpoint from the launch site of an underground nuclear missile. Such behavior has taken me a long way from the path of conventional journalism and liberal politics I walked in Idaho in my middle years, to say nothing of the elite life I enjoyed as a child born into a diplomatic family, raised abroad in colonial splendor, and educated at an exclusive New England boarding school.

The actions of my later years, taken in the company of others, have led to occasional jailings and once to a six-month prison term. Always the feelings have been the same as when I first crossed the line in Boise many years ago. First has come an inner struggle, then a deep fear, then the calm of the action itself, then exhilaration (whatever the outcome), then the sometimes painful satisfaction of having, as the Quakers say, "spoken truth to power." Always when I have crossed the line the ground on the other side has felt good.

# 1

# Growing Up in South Africa

When I was a boy in Johannesburg I used to play a game I called "taking time-pictures." I would look intently on a scene, fixing every detail in my mind, and tell myself I would remember it for the rest of my life.

The game didn't work. I must have taken several dozen time-pictures over the years. Now, a half-century later, I can remember only one. It is a fuzzy view of the wooden fence behind our house on Doveton Road.

More vivid are the memories of things that came uninvited into my childhood. Like the slippery feeling and slightly sour taste of cream sliding down my gullet and the stench of warm cabbage and cauliflower on my dinner plate.

I was a premature baby, born with a rare visual impairment called a congenital coloboma, in which the corneas of both eyes are malformed, looking and behaving as though they were square. How I envy people with ordinary eyeballs that roll easily from side to side. Mine don't do that. Instead of rolling they lurch and tumble. The condition is so unusual that a South African doctor to whom my mother took me as an infant mistook my coloboma for what was then called mongolism. He suggested that I be placed in an institution. She indignantly refused.

Underweight as a baby and later as a child, I was made to take cream in my porridge and to eat vegetables cooked in the unforgiving English style. To this day I cannot drink cream without throwing up.

Despite the best efforts of my mother and a succession of nurses to whom my care and feeding was consigned, I remained sickly and scrawny throughout my youth, a prey to every childhood disease: measles, mumps, diphtheria, scarlet fever, croop, asthma, boils. When I entered the ninth grade at the age of fourteen I was, at barely over ninety pounds, the smallest boy in the school.

Sickly, small for my age, fitted as a child with glasses as thick as milk bottle bottoms, I also had an identity problem unintentionally created for me by my older brother, Christopher, when my parents brought me home from the hospital. Only two, Chris was unable to pronounce my name— Samuel Hamilton Day, Jr. What came out of his mouth was "Sass," which soon evolved into "Sassie." My mother fell in love with the nickname, so it stuck.

For the first years of my life I thought Sass was my real name. In the third grade I won a swimming race, due entirely to the fact that the teacher in charge misjudged my handicap and let me swim almost to the finish line before signaling the others to begin. At the awards ceremony I didn't recognize my name when the judge called out Samuel Day as the winner of the beginners' event. Chris accepted the prize for me.

My mother had an endless fund of Sassie stories. "One day Sassie ate a package of hollyhock seeds," she would tell her friends. "That evening he got a stomach ache, and he came to me, crying, 'Mommy, the hollyhocks are growing!'"

When I left home for boarding school I saw an opportunity to kill the nickname for good. My parents, who drove me to the school, cooperated until the last moment, when the time came for us to part and I burst into tears. Attempting to console me, my mother blurted out, "Don't worry, Sass." My roommate found the name amusing, so it stuck for another four years. Today, almost fifty years later, Sass lives on among my siblings, cousins, prep school classmates, nieces, nephews, and a growing number of their offspring.

I was winsome in addition to being frail. I had curly hair and a magnificent golden forelock. That gave me the looks of a sissy. If I had a single goal early in life it was to prove to myself and others that I was not a sissy.

As a child I played and competed recklessly and ferociously, hoping to establish a tougher Sassie image. I jumped from second story windows, fell out of trees, rode my bicycle heedlessly through traffic intersections.

"Mother, Sassie broke his glasses again," my younger sister, May-flower, would cry out, running into the house to proclaim some horrendous new disaster. I would privately savor the resulting commotion.

Once, while we were playing with slingshots, a friend hit my glasses with a stone, shattering the glass. Our family doctor spent an hour picking the slivers from my eye. Another time I laid open three inches of my left index finger playing with a sickle. At the age of five I broke my arm playing "crack the whip" with Chris. The whip was a piece of rope that connected his bicycle to my sister's tricycle as he pulled me around the tennis court of our Johannesburg house.

Such excesses in derring-do were probably my attempts to compensate for the physical and psychological handicaps a cruel fate had dealt me. They were also the survival tools of a young boy coping with a life of lonely privilege in the Union of South Africa.

My father, Samuel Hamilton Day, was a diplomat, and Johannesburg was his first foreign post. Born in California, educated in the law, and sent overseas as an army officer in World War I, he remained in Germany after the war to assist in the hunger relief work of Herbert Hoover, whom he greatly admired as a businessman and humanitarian.

In 1923, after his marriage to Margery Willis Critchlow of Salt Lake City, he followed Hoover to Washington, D.C., where Hoover had been appointed Secretary of Commerce. Chris was born there on June 6, 1924, while my father was preparing for a career in the Department's overseas trade development program. When my father was transferred to the Philadelphia office, the family moved to suburban Swarthmore. I was born October 3, 1926, at a hospital in the nearby town of Media, Pennsylvania. Nine months later we were on a boat to South Africa.

As members of the diplomatic community (my father was U.S. trade commissioner in Johannesburg) we enjoyed a privileged life in that most colonial and socially stratified of countries, still a part of the British Empire at that time. We belonged to the white, English-speaking class which ran the country and lived in the lap of luxury. Below us were the Dutch-speaking Afrikaners—dirt farmers and blue-collar workers whom our people looked down upon as white trash. Below them—far, far below—was South Africa's vast majority: the Indians, the mixed-race "Cape Coloured," and, at the bottom of the heap, the blacks.

South Africans had a peculiar way of distinguishing the races for purposes of segregation in those days. Bus stops, railway cars, and park benches all were marked accordingly.

We were "Europeans"; they were "Natives." Native was the neutral, value-free South African equivalent of what Americans call negro, colored, or black. The denigrative form of the term was "kaffir," the African word for nigger.

At least half a dozen natives worked for us at the first house I can remember—a large, two-story mansion with servants' wing, expansive grounds, and imposing circular driveway, in Johannesburg's exclusive Park Town section. We had a butler, cook, gardener, and several helpers, most of whom lived on the premises. Like other women of her social position, my mother supervised the domestic staff. Gregarious, cultivated, well-read, and fond of entertaining, she enjoyed managing the servants as she enjoyed other aspects of the diplomatic-colonial life.

In addition to the servants there were the nannies. The move to South Africa brought freedom from the burden of day-to-day child care for both our parents. First Chris, then I, then Mayflower (born in Johannesburg on August 25, 1928) were turned over to the tender mercies of a series of live-in governesses, whom we called nurses. While Mommy and Daddy went their separate way, the nurses got us up in the morning, fed us in "the children's dining room," took us to the zoo and the park, bandaged our wounds, and tucked us in at night. For most of my childhood I had only fleeting contact with my mother and father except on summer holidays and on Thursday, which was the nurse's day off.

First came Nurse Walker, a dim figure from my earliest childhood whom I remember as "Nanny Wabagee"—the closest I could come to pronouncing her name. Then Nurse Hatting. Then a succession of fraus and frauleins, recruited from a pool of women who had come to Johannesburg from depression-ridden South West Africa (now Namibia), the German colony taken over by South Africa under a League of Nations mandate after the Great World War. They were kindly but also thorough and strict. Most of them also were ardent Nazis.

I can still remember some of the songs we sang in German on our early morning hikes on the *koppie* behind our house on Pallinghurst Road:

*Our flag is flying in the wind;*
*Our flag is on the right side;*
*We are marching for Hitler*
*For freedom and bread...*

Frau Schultz, Fraulein Schumacher, other names I can no longer remember—they read us books and took us for walks and saw to our early political indoctrination. I learned from them that Communists were bad because they made you share your toothbrush, that the Jews were trying to take over the world, that the kaffirs were little better than apes. Sad to say, the religious and racial bigotry that I absorbed with my nannies' milk fitted all too neatly with the stereotypes accepted by my family, school, church, and playmates.

The neighborhood kindergarten I went to was a girls' school—St. Katharine's—that accepted boys in the first two grades. I wore the school uniform of navy blue short trousers, a blue hat with floppy brim, and blue blazer with the school initials, S.K.S., sewn on the left breast pocket. At St. Katharine's I learned to tie my shoes and brush my fingernails so they would pass muster when the principal, Ethel B. Fielding, lined us up for inspection each morning.

"Writing has definitely improved," wrote Miss Fielding in her graduation report on me at the end of 1935. "Drawing only fair; too untidy and presses too hard."

I hated St. Katharine's because it was a girls' school and because my older brother and his friends teased me with a ditty that parodied the school's initials: "Singing Kaffir Sausages."

After two years I was old enough to go on to a proper school—the Ridge Preparatory School, an exclusive private school for boys modeled on English public schools like Eton and Harrow. We wore grey uniforms with the school emblem—R.P.S.—neatly emblazoned in red on the school cap. No one made fun of us. Equally important, the Ridge School enabled me to suppress Sassie for a while. Following the English public school custom, students addressed each other by their last names. If brothers happened to be in attendance together, as was the case with Chris and me, they were ranked and addressed according to seniority. Thus, during our years at the Ridge, Chris became Day-1 and I Day-2.

"Hey, come out and play, Day-2," a school chum would yell from the garden gate. My mother thought that was cute. She sewed the name on my nightgown. Day-2.

At the Ridge each boy was assigned to one of three "houses"—fraternities organized by the school to promote loyalty and competition. A house had no meetings or activities or location, as a club might. It was simply an affiliation. But our lives at the Ridge revolved around them.

Each house was assigned wall space in the assembly hall where we gathered for prayers, hymns, and announcements at the start of the school day. There the houses displayed the trophies and other awards won in intramural competition.

The houses were named for heroes from white South African history. Most prestigious of the three was Rhodes House, named for Cecil Rhodes, the Nineteenth Century empire builder who had spread Britain's Union Jack from Cape Town to Cairo. Rhodes House was the perennial leader in my time. Its trophy shelf bristled with silver cups won on the athletic field—in cricket, football, rugby, track. I hated and envied Rhodes.

I was a Botha man, assigned as my brother was to the house named for Louis Botha, an Afrikaner general who threw in his lot with the British after the Boer War and thus attained respectability in the English community. Botha House had the next best athletic record at the Ridge. The loss or gain of a silver cup on the Botha shelf was a major event in my life. I loved the name of Botha and was fiercely loyal to it. This treasured association from my boyhood lingered into middle age, stirring up mixed feelings when, many years later, the name of Pieter W. Botha, prime minister and later president of the Republic of South Africa in the 1980s, became synonymous throughout the world with *apartheid,* repression, and police state brutality.

The third house was Tulbagh, named for an obscure Boer War general also romanticized by the British. With few cups to its name, Tulbagh was looked upon with pity and contempt.

The competition which dominated our lives at the Ridge carried over from the playing field to the classroom. In addition to the customary grades issued on report cards at the end of each term, teachers would occasionally award a star for outstanding scholastic performance, such as an exceptionally well-written essay. Such an award meant the placing of a star opposite your name on a roster attached to the wall just below the shelf that held your house's athletic awards. Stars were highly prized and rarely given. Winning a star ranked only slightly below winning a cup for Botha. As a boy with few athletic gifts, I found fulfillment in the star system. It enabled me to keep my head a little above obscurity, and, quite incidentally, it fanned my first flickering interest in learning.

The Ridge School offered a good classical education. From the first grade on I studied Latin and French as well as English, arithmetic, and history. The school offered an optional course in Afrikaans, the language of most white South Africans, but few of the Ridge's wealthy, English-speaking parents thought their children would have much need of it, even though then, as now, the government was officially bilingual.

I learned history from a European/South African perspective, beginning with the exploits of Fifteenth Century Portuguese explorers—Vasco da Gama, Bartholomeu Dias—who rounded the Cape of Good Hope in their search for a sea route to India. We studied the successive colonization of the Cape by Dutch, French, and English settlers; the "Great Trek" of the Cape Dutch, the *Voortrekkers,* hundreds of miles north into the interior of Africa in the 1830s to escape British oppression; the bloody but triumphant battles of the Boers against Zulu chieftains—Dingaan and Tschaka—later romanticized by white South Africans as noble savages in the same manner that white Americans have rehabilitated Sitting Bull, Crazy Horse, and Chief Joseph. We learned of the discovery of diamonds at Kimberley and gold in the Witwatersrand; the British commercial exploitation of these new-found mineral resources; the Boer War, the peace of Vereeniging, and British absorption of the last Boer homelands into a new Union of South Africa governed by an uneasy Anglo-Boer alliance led by soldier-statesman Jan Christiaan Smuts, a world figure widely respected at home and abroad.

With our Latin declensions and our Anglo-South African world view we also absorbed a disciplinary code. The school offered a choice of punishments for breaking the rules. You could choose between being caned by the headmaster or composing a long statement of contrition. An aggrieved teacher might say, for example, "Alright, Day-2, six with the stick or a six-page essay." That meant I had to report next morning to the headmaster's office—prepared to receive six lashes with a bamboo cane on my bottom as I bent over his couch, or to turn in a long, handwritten essay. Needless to say, few of us risked the scorn and ridicule sure to come from choosing the essay.

I once got four with the stick for chewing gum in class. That evening I proudly displayed to my older brother the four red welts on my "B.T.M." Another time, a teacher who caught me trampling on some classroom desk tops in my cleated football boots caused me deep humiliation by giving me no choice of punishment. "Alright, Day-2," he said. "That will cost you a three-page essay."

The code that mattered most at the Ridge was not the one administered by the school. It was the code imposed by the older boys. Like their counterparts at Eton and Harrow, the senior students at the Ridge—boys

7

in their early teens—exercised a tyranny over the younger ones that was passed on from class to class.

As a youngster of nine or ten I grew accustomed to being pushed into a malodorous urinal that stretched from wall to wall in the basement room where we took our showers after returning from the playing field. That was the way the new boys learned their place. Younger boys could expect to be sneered at, punched, or have their trousers pulled down simply for approaching within striking distance of a senior. The most common way of asserting authority was by kicking—administering a swift kick in the pants, without provocation, to any unsuspecting younger boy who happened by. Like other students, I soon developed a knack for keeping out of the way of seniors.

I suppose this tyranny of the upper boys—sanctioned by adults—was intended to teach us respect for seniority and authority. Perhaps it was also a way of grooming leaders. But from the bottom up it looked like nothing more than random bullying. There was no defense and no recourse. To complain was futile; to fight back was suicidal. The worst possible response was to break into tears—to risk letting word get around that Day-2 had "blubbed."

From an early age I learned to keep a stiff upper lip. Crying, or revealing vulnerability in any other way, simply was not done in my school. Nor was it encouraged in my family. The frauleins regarded emotionalism as a character defect in boys. My father prided himself on his stoicism. "Just make the best of it," he would say. My mother always seemed uncomfortable with tears. Chris was no help to me in school—the code forbade him even to be seen with his younger brother. And then there was my younger sister, Mayflower. A girl.

Even more unforgivingly, the code separated me from Mayflower as it did Chris from me. To be observed in willing company with a sister was even more compromising for a boy than to be seen showing affection for a brother. Chris and Mayflower and I had fun together on rare occasions— on holidays on the beach at Umkomas on the palm-lined Indian Ocean coast of Natal, or at "Nevadavaal," the Vaal River farm of our Aunt Bea and Uncle Scotty, American friends who had emigrated from Nevada. At such places we were beyond the reach and influence of our contemporaries. But in Johannesburg we practiced survival of the fittest.

Chris's territory was the lower part of the backyard, where he raised pigeons and guinea pigs in sturdy wire cages built for him by our father.

I was allowed to watch, but seldom to help, as Chris went about his daily ritual of cleaning the cages, filling the feed bins, and grooming his pets. My turf was the upper yard, where my friends and I would gather after school to skid our bicycles on the gravel driveway and play "kick the can" on the lawn. Mayflower, a pre-schooler for most of our time in South Africa, remained in the secure custody of our nannies, seldom seen or heard by us. To our parents we were the objects of benign neglect. Our father, an outdoorsman at heart, loved the wild South African countryside and was frequently gone on hunting and fishing trips. Our mother was a social lioness, busy with affairs of the Martha Washington Club (for American diplomatic and business wives), with charity benefits for the native hospital in Soweto, and with a full schedule of parties and receptions.

The isolation of the individuals within our family mirrored the social stratification in the world beyond our home, a condition that was later to be called *apartheid.* In my ten and a half years in South Africa I never knew or even spoke to a "native" except the servants in our household— Enoch the gardener, who carried me home on his back one day when I lost my way from school; Dick, a middle-aged head house boy who exposed himself to me one day in the kitchen (prompting me to run to the closet where my father kept his pistol and to point it at him), and many more. Nor did I ever know an Afrikaner boy, although my brother's closest friend, Johann Rissik, was from a Boer family that had become anglicized. Neither the races nor the languages mixed in our world.

The prejudices of school, family, and social class also extended to Jews. Johannesburg had a substantial Jewish community, rooted in the gold and diamond mining industries and in the city's commercial establishment. Antisemites referred to the city as "Jewburg." All but the most wealthy and patrician Jewish families were excluded from the English private schools, the country clubs, and our neighborhood. These attitudes inevitably rubbed off on me. I grew up believing that to be Jewish was to be cursed with a fate worse than death. Jewishness seemed to me to be a psychological death sentence. I felt sorry for the Jews, especially those few who happened to be my friends.

Felix Schneier was Jewish. He lived in a large house across the alley from ours. His parents had a couple of Dobermans. One day, when I was about nine, while at the Schneier house waiting for Felix to finish lunch, his mother gave me a chicken leg to nibble on. One of the dogs lunged at the bone, knocking me to the ground. I came out of my daze a little later in a nearby bedroom, my mouth full of blood and my eye tooth neatly uprooted by the force of the impact.

Curiously, a physical accident also stands out in my memory of another Jewish friend, John Israel, a classmate at St. Katharine's School. He and I collided one day while riding our bicycles, breaking the bone in John's nose. His parents took him all the way to England (15,000 miles and two months round-trip by ship) for corrective surgery.

Most of my friends were white Anglo-Saxon Protestant South Africans. Richard Lay, who, with his older brother Geoffrey, also attended the Ridge School, was the son of a pharmacist who lived in the next block. We were Day-2 and Lay-2. Our code name for cigarettes was "turtle doves." We would steal them from the silver cigarette box in the living-room of my home and puff them behind the backyard fence. They were Chesterfields—unfiltered. Then we'd drop our pants and pee on the fence to see who could reach the highest.

Lay-2 excelled not only in these feats but also as an actor in school plays. I can still remember his golden soprano tones in Shakespeare's Tempest:

*Where the bees suck there suck I;*
 *In a cowslip's dell I lie;*
*Merrily, merrily shall I live now*
 *Under the blossom that hangs on the bough...*

Occasionally an American boy would enter our circle, injected into it by my mother as a favor to his parents, newly arrived in Johannesburg's American community. The presence of such newcomers tended to have an unsettling effect on me. It brought to the surface my own ambivalent feelings about nationality. What was I? American? English? South African?

I knew, of course, that I was an American. I remembered the United States from a long trip the family had taken by train and ship in 1934, when I was seven, from Johannesburg to Salt Lake City, where Mayflower had gotten her hand caught in Aunt Betty's clothes wringer, and where I had been awed by a newspaper headline proclaiming the death of the notorious gangster John Dillinger, shot down by FBI agents in Chicago. In South Africa, I liked to accompany my mother to my father's office in downtown Johannesburg, where the American flag behind his desk told me he was an important government official. I realized that someday we would be returning to the United States for good. But that seemed a long way off.

In the meantime, I looked, sounded, and felt South African. In my heart of hearts I was British. And a Tory.

The things I came to like best as a boy were British: bacon and eggs with toast and marmalade for breakfast; tea in the morning and afternoon, roast beef with Yorkshire pudding on Sundays, British cars, British motorcycles, British ocean liners, British sports, British adventure books, and, above all, the British Royal Family.

In 1935, when I turned nine, King George V and Queen Mary observed the twenty-fifth year of their reign—the Silver Jubilee. The anniversary was enthusiastically celebrated in South Africa, and throughout the Empire, with parades, fireworks, and concerts, and with the issuance of commemorative coins, mugs, plates, and postage stamps. The Jubilee left an indelible mark on me, shaping my first formative political impressions. In my boyhood I came to regard this handsome, bearded monarch as the prototype for statesmanship, a model for lesser lights like General Smuts, Franklin D. Roosevelt, Neville Chamberlain, and Adolf Hitler.

My loyalty to the Royal Family only quickened the following year when George V died, to be succeeded by his dashing son, the Prince of Wales, as Edward VIII. Then came Edward's abdication crisis, the selection of a new royal couple, and, finally, in May of 1937, the coronation of King George VI and Queen Elizabeth. The drama in far-off England stirred my boyish imagination and ushered me into a new world of great events beyond the boundaries of my childhood.

"Tell Mom to cut out the picture of King George in the Rand Daily Mail," I wrote my father in a letter from Nevadavaal at the age of ten. "Tell Mayflower that I am itching to have a game of soldiers."

And to my mother: "I am drinking a glass of milk every meal, including tea time....Uncle Scotty gave us each a whip and we are whipping the donkeys. We are having a lovely time."

In December 1937, two months into my twelfth year, I sat on a steamship bunk one night absorbed in a series of newly issued British Empire coronation stamps given to me by my parents on my birthday. The stamps were beautiful beyond belief, portraying the handsome bust of the new king and queen engraved in blue, green, grey, magenta, and other colors beside the names of Britain's colonies and dominions around the world: Bechuanaland, Borneo, Ceylon, Burma, Sierra Leone, Nyasaland, Southern Rhodesia, Kenya, Uganda, Tanganyika, and, printed alternately in English and Dutch, my own South Africa/*Suid Afrika*. The stamps bespoke a stability and permanence that was soon to crumble—not only for the Empire but for me, too. My father had been reassigned to home duty in Washington, and we were on a boat headed for America.

# 2

# Coming Home

The scene to which our family returned in Washington at the end of 1937, after ten years abroad, must have been as unsettling for our parents as it was for the three Day children. My father would have preferred to remain in South Africa, where he knew and loved the people, the country, the climate, the way of life. He had done a conscientious job of promoting American business interests in a market historically dominated by the British. He had helped U.S. mining supply companies and other corporations (Caterpillar Tractor, Otis Elevator, Standard Oil) gain a toehold in South Africa. Decades later, after *apartheid* had burst upon the American political consciousness, the courting of U.S.-South African trade relations was to fall from grace. But this was the 1930s, when more exports meant more jobs for unemployed Americans, and when the United States was a country no less racially segregated than South Africa. At fifty-one, my father had looked forward to finishing his career in South Africa, perhaps eventually attaining the rank of ambassador.

But bureaucratic clouds had arisen. As a protege of Herbert Hoover he had fared well professionally until the Great Depression, when being one of "Hoover's boys" was no longer a political advantage. Further complicating matters, the foreign trade operations of the Department of Commerce were phased out in the 1930s and merged into the U.S. Foreign Service, part of the State Department. My father became U.S. commercial attache at the consulate in Johannesburg, which reported to the U.S. legation in Pretoria, the capital. He had lost his special connections in Washington. Friends persuaded him to accept home assignment with good grace and to take advantage of the opportunity to cultivate new connections at the source of power.

The change was also an abrupt one for my mother. She lost her household retinue, the expansive physical accommodations to which she had grown accustomed, and her status as a big fish in the small pond of Johannesburg cafe society. There was also the gnawing problem of what to do with the children in the absence of built-in child care services. But, at thirty-nine, Mother was energetic, resourceful, and ready to take on Washington. She rented a house on Newark Street and enrolled Chris in the Sidwell Friends School. For the first time in our lives Mayflower and I found ourselves in school together—she in the third grade and I in the fifth at John Eaton, a public school a few blocks from our home.

The strange new school made companions-in-arms of my sister and me. A few months after our arrival she asked me to protect her from a boy in her class who had been pulling her pigtails and teasing her in other ways. I rose to the challenge.

"Stop bothering my sister," I told him on the playground next day.

"Oh yeah," he replied. "You wanna make sumpin out of it?"

Not sure what that meant, I answered, "No, please just leave her alone."

The next day, when the teasing continued, I stopped him again and repeated my request, to which he again responded in the same manner.

"Yes, I'd like to make something out of it," I replied, quite formally, raising my fists in the way I had learned in boxing lessons at the Ridge. A couple of blows were exchanged and the boy ran away, blood dripping from his nose.

The brief act of brotherly solidarity was enough to get Mayflower's tormentor off her back. It also helped strengthen the early bond between my sister and me.

From Newark Street we moved to a bigger house deeper into Georgetown and from there to a more elegant house just off Dupont Circle—three houses and three schools in barely two years. Chris disappeared into a forbidding teen-age world of dates, dances, and early morning newspaper delivery routes, and Mayflower had dropped out of my sight again, leaving me to cope alone with new teachers and new classmates.

While I was in the sixth grade at the Andrew Jackson School I helped my friend John Baxter build a red wagon, which we named in honor of his girlfriend, Edna. We took the wagon across Rock Creek Park to a hillside in the black section of Washington. (The city was still strictly segregated in those days.) A swarm of black kids quickly surrounded us, whereupon John took off, leaving Edna in my charge.

Holding onto the wagon with one hand and raising my other fist, I cried out, recklessly, "I'll fight any one of you—but only one." A big boy about twice my size stepped forward.

Just then, miraculously, a passing truck driver noticed my predicament and brought me home with the red wagon.

In the seventh grade, at Gordon Junior High School, I lost a couple of schoolyard fights, and with them the last shreds of my self-confidence in boxing. The year—1939—was a discouraging one for me. Visited by one childhood illness after another, I spent much of the year in bed and was finally taken out of school altogether to recuperate at the home of an aunt and uncle in Virginia, where I whiled away the hours in the warm sun, fishing for crabs with bacon rind tied to the end of a piece of string.

While it brought loneliness and boredom to me, 1939 was an exhilarating year in some respects. The war clouds were gathering in Europe. Through the fall of 1938 and into the winter of 1939 I listened, often from my sickbed, for the familiar NBC radio chimes proclaiming some development in Europe: "We interrupt this program to bring you a news bulletin from our Berlin bureau...Herr Hitler has...."

I began devouring the *Washington Post* every day for news of the growing crisis—from the Sudetenland to Munich, to Danzig, to Memel. I clipped newspaper photographs of soldiers filling sandbags and installing antiaircraft batteries in the parks of London. I cursed the faint-hearted Chamberlain and his rubbish about "peace in our time." Peace was the last thing I wanted. I cheered the sight of the King and Queen inspecting the fleet at Portsmouth and Scapa Flow. The debate over American neutrality distressed me. I thrilled to the prospect of a great world war, with Britain, the United States, and South Africa marching together to victory.

On August 30, 1939, Hitler invaded Poland. A few days later Britain and France declared war on Germany, fulfilling my fondest boyhood hopes. World War II had begun. I followed the course of the war every day for the next six years.

Five months later we were on a train to my father's next Foreign Service post—Toronto, Canada.

I lived in Canada barely a year and a half, from February 1940 until September 1941, when I was sent off to boarding school in the United States. That was enough time for me to perfect the Boy Scout skills of lighting campfires and smoking cigarettes.

The Boy Scouts, who met weekly in the basement of Forest Hill Village School under the tutelage of Scoutmaster Hart Phips, defined and shaped my life in Canada. Ours was a neighborhood troop made up of boys who also went to school together. In the morning, before classes, we played a mass production form of marbles in which huge sacks could be won or lost in an hour's shooting. In the afternoon we swatted hockey pucks across the flooded rink behind the school. On Saturdays, whatever the weather, we disappeared on our bicycles into the nearby woods, our backpacks stocked with raw beefsteak and potatoes, Coca-Cola, candy bars, cigarettes, and girlie magazines. Then in my early teens, I was still small for my age but strong and scrappy and ready for any adventure. It was an idyllic time for me. I was back in my element as a heavy-hitting participant in a rough-and-tumble pack of boys.

In 1940 I wrote my mother, who was visiting friends in New York at the time:

> I went on the troop hike today, there was a grass fire and some one accidentally flipped my sweater into the flames. I didn't care much however, because it was an old Ridge School sleeveless one. (It is ruined). It was on the whole a successfull hike.

Meanwhile, the war went on. I followed it as intently as my Canadian friends. Germany invaded Denmark and Norway in April 1940, and I despaired as British troops were forced out of one rocky fjord after another. Then came the blitzkrieg in the west, Dunkirk, the fall of France, the Battle of Britain.

As an American in wartime Canada I felt humiliated, embarrassed, apologetic that my country would not join the fight. I had no patience with the isolationists who were obstructing President Roosevelt's efforts to get us into the war on Britain's side. My despair grew as the long list of Allied reversals lengthened into 1941—Hitler's invasion of the Balkans, his crushing of the plucky Greeks who had so bravely stood up to Mussolini, and his airborne conquest of Crete; Germany's triumphs in North Africa, and, finally, the invasion of Russia and the relentless surge of Hitler's panzer divisions to the gates of Moscow and Leningrad. What was the matter with my country? I asked. Would we never get into the war?

On September 14, 1941, I left Canada to return to school in the United States. Eighty-four days later, on December 7, the radio in my dormitory brought news that sent my spirits soaring. The Japanese attack on Pearl Harbor had plunged America into World War II. What I didn't realize at the time was that it also signaled the dispersal of our family.

# 3

# Prep School

A few days after the Japanese attack on Pearl Harbor the white-haired, grandfatherly principal of Phillips Exeter Academy, Dr. Lewis E. Perry, announced at morning chapel that the school would be going on a war footing. Henceforth, he declared, there would be no more peacetime frills. One of the luxuries to be dispensed with was daily maid service in the dormitories. From then on the boys would have to make their own beds.

A stir went through the student body, a sea of coats and ties and upturned faces in the great hall of this historic old preparatory school for America's aristocratic young.

"Are there any questions?" Dr. Perry asked.

A hand went up at the back of the hall.

"Please, Sir, may we bring our own maids?"

The Exeter I entered as a boy of fourteen, alone for the first time, was an imposing, grown-up place. The other boys, even those my age, were not only bigger than I but also seemed older and more polished.

My first roommate, Leonard Zartman, spoke in a rich baritone and had a chin that required shaving. He cast a disparaging look at the wall posters I had brought with me from home—scenes of Spitfires and Hurricanes blasting German Messerschmitts from the English skies. He suggested gently that we replace them with pictures of his own: prints of horses and sailing ships and hunting dogs flushing quail and pheasants from the brush.

Founded in 1781 in southern New Hampshire about ninety miles from Boston, Phillips Exeter was a training ground for the Ivy League, like its sister school, Phillips Andover, just across the Massachusetts line. Exeter (the red and grey) sent its sons to Harvard, Andover (the blue and white) to Yale. What got me and my older brother into Exeter was neither blood nor wealth nor scholastic achievement; as American children reared abroad, we helped the school's admissions program fill its self-imposed quota of students from families beyond New England and the Middle Atlantic states.

At Exeter I was lonely and homesick, especially during the first year. I tried to cover up my feelings in my letters home:

> On Saturday morning after chapel, Mr. Perry, the principal, asked me if I was liking Exeter, my answer was of course in the affirmative, which is getting to be true. I am liking Exeter alot better, but the work is also getting alot harder. I think I am going to have some trouble with French.

Spurred by Mother's insistent demands for more information, I began a weekly correspondence that continued not only through Exeter but for the following forty years.

> I received yours and Mayflowers letters today, I was disappointed to learn that you didn't think that my letters were newsy enough. I am, however, hoping that this will meet your approval.
>
> The reason I didn't describe my stay in the infirmary was because I was afraid that I might have alarmed you; I simply went to the infirmary because my throat was feeling soar. There the doctor took my temperature and gave me some pills, nose drops, and salt water after politely informing me that I had a slight fever.
>
> I was then ushered into a sun parlor, by a middle aged nurse, where I remained for the rest of the day. I was released at about 5:30.
>
> I will answer the rest of your questions tomorrow, due to the fact that it is almost 10:30 (my maximum bed-time).
>
> Wednesday:
>
> I will now proceed to answer all your questions in the order in which they came:

1. I have joined Phillips Church because I know of no-one who goes to Christ Church, and I believe that the Phillips Church sermons are just as interesting.

2. I did not join the Outing Club because of lack of time as I have previously mentioned. It is really a choice between Latin and hiking.

3. I am liking soccer very much and I am finding that my old skill is coming back to me (kaff-kaff!)

4. Chris made a hero of himself in the game by making several excellant kicks. He was a full-back, so naturally he didn't score any goals, but he prevented alot.

5. I am liking my room mate very much. The other day, his mother sent us some andirons and a fire screen.

6. I haven't seen or heard of Chapman, but I know Charlie Officer very well.

7. The boy who stood next to me in line, sits next to me in chapel, so I see quite alot of him.

Incidentally, I am having absolutely no trouble at all about getting friends, I wish I could give a few of them to Mayflower. Most of them are pretty nice guys, and, to the best of my knowledge, none of them are Jews....

We were at Exeter to be socialized as well as educated. I wore a coat and tie to class—the coat usually of tweed or camelhair with leather elbow patches. In the dining halls we ate on china and were waited on by white-coated scholarship students whom we were expected to tip at the end of the term. On autumn Saturdays all 750 of us would troop to the football field at the far end of the campus. Games with Andover were the highlight of the year. Whenever we beat our archrival school I would wait long and patiently for my chance to pull the rope of the school bell in the tower atop the Academy Building, ringing my exultation to the heavens. As a veteran of Botha House at the Ridge School in Johannesburg I understood and valued team spirit.

After our first year at Exeter we were considered to be mature. It was then that we could move into dormitories with "butt rooms"—lounges where smoking was permitted. Most of us became smokers by the second week of our "lower middle" (or sophomore) year, often encouraged by free butts from other students supplied with free cartons by the tobacco companies. At Exeter I puffed on cigarettes to be sociable, as I had since the age of eight, but did not become a serious smoker until my third year, when my lungs had developed sufficiently to permit me to inhale without discomfort. Once addicted, I smoked heavily for almost four decades, sometimes up to four packs a day, before quitting on January 3, 1981.

A heavy endowment and high tuition fees enabled Exeter to offer peerless opportunities for learning. We had gifted teachers, a classical curriculum (requiring four years of English; three years of Latin or Greek; three years of math; three years of French, Spanish, or German; two years of history, and two years of science), an excellent library and good science laboratories. The school's greatest pride was a teaching system known as the Harkness plan, in which classes were limited to twelve boys sitting with their teacher around a large table. The system encouraged, even demanded, interaction between teacher and boys, and individual participation by each student.

It was as a freshman at the round table of William Bates, an English teacher, that I acquired my first taste for writing.

One day, early in the term, Mr. Bates handed out sheets of paper and asked us to do a paragraph of descriptive writing on any topic. I wrote something recounting some adventure from the previous summer, then realized from the ensuing discussion that I had missed the point. The assignment called not for a narration but a *description*—like, for example, the sight and sound of autumn leaves rustling in the wind. The next day, when he asked us to try again, I composed a passage drawn from my musings in the dining hall kitchen, where I worked at that time as a scholarship boy. My paragraph was based on an imaginary scene in which a young boy operating a bread-slicing machine accidentally cut his finger off. It was a short paragraph that painted a picture of deep red blood spurting from the severed artery and spraying the white bread loaves in delicate shades of pink.

Collecting the papers, Mr. Bates shuffled through them, reading casually, until he came to mine. He stopped, read it to himself a second time, then read it to the class. Then he read it to us again.

"Mr. Day," he said. "you should do more writing."

In the Exeter of my time there was a debit side to this magnificent, multi-million-dollar educational establishment. The problem was that learning had to be bootlegged. Any serious attempt by a student to take advantage of the teaching, the round table, the opportunities for learning and self-improvement tended to be regarded by his peers as a violation of the student code. The term for this sort of behavior was "sucking." From time to time, when a student seemed too eager in discussion or lingered too long after class he would be put on notice by the hissing sound of other boys softly but audibly sucking in their breath.

Sucking meant any show of serious interest in learning. A few strong and determined young men at Exeter—the "greasy grinds"—braved ridicule and ostracism in order to take full advantage of the school's educational opportunities. I was not one of them. In subjects that interested me most—English, history, and languages—I participated as fully as I dared. But mostly I went with the flow.

At Exeter in the war years the flow was athletic. This was a jock school. The ultimate status symbol was the athletic letter, a capital E, awarded for playing against Andover on a varsity team. You wore it on your sweater inside-out in order to give the impression that the letter was really no big thing to you. Not just any letter would do. It had to be a letter in a major sport—football, basketball, or track—or at least in a second ranked game like baseball, lacrosse, or hockey. Exeter also awarded letters for fencing and other nonprestige activities, but the discerning student soon learned to keep them in his drawer.

As a ninety-eight-pound runt with thick glasses, my only shot at athletic distinction at Exeter lay in wrestling and boxing, where I could compete with boys my size. The coach encouraged me to put on some weight and try out for the 121-pound class, the lowest of the wrestling entry levels. I stood some chance of making the varsity wrestling team eventually, but at the beginning of my second year I succumbed to my mother's entreaties to give up the sport. She feared it would ruin my posture.

My frail health was a source of continuing concern to my mother. Consciously or unconsciously I played into her fears in letters recounting my exploits on the wrestling mat.

> We had another wrestling class today in which I got beaten up....
> ...I think I might quit wrestling because every time I go there, I get tossed all over the mat. This is because I am the lightest boy there by 20 lbs. However, if I stick, I think that I will learn how to wrestle, and after all, I don't care if I get bumped around, just so long as I get some good out of the course....

And again:

...Well, I had my match with Dingwall today. We wrestled it in the middle of a varsity wrestling match with Dartmouth. After we walked into the gym amid thunderous applause, we waited about 45 minutes while the varsity wrestled. When our time came to wrestle, Dingwall and I peeled off our sweat shirts and strode on to the mat. (I was already exhausted from nervousness). We then shook hands and began to wrestle. Toward the end of the first period, Dingwall made a dive for my legs and feet. I miraculously side stepped and got on top of him, thus gaining two points.

The second period opened with me on top of him. He soon escaped and got on top of me, however, (gaining two points for himself) from which position I soon escaped and got on top of him (two points for me).

The third period opened with Dingwall on top of me, but I luckily escaped and got on top of him (2 points for me) in which position we stayed for the rest of the bout.

Coach Mahoney decided to call it a draw so everyone was happy.

I have never been so tired in my life as I was in that fight....

Following the Dingwall bout my mother took the offensive. That summer she sent me to a place called the Whitney Homestead in Stow, Massachusetts, for a few weeks to take lessons from F. Matthias Alexander, a teacher of posture in whom she placed great confidence. For almost a month I endured the ministrations of "F.M." and his assistant, Miss Goldie.

My mother had become a devotee of "the Alexander method," a technique of breathing, relaxation, and body control somewhat akin to yoga. During our stay in Canada she had encountered "F.M." and his retinue, who had come over from England after the outbreak of the war, and she had gone to New York to take lessons from the master. She also had developed a close friendship with Goldie, a well-meaning but overbearing Englishwoman who reminded me and Mayflower of our nannies in South Africa. From time to time Mother would attempt to instruct us in the Alexander technique, sometimes with Goldie's help, usually to little avail. We joked with each other and privately resented Mother's intense interest in this curious old man and his puzzling rules for "keeping the head forward and up." Distressed by my accounts of mayhem on the wrestling mat at Exeter, it was natural that she should turn to her mentor for help.

My letters from the Whitney Homestead reflected exasperation:

> ...I am doing fairly well with my lessons, although I don't really know.
> These lessons aren't anything like I imagined they would be. Mr.
> Alexander stands over me and fiddles around with his hands. Occasion-
> ally he tells me to shorten or stiffen my neck, but most of the time I
> haven't the faintest idea as to what he is trying to do so consequently
> there isn't much I can do to help....

And again, especially after my stay at the Alexander school was extended beyond the initial two weeks:

> On Friday, I learned to my utter dismay and disgust that I had been
> sabotaged by my own family. What on earth did you think that F. M.'s
> reply would be? Surely you didn't expect him to say: "I feel it would
> be useless for Sam to stay here any longer. I have imparted all my
> knowledge to him and there simply isn't anything more I can teach
> him."
> Goldie has undertaken the job of teaching me how to write. She has
> also asked me to write a theme for the school newspaper. So I am right
> in the middle of the finished copy of the theme when she comes along
> and asks me if I know anything about paragraphs. And then to add injury
> to insult she shows me how to hold the pen and how to move my fingers.
> The result is that one of my best themes is crazily written and looks like
> a mess....

The influence of F. Matthias Alexander did not end with my completion
of the course at the Whitney Homestead. He wrote a letter to my mother
strongly urging that I discontinue wrestling: "The exercises given him to
develop his shoulder muscles have done much harm—these exercise
mongers should be put into prison or a mental home."

Upon my return to Exeter for my sophomore year I found myself
squeezed between two conflicting schools of physical exercise:

> I just got back from my physical examination and I am disgusted.
> The posture man took a look at me and said I needed improvement
> and offered to give me exercises. I asked him what was specifically
> wrong with me and he said I still had a hollow back. When I told him

that I had been to an expert, he expressed surprise that I had not been given any exercises to do.

He also stated that my swimming was poor and offered to give me lessons in swimming, too.

I did not flatly refuse to take his posture exercises. Instead I decided to get a letter from you to him via me explaining the matter. A letter from Mr. Alexander would greatly help too. If he should start to work on me before your letter arrives, I will refuse to be operated upon.

I really was disgusted: he turned me around, took one glance at my profile and said I had a hollow back. He payed no attention to the relative position of my head, or the breadth of my back. If I had been as stiff as a board it wouldn't have made the least difference. I did not argue or explain the Alexander technique to him because the situation was so rushed and stupidly organized.

Small size, poor eyesight, and questionable posture were only part of my physical problem at Exeter. I was also a nonshaver, one of the fast-dwindling handful with no hint of approaching facial hair. By contrast, one of my classmates, a big fellow named Winslow Lovejoy, shaved once and sometimes twice a day. To make matters even worse, my voice had not yet changed, a fact brought home traumatically one day when Mr. Bates, the English teacher, recorded the voices in our class and played them to us. The pitch of my voice was something to which I had never previously given thought. It mortified me to discover that I sounded like a girl.

Years passed before I overcame the inferiority complex induced by these physical inadequacies. In the meantime, I cultivated a husky rasp to make my voice sound deeper, scraped my face frequently with a razor blade in hopes that this would stimulate the hair follicles, and told myself to make the best of it. But Exeter was not a happy place for me. Lonely, insecure, preoccupied with the problems of adolescence, I had few close friends. My brother Chris, two years ahead of me, was forbidden by the code from making more than a fleeting acknowledgment of my presence on those few occasions when I caught his eye as we trooped out of chapel on the way to morning classes.

In the spring of 1942, following U.S. entry into the war, my father was transferred from Toronto to Leopoldville, in what was then the Belgian Congo.

It was an unsettling development for me, as I wrote my mother in a letter from Exeter:

> ...The tragic news of Dad's transfer struck me like a bombshell today! I was very much surprised and shocked. There seems to be one main thing that dad forgot to tell: that was "Why is no other member of the family allowed to go to Africa with him?" I should think that it would be a good idea if you and Mayflower could go with him. There would, however, be a snag to that: Chris and I would probably not see you for about four years. Chris and I talked the matter over but we did not get very far. Neither of us think that it would be a very good idea for you to live in Exeter, but we decided that it wouldn't be so bad if you lived about ten miles away, on the coast. We both also thought it wouldn't be so bad if you and Mayflower went to California or Utah to live. However, if you and Dad are coming down next week to see about getting a house down here, you must be pretty dead set on it.
>
> I do not think that you would enjoy this town very much: It would seem awfully quiet and dull after living in the city all of your lives. Besides that difficulty, which is not entirely insurmountable, is that Exeter offers no attractions such as beautiful scenery, lakes, rivers, or mountains. The sea is too far away to be seen or enjoyed frequently and there is no cool ocean breeze. I am sure, however, that when you come down, we will be able to discuss the matter to much greater length.
>
> Of course, the place where I would like to live most is in Toronto, but I can see how that would not be possible, now that we have no more "pull" there.

My father was to spend most of the war years looking after U.S. strategic interests in Central Africa and helping to repatriate Allied sailors stranded on the coast of Portuguese Angola by German submarine attacks. My mother closed out our home in Toronto and moved to Wellesley, Massachusetts, near Boston. In the fall of 1943 she joined him in Africa, leaving me and Mayflower (now in boarding school near Boston) in the custody of old friends as legal guardians. Chris, now nineteen, had graduated from Exeter and was enrolled at Harvard in a Navy officer training program.

Throughout the years at Exeter my deepest and most abiding interest was the war. I followed it every inch of the way from Pearl Harbor to Bataan to Guadalcanal to El Alamein to Stalingrad to D-Day and beyond. When morning classes were over I would hurry to the school library to read the *New York Times* and the *Boston Herald*. I read the war news every day. My enthusiasm for the war knew no bounds. I wrote home:

> ...I have gone on a patriotic splurge and I have bought $1.00 worth of defense stamps instead of going to the grill. From now on I am going to spend 50% of my allowance on defense stamps....
>
> ...Today I went down town and bought myself a harmonica. I have been playing all afternoon and now I can play: "Deep in the Heart of Texas" and "God Save the King."...

In the summer of 1943 I had a job tending a large garden in Wellesley. The garden had a big flowerbed that matched the triangular shape of the island of Sicily, invaded that summer by the Allies. Day after day through July and August I spaded the flowerbed from end to end, joyously following the routes of Patton's and Montgomery's victorious tank columns.

In the summer of 1944 I began my senior year at Exeter in the Anticipatory Program, a wartime measure to hasten graduation of seniors eligible for the draft. By going to summer school, I and other AP students would advance our graduation from June to early February 1945.

Through the fall and into the early winter of 1944, as the members of the class of "1945-AP" turned eighteen, each would take the train to Boston for his Selective Service physical examination, to be followed a little later by the inevitable notice of induction. Some chose the Navy, some the Marines, and some hoped for a place in the vast armies that were then girding for the final assault on Hitler's Third Reich.

On October 3 I turned eighteen and registered for the draft. Six weeks later I was ordered to report for my physical. On the appointed date I climbed on the train, waving to friends who had come to the station to see me off. It was in mid-December, during the Battle of the Bulge, a dark hour in the war.

As I waited my turn in the long lines of half-naked men I prayed for a break from the Selective Service doctors, for understanding and sympathy, for their compassionate realization that a young man with a sound body flawed only by a strange malformation of the eyeballs could still play a useful role in uniform. This was not something I felt I could tell the examiners. So I only hoped and prayed.

A grimace on the face of the doctor who checked my eyes told me that my hopes would be in vain. At the end of that long afternoon in Boston a clerk stamped my papers with large red letters. I can still see and feel the words as though they had been inscribed in my own blood. "Unfit for Military Service."

# 4

# Reading for Honors

It would be difficult to imagine two learning institutions more different than Exeter and Swarthmore, the college into which I drifted in March 1945. One was a proving ground for sons of the upper classes—patrician, snobbish, anti-intellectual, steeped at that time in the values of the locker room. The other was a social melting pot, a bubbling cauldron for bright young men and women of every race and social station. It was mere chance that took me from one school to the other.

I had not prepared for entrance into any college, hoping instead to be marching off to war from Phillips Exeter. When Selective Service dealt me the shattering blow of classifying me 4-F, a scant six weeks before graduation, I turned to college as an unwelcome alternative. Swarthmore suggested itself because my parents as well as my wartime guardians, Irene and Alden Thresher, were old friends of the dean of admissions and could smooth the way for me. I was readily admitted to the college.

A small Quaker college founded in 1864, Swarthmore sprawled across broad lawns and wooded hills in the town of that name on the Pennsylvania Railroad's Paoli line, a half-hour from downtown Philadelphia. When I walked for the first time from the station up a tree-lined footpath to Parrish Hall, the administration building, I was one of only a handful of freshmen admitted at the start of that spring semester. We hit it off immediately.

Barry Caesar and Sam Todes from Philadelphia; Sid Mitchell, Betty Hunter, and Arthur Levin from New York, Wendy Hackett from Provincetown—three Jews, three WASPs, and a black—we were an unlikely but solid clique forged during freshman orientation. We took courses together, cut classes with gay abandon, sprawled on the grass in the warm spring sunshine, took the bus into nearby Chester for submarine sandwiches, and downed countless pitchers of beer at Plushy's, the student watering hole. I exulted in my newfound freedom, in escape from continuing reminders of my shame and embarrassment for being physically unfit, and in the vicarious thrill of victory over Germany in May of 1945. At the end of the semester I was placed on academic probation for poor grades.

No matter. I played through the early summer, attaching myself to a cousin, Jessica Tyndale, who had an apartment in New York and worked in the shipping business. Jessica, about ten years my senior, treated me like a grownup. She let me stay with her, smoked cigarettes with me, taught me how to mix drinks. A Phi Beta Kappa graduate of Cornell University, Jess had gone to New York in the depth of the Depression, found a job as a clerk, worked her way up, and was eventually to become an international financier of the first order, engineering major business deals in Europe and the Middle East. (The small island of Jessica, a spit of sand near Bahrein in the Persian Gulf, was named in her honor by its admiring owner.) Genteel, compassionate, generous, Jess became something of a fairy godmother to me in my Swarthmore days and afterwards.

Jess also cultivated my budding interest in left-wing politics. The political belief system I brought to Swarthmore was essentially that of Rudyard Kipling. Nothing had arisen in my upbringing in South Africa and Canada or in the books I read at Exeter to challenge the Anglo-American imperial world view I had absorbed as a child. My enthusiasm for the momentous battles of World War II only deepened that outlook. The heroes of my teen-aged years were the victorious Allied generals of that war. I also admired Franklin D. Roosevelt, the wartime president, and thought he should have been appointed president-for-life. I mourned his death as though he were my own father. I was appalled at the ingratitude of the British electorate for turning Winston Churchill out of office in 1945, so soon after the end of the war in Europe. But at Swarthmore these unexamined notions underwent the skeptical scrutiny of fellow students more politically sophisticated than I. I encountered Marx and Lenin and Mao for the first time, read about capitalism and socialism, learned first hand from classmates about discrimination against blacks and Jews, knocked on doors in the slums of industrial Chester in search of votes for a Swarthmore professor who ran for Congress my freshman year. My cousin Jess, who, with her late husband Dale, had been a Communist during the Depression, helped steady me in this hurricane of new ideas.

For me, Jess was more than just the ultimate in social and intellectual sophistication. She was also a political model. By the mid-1940s, when I came to know her, she had moved far beyond communism and pink-collar poverty. She was well on her way to becoming a high financier. But she remembered her roots and empathized with the victims of oppression and injustice. She was a capitalist with a social conscience. The liberalism I absorbed from Jessica Tyndale, with additional input from Swarthmore, became the political compass that would guide me for a quarter of a century.

I was never much more than an average student at Swarthmore. But toward the end of my sophomore year the encouragement of a political science teacher, Bryce Wood, began to make me a serious student. In a sophomore class in International Relations Wood recognized my flair for writing and suggested I apply for entry to the Swarthmore Honors Program, available to students in their last two years. "Reading for honors," as they call it, is an intensive program in which you study just two subjects at a time. In each subject you meet your professor with six or seven other students just once a week at a seminar, usually in the evening at the professor's home. You spend most of your time studying independently at the library and preparing a paper to be dissected by the professor and students at the next meeting. At the end of two years you are thrown to the mercies of outside examiners (scholars from around the country) for a full week of written tests and oral interviews in all eight subjects. The honors program is immensely stimulating but also a brutal passage. I was accepted on probation.

As a major in political science minoring in history and economics, I applied myself diligently as an honors student. I read neither as rapidly nor as comprehensively as other students. Nor with the same discipline. The newspapers in the periodicals section of the Swarthmore library were a constant trap for me. I'd arrive in the morning with an armload of books and by mid-afternoon still be immersed in the *New York Times, PM,* and the *Daily Worker*. But in time I acquired the knack of gathering relevant material on a given subject, assembling it in logical order, and turning out a paper of the right length reflecting a point of view that usually interested the other students. I seldom showed much erudition. But I usually wrote good papers.

As seminar followed seminar and semester followed semester I came to hold my own in the Swarthmore honors program. But it was never easy for me.

I wrote my parents complaining about my readings ("endlessly long and difficult") and coursework. Several of my papers were inadequate—a fact that did not escape the attention of my peers. One paper, I noted darkly, was "ripped to shreds...systematically mutilated word for word, and then buried." Near the end of my first term in honors, I was close to despair. "If you don't happen to have a mighty reservoir of grey matter," I wrote, "maintaining the pace becomes a dull, heavy grind...."

I managed to survive the early hurdles of the honors program, but the pressure of such intensive study took its toll. In the fall of 1947, I planned to take a semester off the following spring in order to visit India, where my father was concluding his diplomatic career as economic counselor to the U.S. Embassy at New Delhi. In December those plans took on an unexpected note of urgency.

Dear Mother and Dad,

I am writing now under very strong emotional strain—and one of the chief reasons for this letter, I have no doubt, is to provide an outlet for it. But I feel that once the strain has worn off the feelings that I express here, and the decision that I have had to make, will not have altered.

Though I have given no indication of it in my past letters, the case is that I have for the past two months been in love with a girl here at Swarthmore—Marian Ham. Perhaps I am mistaken in calling it love—I really don't know enough about myself, or her, to tell. But it has nevertheless been an infatuation so strong that it has come to dominate me completely, and at all times. The attraction may be nothing more than a product of my adolescence or my peculiarly sanguine and romantic temperament; but I have thought about it endlessly and I have come to the conclusion that it cannot be dismissed as a fleeting mood or a passing fascination.

Our relations had been unnaturally stiff and inhibited, because of my timidity and hesitancy in view of the great stakes involved, until last night, when my great frustration, which had become unbearable, led me to bring about a denouement. To make the story short, she is in love with a man in Chicago—and I can tell from the way she talks that it would be fruitless and cruel for me to assert myself. There seems to be no way out for me that is even tolerable—and I say quite plainly that I am utterly crushed. There seems to be no doubt of the fact that the other man can make her completely happy, whereas I cannot. And I know that I cannot bear anything less than her complete love. In view of this I have decided to leave her and Swarthmore, and all the other associations, until I am able to forget her. If the trip to India does not work out I shall seek some other change of environment—probably the merchant marine. She graduates in June, so I think I should be able to return in safety in September—broadened and recovered.

I hope that you can react to this sympathetically and with understanding. I know that you will have observations and suggestions to make, and there will be time to make them. I know that it is a rash course which I have selected, but it is the only alternative. To stay on at Swarthmore while she is here would be unthinkable. The rest of this semester will be a dull, weary struggle. I just haven't got it in me to attend to my work under the circumstances. Please don't blame her for this.

Love, Sass.

Marian was an English major half a year ahead of me in the Swarthmore honors program. We met at the beginning of the fall semester in an English history seminar that brought us together one evening a week. For me it was love at first sight—but it was a love that lived only in my fantasies. Unpracticed in romantic relationships (I had never kissed a girlfriend on the lips), I kept my feelings to myself in the vain hope that she would lead the way. Drawn to her but terrified by the fear of rejection, I lived in simultaneous anticipation and dread of a chance encounter in the library, a corridor, the college recreation hall. Soon our weekly seminars became nightmares for me. I reached such a point of paralysis in these meetings that I couldn't find the voice to present my papers to the others, as was the custom, and had to ask that they be read for me. I feigned laryngitis. My growing incapacitation finally drove me to take matters in hand. Screwing up my courage, I invited Marian to the Christmas dance. Afterward we repaired to the steps of the Clothier Memorial tower, a popular trysting place. Weak with fear, I confessed my love, wondering and dreading what her response would be.

"Oh dear," she replied. "I was afraid of that."

With help from Marian, who did her best to let me down easily, and with encouragement from my father, who spent most of an evening composing a letter of advice ("You'll get over it"), I managed to struggle through the remainder of the semester. At the end of January I took leave of Swarthmore. Six weeks later I was on a boat headed for India.

# 5

# India

Three strands formed the thread of my trip to India, from early March to mid-September of 1948. First, the journey let me relive the adventure and carefree abandon of ocean travel. As a child, on long trips between the United States and South Africa, I had reveled in the sights and sounds, the smells and sensations of shipboard life—the roll and pitch of the deck, the blue waters parting at the vessel's prow and frothing in its wake, the salt spray tingling in my nostrils, the sense of being suspended in the limitless circumference of sea and sky, the deep and comforting throb of the engines.

Three years earlier, in the summer of my freshman year at Swarthmore, on a trip arranged by cousin Jessica in New York, as was this one, I had worked my way on a wartime freighter to South Africa for a brief reunion with my parents in Johannesburg. (I relaxed as a passenger on the way out and worked as a dishwasher on the return trip.) Eleven days out, as we were rounding the hump of Brazil, the ship's radio crackled the news of the dropping of an atomic bomb on Japan. A week later, in the South Atlantic, we celebrated the war's end with such copious quantities of alcohol, brought aboard at Trinidad, that I have never since enjoyed the taste of rum.

Now, headed for India, the old thrill of ocean travel and the prospect of foreign adventure surged within me again as our tramp freighter, commanded by British officers and crewed by Pakistanis, backed away from a Brooklyn pier and plodded east across the Atlantic to the Straits of Gibraltar, past the muddy mouth of the Nile, through the locks and lakes of Suez, and into the sun-baked Red Sea. Traveling with me on the five-week voyage were an American couple returning to India with a tractor for their mission farm in the foothills of the Himalayas. We struck up a friendship and I looked forward to helping them assemble the tractor parts on the dock at Bombay and drive the vehicle several hundred miles as far as New Delhi, where my parents would be awaiting my arrival.

The second strand of my Indian sojourn was my coming together again with two people—my parents—for whom letters had come to be our only communications link. Begun in boarding school as dutiful weekly reports, the letters became my way of "going home" during the separations of the war years and beyond. I would write home every Sunday night—a practice that was to continue through four decades, until my father's death in 1982 and my mother's incapacitation from a stroke a few years later. It was my mother who usually wrote in response, with my father chipping in when some important occasion required it. Sometimes, depending on the distances, it would take a month or six weeks to get a question answered, especially during the war.

The disjointed, one-dimensional nature of our communication became the norm for us. For me, the letters came in time to be the reality of our relationship—more natural than our rare reunions. On the trip to South Africa in 1945 I had been shocked by the sight of the two greying strangers—my parents—who greeted me on the train platform in Johannesburg. "Gee, they look old," I told my brother on my return. In India, three years later, the reunion was to be awkward, even painful, once again.

At a stopover in Karachi I left word at the American embassy that my arrival in New Delhi would be delayed by the tractor trip. On my arrival in Bombay a few days later an emissary from the consulate brought an anguished greeting from my mother and father, both appalled at the thought of such a long journey under the hot sun in the scorching heat of the north Indian plains. For a week we battled back and forth by telephone and letter, my mother and I, in a struggle reminiscent of our contest over wrestling at Exeter. The standoff ended abruptly when she fell ill with cholera, necessitating abandonment of my tractor plan.

Arriving in New Delhi by train, and entering my parents' house in the well-to-do embassy area of the Indian capital, I found a scene not unlike the one I had known in Johannesburg: finely appointed rooms, a spacious garden, servants' quarters, and a small army of bearers, sweepers, cooks, drivers, and other helpers to do the work. But this time I was prepared to be a visitor in my parents' home. Like an old acquaintance who had dropped by for a short stay, I pitched in during the emergency, helping run the household while my mother recuperated, and even standing in for her at social functions.

My arrival in India followed the departure of my younger sister, Mayflower, who, between boarding school and college, had accompanied our parents to India in the fall of 1946. The glamorous daughter of a diplomat, sought after and pampered by young aides-de-camp of India's last viceroy and first governor general, Lord Louis Mountbatten, Mayflower had set a social pace impossible for me to follow. Nevertheless, I plunged into the cocktail parties, dances, embassy receptions, and gymkhana club poolside soirees that characterized the capital's giddy social whirl during India's first year of national independence.

I also attempted the more difficult task of trying to get closer to my father, then in the final year of his Foreign Service career. It was a time of disappointment for him. His reassignment from Johannesburg to New Delhi after the end of the war had dashed his hopes of crowning twenty-five years of service with an ambassadorial appointment. (The South African post went instead to a Marine Corps general with political connections in Washington.) As economic counselor to the embassy in New Delhi he had high rank but no real outlet for his long experience in southern and central Africa. To top it off, a few weeks before my arrival he had narrowly survived a hunting accident that left his cheek bone pitted with bird shot (and, at my mother's insistence, brought an end to his lifetime shooting hobby). There seemed few openings for me in the world of this preoccupied old man, forty years my senior. He had always been a remote figure to me but was later to open up and blossom as a grandparent, in his retirement. For a while I worked in a clerical job, cataloguing films, he secured for me in the U.S. Information Service office in New Delhi. With my mother and an entourage from the embassy, I accompanied him to a United Nations regional economic conference at a mountain resort in southern India. He headed the U.S. delegation. I watched as, clearing his throat to ease the nervousness, he parried the thrusts of the Soviet delegation, and I tried to picture myself in that position.

Thoughts about my own future made up the third strand of my Indian journey. My older brother, Chris, had graduated from Harvard as a naval cadet and begun a career in the shipping business. By this time my own college graduation was only a year away. The Foreign Service had begun to loom as the most likely career choice for me. As I had drifted into Swarthmore three years earlier, now I was drifting toward the diplomatic service.

I had conversational gifts, a taste for travel and life abroad, and the self-confidence from having been born into the diplomatic corps, all of which augured well for a career with the State Department. Further, I had focused my Swarthmore studies in an appropriate field—politics, economics, and international relations—and was developing a keen interest in those subjects. These were the birth years of the Cold War—the Truman Doctrine, in which the United States replaced Britain as the guardian of the eastern Mediterranean; the Marshall Plan to rebuild Europe in the image of western capitalism; the historic article in the magazine *Foreign Affairs* in which George Kennan, writing under the pseudonym of "X," laid out the strategy of "Communist containment" that came to be the anchor of U.S. postwar policy toward the Soviet Union. Under the continuing tutelage of Bryce Wood, the professor who guided me into the Swarthmore honors program, I witnessed the birth of those and other historic happenings in the early postwar era. I followed them with the passion of a scholar. As an earlier teacher, William Bates at Exeter, had ignited my self-confidence as a writer, so Bryce Wood of Swarthmore gave me a sense of belonging in the study of international relations.

Like other liberals of the early postwar years, Bryce Wood also had a hard edge. He held an unrelenting distrust of the Soviet Union and communism, and he communicated it unhesitatingly to his students. This gave me problems in the beginning. Like many other Swarthmore students, I savored the lingering aura of the wartime alliance with the Soviets, scorned the Truman Administration's increasingly strident anticommunism at home and abroad, and warmed to the more progressive stance of Henry Wallace, Franklin Roosevelt's one-time secretary of agriculture, who revolted against Truman's anti-Soviet hard line. But Bryce Wood's influence was formidable. My final conversion to Cold War liberalism, in full support of U.S. "containment" policy, was completed—and was to continue for twenty years—following the Communist coup which unseated the pro-Western government of Jan Masaryk in Czechoslovakia in 1948. To me and to many others at that time, this was the last straw.

But the spell of Bryce Wood was also tugging me in another career direction, as were other circumstances in my life. An avid reader of and believer in the *New York Times*, as was I, Wood also whetted my interest in journalism. So, too, did a New York friend, Rudy Stewart, who was later to marry my cousin Jess. Rudy's own career as a *Times* reporter had soured, but he remained a booster of the newspaper. With Jess and Rudy on vacations from Swarthmore I met reporters for the *Times* and hobnobbed with them at a bar around the corner from the *Times* building. In the years preceding my trip to India, and in India itself, as a career decision approached, I began picturing myself as a writer, perhaps a foreign correspondent, for a newspaper or magazine, especially a prestigious one like the *New York Times*.

After the U.N. economic conference at Ootacamund in India in June 1948, I detached myself from my parents. For a month I took a room in a hotel in the southern city of Bangalore. I walked the streets, read newspapers in the coffee shops, absorbed the flavor of the bazaar, and made notes in my journal. For another few weeks, until early August, I hitched a ride with a friend, Kurt Wentzel, a photographer for the *National Geographic* magazine. With his assistant, Francis Leeson, we roamed the provinces of Bangalore and Mysore in a converted Army ambulance, taking pictures of elephants, temples, weddings, blacksmith's shops, and other pieces of the kaleidoscope of Indian country life. On the forty-five-day voyage home I put my journal entries into a scrapbook to pass the time:

> One warm July evening we were walking through the streets of Mysore with a Brahman friend when we came upon the temple in front of the Maharaja's palace, where a special "puja" was being performed in observance of a local festival. Indicating to the priests, who were friends of his, that we were o.k., the Brahman took us in for a look-around.
>
> Outside of the temple, which was a fairly small, stone building, dedicated to Hanumanji, the Sacred Monkey, there were swarms of beggars—cripples mostly—lying on the pavement with their tin pots beside them, calling out to the passers by for "backsheesh." I noticed two sadhus—men dressed in the robes of medieval monks, who wore the peaked joker's cap of a medieval clown. Their clothes were a brilliant orange and white, their faces were painted, and they were chanting shrilly, plucking on huge, gourd-like banjos. As we went in, a priest stepped out and hurled two coconuts on the ground. There was a mad scramble and a feverish bickering for the pieces.

Inside, there was the smell of burning incense, crushed marigolds, stale coconuts, and sour milk; along the damp walls, framed pictures and cheap prints of Hanuman—depicted in a number of formalized attitudes. In prominent places, there were a number of his brass and clay statues.

A bare-chested Brahman priest rang a bell sharply to summon the god's attention, and ladled out a spoonful of holy water for us to drink with our hands. Perfunctorily he tore off a few inches of moist, withered flowers from a long, threaded chain that was at hand, and gave them to us. We circled our right hands two or three times over a flame, gave him a rupee, and that was all. We were cleansed.

My batteries recharged by the trip to India, I returned to Swarthmore in the fall of 1948 and plunged into my final year of studies. The work went well, and, on June 6, 1949, I was graduated with high honors. The graduation guests included Marian Ham, who, following her own graduation the previous spring, had magically reappeared in my life. While I completed my senior year, she taught at a school in nearby Wilmington, Delaware, an arrangement that permitted frequent visits, culminating in our engagement just before my graduation. We planned to marry about the time of my entrance into the United States Foreign Service.

# 6

# Cub Reporter

It was literally the toss of a coin that launched my career as a journalist. When I went to Washington in the fall of 1949 it was to take the written examinations for the U.S. Foreign Service. I had decided to follow in the footsteps of my father, who had come home from India the previous year and, at sixty-two, had retired with my mother to a farm on the Virginia shore of Chesapeake Bay. In my last year at Swarthmore I had prepared myself for a diplomatic career by taking seminars in International Relations and U.S. Foreign Policy. Over the summer I had boned up on my French.

After taking the written test, which extended over two or three days, I looked around Washington for temporary employment to tide me over until winter, when the results of the exams would be known. I applied at several places. Ironically, two offers came through on the same day. One was the position of clerk-typist in the State Department's Far Eastern Bureau. The other was a job as a copyboy on the *Washington Evening Star*. The choice mattered little to me, so I flipped a coin. It came up copyboy.

The *Star*, a family-owned property which called itself Washington's hometown newspaper, was the biggest and most prestigious of four dailies serving the Washington metropolitan area at that time. Politically, it stood between the liberal *Washington Post* and arch-conservative *Times-Her-*

*ald*, an affiliate of Col. Bertie McCormick's neanderthal *Chicago Tribune*. The fourth daily in town was the tabloid *Daily News*, a Scripps-Howard paper. (Of the four, only the *Post* survives today.) While paying some attention to the White House, Congress, and other federal power centers in Washington, the *Star* focused more on the local news of Washington and suburban Maryland and Virginia. From its busy third-floor newsroom in a wedge-shaped building on Pennsylvania Avenue in downtown Washington, the *Star* dispatched legions of reporters to dig for news not just in the courts and police stations but also in the neighborhoods.

The Star's intense interest in neighborhood news (mostly as seen through the eyes of the city's white property owners) was such that even the lowliest of copyboys (no girls were hired for this work in those days) had an opportunity to participate. Thus, in addition to our ordinary daytime duties of sorting mail, carrying messages, and fetching coffee and cigarettes for the reporters and editors, I and the dozen other copyboys were given a chance to practice reporting and writing on our own at night. As cub reporters working on assignment, we covered meetings of the city's myriad "citizens' associations," a network of neighborhood improvement groups. Returning to the newsroom after a meeting, we would compose our stories under the tutelage of an assistant city editor who served both as teacher and editor. A patient assistant editor named Norman Kahl taught me my first tricks of the trade.

Editors and readers, I soon learned, like a snappy lead that focuses on specifics or teases the imagination:

> Spring has brought a colony of ticks to Brentwood Terrace.
> Told that wooded patches in the area are "infested" with the pests, the Brentwood Terrace Citizens' Association last night passed the warning on to residents of the community. The group will ask John W. Batson, Superintendent of the Trees and Parking Division, to send tick experts and spraying equipment as soon as possible....

> The Metropolis View Citizens' Association has taken steps designed to safeguard its area in case of war and at the same time to provide refreshments for next season's meetings.
> Last night the association decided to appoint block leaders who will form the nucleus of a civil defense system in the area in case of an "emergency."

Pending the emergency, the block leaders will have the duty of persuading more members to pay their dues so the association will have a refreshments fund by October....

Looking for an angle that would please Norman Kahl and guarantee the story a prominent headline and good position in the paper, I sometimes overreached. A reader clipped the story about the Metropolis View Citizens' Association's plans for refreshments and World War III, and sent it to the *New Yorker*, which reprinted the first paragraph with this comment: "It pays to look at the whole picture."

Determined never to come home from a meeting empty-handed, I learned to contrive an acceptable report even when nothing had happened:

> For the first time in at least 21 years the Chillum Heights Citizens' Association has failed to meet for the lack of a quorum.
> Olaf P. Solem, president, referred to the group's long record, as he blamed last night's low attendance on the cold weather and on sickness in the neighborhood....

At bottom, the business of the citizens' associations went well beyond tick infestations, civil defense, and twenty-one-year quorum records. These were organizations of white citizens living in the racially segregated District of Columbia. The *Star* gave voice to their campaign of resistance to the encroachment of blacks into white neighborhoods. (No coverage was given to the meetings of black neighborhood groups.) In our stories we copyboys did what we could to highlight the racism of the citizens' associations.

> Herbert P. Leeman, president of the Federation of Citizens' Associations, said last night his group has a plan to "upset" the transfer of Central High School to the use of colored students.
> He told the Citizens' Forum of Columbia Heights the aim of the Federation is to persuade members of Congress to withhold Central High School appropriations in favor of funds for a new junior college for white students.
> But the success of the plan can only be temporary, Mr. Leeman cautioned, unless Congress passes the Kefauver home rule bill, which provides for an elected Board of Education.

> He said the present Board of Education, in voting March 8 for the transfer of Central High School, had demonstrated its incapacity to serve the "better interests" of Washington....

Toward the end of 1949 a letter from the State Department brought the disappointing news that I had flunked the Foreign Service exams and would have to try again another year. I decided to make the most of what had begun as an accidental alternative career. Working on my own time and hoping to attract the notice of higher-ups, I began originating stories for the *Star*. The key to doing this successfully, I soon discovered, was coming up with fresh angles on topics of current interest, such as the rising tide of anticommunist hysteria then coming to a crest in Washington. One such article began:

> A former ambassador to Russia charged last night that "dupes of Soviet propaganda" are doing the work of Russian agents in the State Department...

In July 1950 I received my first byline. It was for a story about the National Art Gallery which began with a tip from a friend of my mother who copied paintings there. More by-lined stories followed. I soon learned that the secret to success in this business was to find stories that had strong human-interest themes or evoked nostalgia.

One story of note concerned a hassle over a statue of Abraham Lincoln removed from a Washington park by order of Congress but later restored to its base as a result of strenuous citizens' protest. The article, accorded a place of honor on the Sunday editorial page on November 4, 1950, might soon have liberated me from the confines of the newsroom copyboy pen and assured me a future as a reporter on Washington's hometown newspaper. But it proved instead to be my last hurrah at the *Star*. On the day it appeared I had already left the newspaper, never to return.

On June 25, 1950, a front-page headline in the *Washington Star* proclaimed the outbreak of the Korean War, an event that was to have profound consequences for me. Rejected for military service in World War II, to my deep disappointment, I had buried that wound and moved on with my life. In time, the sting of physical rejection no longer mattered much to me. But suddenly an unexpected new war presented an unforeseen opportunity for redemption. At twenty-three, I was still of draft age.

Through the summer of 1950, as the fighting raged up and down the Korean peninsula, and as the long-suspended military draft creaked back into operation at home, I waited to hear from my new draft board in Washington. In August came the letter I had hoped for— an order to report for a physical examination. The following month I found myself in shorts and socks in a line of prospective draftees at the U.S. Army Recruiting Main Station in Arlington, Virginia.

Was it possible that this time the Army would overlook the congenital eye defect that had kept me out of World War II? I made up my mind that this time I would do more than just hope and pray.

The physician who shone his flashlight into my eyes was a young man not much older than I. As he moved the light beam to and fro, peering into my cornea, I asked him, straight out, to give me a break.

"The coloboma doesn't bother me at all," I told him. "I can see just fine."

"You mean you want to *go into* the Army?" he asked, looking puzzled.

"Yes."

He paused, made a notation, and told me to move on. I remained in suspense until a few weeks later, when a notice from the draft board informed me that I had been reclassified from 4-F to 1-A. I could hardly believe my good fortune.

Not until the late afternoon of November 1, when, after a second physical examination, I raised my hand with other draftees in a formal induction ceremony at the Army recruiting station, could I be sure that my newly rekindled hopes would not be dashed. Miraculously, the great burden of rejection had been lifted. I was *really* in the Army. I felt great.

Thus began a two-year adventure into which I flung myself enthusiastically. I never got anywhere near Korea. Instead, the Army made me an "information specialist" in an infantry division bound for Europe. My engagement to Marian failed to survive the strains and stresses of separation. Indeed, it had never advanced much beyond puppy love. Following the euphoria of our first romantic encounters, about the time of my graduation from Swarthmore, Marian and I settled into separate lives in Washington—she as a teacher at the National Cathedral School and I as a copyboy, living nearby. We saw each other frequently, but it soon became apparent that our lives and our interests were in flux. I gave her a diamond ring, but we didn't set a wedding date. Our occasional talks about wedding and marriage plans seemed unreal to both of us. Friends sensed my indecision. Once, on a visit to my parents' retirement home in Virginia, my father and mother plunged headlong into the subject, urging in the strongest terms that the wedding be put off indefinitely. I resented their intrusion, but their arguments had an impact. By the midsummer of 1950 I knew that the marriage would never happen. The Army's unexpected draft call brought new uncertainties to our relationship and gave me an excuse for proposing indefinite postponement of the marriage. By the time I left for the Army it seemed clear to both of us that our engagement was doomed. On one of my first leaves home the following year we bade each other a passionate farewell.

In my two years of military service my enthusiasm for soldiering did not make me a good soldier. Untidy, disheveled, inattentive to such military niceties as polished brass and a clean rifle, I did not advance beyond the rank of corporal. But I remained grateful to the Army for having taken me in. My attitude made me a good military propagandist.

> CAMP PICKETT, Va., Dec. 23 — A big lump was in little newspaper carrier Eddie Green's throat yesterday when the troops stood retreat here at Camp Pickett.
>
> Twisting his cap, he stood on a barracks-lined parade ground and looked nervously at the soldiers of the 169th Antiaircraft Artillery Automatic Weapons Battalion, assembled to pay special tribute to him. It was the Christmas season; it was the eve of furloughs for many men, and besides, the troops felt it was time to show they thought Eddie was a pretty swell boy.
>
> Eddie, a 10-year-old third-grader, has five brothers and sisters in nearby Blackstone. He is the youngest member of a small band of newspaper carriers who get up at 4 o'clock in the morning to deliver papers and then come back to camp at night to deliver afternoon papers to the troops of the Forty-third (Victory) Division and other units stationed at Camp Pickett.
>
> Since September, when this National Guard unit was federalized, Eddie has been hustling about 100 papers every day into a dozen mess halls in the divisional artillery area. Through the mud and snow he comes, and some sad times, when the troops are called out early or kept late in the field, he has a lot of unsold papers to carry back.
>
> Yesterday the officers and men of the 169th AAA said "thank you" and "come again" with a $10 bill and a brand-new bicycle....

From the snows of Camp Pickett to the budding woods and fields of northern Virginia, and from the scorching heat of a Mojave Desert tank training center to the autumn rains of Hampton Roads, my army career took me from one adventure to another. I belonged to a small headquarters detachment, composed mainly of young newspaper reporters plucked out of civilian life—Ed Donlon of the *New Haven Register*, Dale Taft of the *Providence Journal-Bulletin*, John Praksta of the *Philadelphia News*, Luther Sigsbee Miller of the *Charlotte Observer*, Alphonse Normandia of the Madison Avenue advertising agency of Batten, Barton, Durstine & Osborn. Our mission was to turn out news releases glorifying our infantry division, commanded by an ex-coal dealer from Hartford, Connecticut. The officer in charge of our unit, Captain Thomas E.J. Keena, a civilian-soldier from the editorial staff of the *Hartford Courant* was a military version of my old Canadian scoutmaster. He tried to be a soldier but felt more at home in the company of his men with a six-pack than a rifle.

With other members of the 43rd Infantry Division public information office, I wrote human interest stories about Army life. We mailed them off to newspaper editors eager for news from the training camps.

In October 1951 came an ocean voyage. A ditty composed by a fellow soldier captured the excitement we felt. I had been ordered to Germany with my unit to stem what our government called the tide of communism. The words of the song went:

*Augsburg, Augsburg,*
  *Ach, what a wonderful town;*
*We're glad we're here*
  *Mit der schnitzels and beer,*
*The music goes round and round....*

We sang the song on the troopship that carried us to Europe and on the train that transported us to the Bavarian towns and cities where we would be taking up duties for our remaining year of military service. In the following months we sometimes sang it for the amusement of German friends who welcomed us into their homes as a new breed of troops that had come not as conquerors but as defenders.

For the most part, we were off on a lark, enjoying a European vacation at the taxpayers' expense. But some of us also fancied ourselves as the vanguard of a new force that would transcend the narrow nationalisms that had plunged the world into the bloodiest war in history. Our new idea was the North Atlantic Treaty Organization—NATO. We felt good about it.

AUGSBURG, Dec. 18 (Special)—Soldiers of the 43d Inf Div are sharing this Christmas with almost 4,000 German children from the homes, orphanages and refugee camps of central Bavaria.

The youngsters are trooping to parties in the division's Bavarian kasernes in groups of 50 to 700.

Many soldiers, meanwhile, have been invited to German homes during the Yuletide....

In the fall of 1952, a hardened "combat correspondent" about to be rotated home, I filed my final story for the *Grape Leaf*, the division newspaper I had edited for much of my army career.

The soldier rubbed a pair of reddened, sleepy eyes and peered up into the darkness.

"What's happening here," he grumbled. "Don't you guys ever go to bed?"

It was a cold, misty morning, two days after the start of "Exercise Equinox." The soldier was a member of a surprised and beaten "aggressor" unit—and he was paying reluctant tribute to a 43d Div outfit which had proved it pays to get up early in the morning....

Looking back on my two years in the Army, I see it as a psychological healing process for me, a restoration of my self-esteem. In later years, especially after the onset of U.S. military involvement in Vietnam, I came to look upon the draft and military service in quite a different light. I came to view the military and militarism as perhaps the greatest of all threats to humanity. But, despite that, I still treasure the sense of belonging, the feelings of solidarity and companionship, that buoyed me in my Army years.

As one who experienced the sense of community that can accompany military life, I understand the emotional spell that military values still hold over many in my generation who wore the uniform during World War II and Korea.

Mustered out of the Army at Fort Ord, California, at the end of October 1952, I began my job search in the San Francisco Bay area, where my parents had settled a few months earlier after selling their retirement farm in Virginia. I had the right to return to my old job as a copyboy at the

*Washington Evening Star*, but, with a scrapbook full of clippings in my duffel bag, I figured I could do better than that.

The Associated Press hired me as a cub reporter in its San Francisco bureau and put me to work on odd jobs: rewriting stories from the metropolitan papers, covering the news beat at the federal courthouse and state supreme court building, and preparing scripts for the AP's radio news wire.

I loved the work, and I wanted more. Energetic, unattached, and anxious to get ahead, I beat the bushes on my days off for stories that would put my by-line on the Associated Press national wire. With encouragement from management and rewrite help from the AP Newsfeatures desk in New York, these efforts produced results.

> SAN FRANCISCO, Aug 8 (AP)—"Here I go—P.J."
>
> That cryptic message, scrawled in chalk on the curb of San Francisco's Golden Gate Bridge, added the name of a graying old man to the lengthening log of those who have sought death and found it in the churning water 220 feet below.
>
> The bridge has been a top tourist attraction since it was opened to use in 1937. But it has also proved an attraction to suicides. At least 126 have slipped over its side for the three-second plunge, to hit the swirling tide at 80 miles an hour....

> SAN FRANCISCO, March 16 (AP)—Wanted: One dozen practical psychologists, willing to work up a daily sweat, and able to bang out "Shave and a haircut, two bits" on the gong of a bouncing cable car.
>
> That's the unofficial way the recruiting department of America's unique municipal transportation system—the San Francisco cable cars—states its manpower requirements.
>
> During the next year the law of averages will reduce the staff of operators by 10 or 12. The city wants replacements who will be true to a spirit of transportation that goes back 80 years....

By the time of the cable car gripmen's appearance on the AP's trunk wire I was long gone from the San Francisco scene—transferred to a remote outpost of the far-flung wire service. My willingness to do stories on my own time had created a union-management issue at the San Francisco bureau. I was more interested in experience and recognition than in the money. Unprepared to assign me to feature stories because of my fledgling status, or to pay me for such work, the AP nevertheless accepted my free-lance stories and put them on the wire. The American Newspaper Guild, which represented reporters and editors in the office, including me, quite rightly objected. The assistant bureau manager, Paul K. Lee, who had encouraged me, was in a pickle. Loathe to cool my ardor or to nettle the Guild still further, he arranged to have me transferred to a town where the union was not so strong. On a crisp autumn morning in October 1953, after an overnight journey by rail and road, I stepped off a bus at Boise, Idaho.

For the next three years I was one of the three AP reporters who covered the news of that vast, sparsely populated Rocky Mountain state from a small office in the capital, feeding endless stories to the dozen or so widely scattered member newspapers and radio stations in Idaho. In those days almost every state office—from the Governor on down—was housed under the dome of the Capitol, just a couple of blocks from our office. Every weekday we scoured the Statehouse and checked our other news sources—the state police, the political parties, other sectors of the establishment—for stories large and small. We practiced formula journalism:

> SILVER CITY, Idaho (AP)—William J. "Willie" Hawes, 79, is the mayor, councilman, police chief, fireman, postman, dog catcher and general handyman of this southeastern Idaho mining town, once a thriving metropolis of the old west.
>
> He holds every public office in the community. He has to, because—though thousands of miners once lived here and dug a fortune from the surrounding hills—Hawes is now the only permanent resident....

> BOISE, Idaho (AP)—Orville Casey can give you a quick answer to one of the burning questions of the 1955 State Legislature—the question of whether the lawmakers should meet longer and more often to get their legislative duties done.
>
> If Casey had his way, they'd be in session 12 months a year.
>
> Casey, 55-year-old blind concessionaire in the Statehouse, has been doing a booming business since the legislators came to town in early January....

One of my mentors in Idaho was Thomas B. Aden, who, as Associated Press correspondent, supervised the Boise bureau. Recognizing my flair for words, Aden assigned me to pore through Idaho's sixty-odd weekly newspapers in search of humorous material for the AP wire. I soon found that the best of the weeklies—a half dozen or so—were gold mines for satire. My efforts evolved into a weekly AP column, "Idaho Oddities," which ran in almost every newspaper.

Five-year-old Davy Coski had no scheduled part in the annual Alpha Grange party in Cascade but he managed to steal the show anyway.

Seated among the guests, Davy piped up in a loud, clear voice, "Grandma, is President Eisenhower here tonight?"

"Why no," replied his grandmother, Mrs. Edmund Kerby. "Why do you ask?"

Davy pointed a finger at John Redmon of Cascade and asked: "Well, then, who's that bald-headed man sitting over there?"

*　　*　　*

John Long of Salmon hurried into the office of the *Recorder-Herald* to cancel the advertisement offering his truck for sale.

"Sold the truck already?" asked the advertising manager.

"No," Long replied. "I just wrecked it."

*　　*　　*

Officers of the Pershing school PTA in Rupert say it'll be a long time before they again try the "market basket project" as a means of raising contributions. The PTA put three baskets into circulation. The first person was supposed to put food or money into the basket and pass it on to a friend. Eventually the baskets—laden with food and money— were to be returned to the PTA. There's only one thing wrong—all three baskets are missing.

Idaho is a conservative state, dominated then, as now, by mining, ranching, and lumbering interests; by banks, utilities, and powerful cor- porations, by the conservative Mormon Church. Idaho's politics in the 1950s were epitomized by those of the self-made rancher and automobile salesman Len B. Jordan, who occupied the governor's office when I arrived on the scene. A fiscal conservative, Jordan believed in holding the line on state services and giving private enterprise full rein. He was an ardent supporter of Idaho Power Company in its successful campaign to build three hydroelectric power dams in the Hells Canyon gorge of the Snake River between Idaho and Oregon. As an Associated Press reporter covering Hells Canyon and other stories of major political and social impact I had to be neutral and "objective," keeping my liberal notions to myself. But I hoped that my reporting at least would provide fodder for editorial dissent.

BROWNLEE DAMSITE, Idaho (AP)—One year after an historic and controversial legal decision sent them into the nation's deepest river gorge, workmen were blasting huge new contours Thursday in the jagged walls of Hells Canyon.

By the end of next week they expect to complete the first major engineering step in the construction of three dams for Idaho Power Co.—the diversion of Snake River through a 2,550-foot tunnel.

Unless lawyers can stop them in the meantime they'll be far enough along a year from now to place new obstacles in the way of public power advocates who'd prefer to see a federal dam in the canyon....

BLACKFOOT, Idaho (AP)—Drive down a shady residential street on the south side of Blackfoot and you'll come upon a cluster of cream-colored buildings amid trees and lawns. It's a quiet scene, as tidy as a college campus.

Five or six elderly women are sunning themselves on the benches. A man is mowing the grass and another is clipping the hedges.

Perhaps you will notice a nurse in starched white uniform.

This is State Hospital South—the home of some 800 men and women under treatment for mental disorder, from the mildest type of personality quirk to more severe forms of brain disease.

This is the institution which won recognition from the American Psychological Assn. last year as one of the most progressive mental hospitals in the nation.

And this is also the place where multitudes of human beings for years were systematically tortured, starved and neglected—and sometimes beaten to death—in filthy, foul-smelling dungeons.

It was just 10 years ago Thursday that the citizens of Idaho took the step which was to break a link with the past and put Blackfoot on the road toward sane treatment of the so-called "insane"....

The bulldozers in Hells Canyon, the turmoil at State Hospital South, and other stories hinting at Idaho's underlying social problems had whetted my appetite for investigative reporting. But my stories for the AP were peripheral or historical treatments that just nibbled at the edges. I longed to probe deeper and become more personally involved than Associated Press standards would permit. I would soon get my chance.

# 7

# The Lewiston Morning Tribune

One Sunday afternoon in the fall of 1955 I looked up from my typewriter in the Associated Press bureau in a corner of the *Idaho Statesman* newsroom in Boise to examine a sheet of paper placed on my desk by a *Statesman* editor. "Here," he had said, "it looks like a story for you." What I found was a news release written by an organization of deaf people at a picnic in a Boise park. It contained a statement calling the superintendent of the State School for the Deaf and Blind a thief.

In those days it was the custom of the *Statesman*, Idaho's most influential newspaper and probably its most profitable, to depend on the Associated Press for coverage of significant news in its own community. ("That's what we pay you people for," said James L. Brown, the newspaper's despotic general manager, who employed one of the smallest news staffs in the state.) So it fell to me, as the only AP reporter on duty that day, to judge the newsworthiness of this item.

Ordinarily a news organization like the AP would look askance at a diatribe against a public figure scribbled in longhand at a Sunday picnic. Especially one that accused the official of criminal wrong-doing. But this was not an ordinary situation. The school superintendent, Burton Driggs, had been under fire for weeks from organized deaf and blind groups all over the state. They accused him of running a substandard educational program for Idaho's blind and deaf children. With charges and counter-charges flying almost daily, the controversy had become a running story, reported by both wire services and all the state's newspapers.

Scanning the news release in search of something fresh, my eyes fell on a passage accusing the superintendent of using public resources for his own purposes. It sounded vague. I wondered what it meant. I thought of trying to contact the authors for an explanation, but they had left no telephone number and, after all, they were deaf; it might be hard to get an answer. Mulling the matter over, I decided to take a chance. The accusation seemed general enough to be safe. Little time remained for further reflection because of the approaching 6 p.m. deadline for the southern Idaho edition of the *Salt Lake Tribune*, which had taken an interest in the controversy. So I went to the teletype machine and banged out a story. It was a mistake.

Next day I learned that a member of the deaf club had come to the AP office after my departure and had retracted the statement on the insistence of Burton Driggs. The AP killed the story—but too late for the *Salt Lake Tribune*, which went to press with my libelous account. Later the superintendent sued the newspaper for $100,000 and settled out of court for $15,000. It was a painful lesson for me.

The libel suit was not the only damaging fallout for me from the controversy over the State School for the Deaf and Blind. Idaho's newly elected governor, Robert E. Smylie, sensitive to pressure he was getting from the organized deaf and blind groups over the school issue, accused me of "scurrilous reporting" on his behind-the-scenes meetings with the protesting groups. It was a groundless accusation, but the governor's complaints and continuing hostility came to the notice of my superiors in Salt Lake City, further dampening my career prospects with the Associated Press.

My troubles with the AP doubtless could have been surmounted had I chosen to persevere. I liked the life of a wire service reporter—the fast pace, the wide variety of stories to be covered, the opportunity for travel. I welcomed the challenge of having to produce clear, coherent, and sometimes complex copy under fierce deadline pressure. While I was never as fast as some AP reporters, I could write as well as most of them, especially feature stories requiring extensive research. I was energetic and ambitious. As I had done earlier at the San Francisco bureau, I dug up feature stories in Idaho for the national trunk wire. I hoped some day to be transferred to the AP Newsfeatures desk in New York. That was home base for an elite group of AP writers who produced "in-depth" stories from around the country. But by 1956 my life was entering new waters. In addition to my frayed relations with the AP high command, a couple of considerations were impelling me to sink roots in Idaho. One was the pull of an unusual newspaper in northern Idaho which promised professional and political fulfillment unavailable to me at a news service such as the AP. The other attraction was a budding romance.

I first met Kathleen Hammond on my news beat in the Idaho Statehouse. A schoolteacher who had become administrative assistant to the state superintendent of public instruction, Alton B. Jones, she was friendly and helpful to me, as she was to other reporters covering the Capitol. I knew her initially only as a good news source. She had an easier way with the press than her boss, who was inclined to be overly protective of his public image. One day, in May of 1955, making my Statehouse news rounds, I found Alton Jones' office staff in a state of shock. Kathleen's husband of only a few months, Wendell Sims, had died in his sleep of a heart attack.

It was not until the following year that Kathleen and I began meeting socially. What brought us together was my discovery that she was a crypto-Democrat in a Republican office. I learned this when she called me one day at the AP office to inquire about the arrival time of Adlai Stevenson, the Democratic candidate for President, then planning a campaign swing through Boise. After our first date I brought her into my social circle of party-going singles and young couples. Following a whirlwind courtship I proposed marriage to her on a trip to introduce her to my parents in California in the fall of 1956. (They gave their unstinting approval.) We set the wedding for the following March, and a few weeks later I left the Associated Press to join the staff of the *Lewiston Morning Tribune* in Lewiston, Idaho.

The road from Boise to Lewiston is 185 miles of twisting, bucking pavement chiseled from the pine-scented canyon of the Payette River and the great, bare cliffs overhanging the mighty Salmon. In the 1950s, before bulldozers straightened out the kinks, the road spiraled like a corkscrew from the Salmon River gorge up Whitebird Hill to the deep black soil of Camas Prairie, rich with wheat and peas and lentils, then plunged down the western face of the prairie into the deep canyon of the Clearwater River as it rushed to meet the Snake. I traveled that spectacular road for the first time, like a migratory bird, in response to a pull that began tugging on me soon after my arrival in Idaho. I wanted to see the *Lewiston Morning Tribune*.

A liberal young Easterner exiled to a political and journalistic Siberia, I had begun to suffocate in the stodgy, monotonous conservatism of Idaho politics and journalism. My lifeline to sanity as a journalist and political liberal had become the *Tribune*, and in particular its managing editor and editorial writer, William F. Johnston, who went by the initials BJ. In three years with the Associated Press in Boise, the highlight of my workday had come to be my lunchbreak with the *Tribune*, absorbing BJ's gift for marshaling facts and arguments in editorials that cut like a beacon through the timid, pallid, conforming crowd-mindedness that characterized the rest of the Idaho press.

A big, football-playing, elk-hunting, backwoods intellectual who had won his spurs as a student editor at the University of Idaho, where he led a campaign to break the social and political power of the Greek-letter fraternities, BJ had been the voice of the *Tribune* since 1949. In the 1950s his was one of the few journalistic voices raised in Idaho against the anticommunist smear tactics of its two United States Senators, the blatant antiunionism of its corporate barons, the neglectful policies of its public agencies toward the weak and the poor, the readiness of its pliant state officials to turn over public resources for private exploitation.

While other mainstream editors and politicians in Idaho stood by in silence or joined the witch hunters in the era of red-baiting Senator Joseph McCarthy, BJ let them have it with both barrels:

"Honest, sincere citizens have succumbed to the totalitarian theory that the way to combat ideas they don't like is to put people in jail. They have borrowed this page of the Communist handbook to fight Communism. They have discarded the oldfashioned American notion that every idea must compete freely on its merits in the market place of public opinion if free citizens are to decide freely what is the truth.

"Well, I'm not buying any part of it. Thomas Jefferson said it well enough for me:

"'I swear on the altar of God eternal hostility to every form of tyranny over the mind of man.'

"In my book that covers the McCarthys, the Jenners and every self-appointed thought policeman up and down Main Street of Lewiston. If you think this means I have 'something to hide' go ahead and turn me in to Jumpin' Joe."

I loved it.

It was also BJ's editorial voice, going to the heart of matters, that seemed always to invest meaning and purpose into our reportage from the capital—the fight over Hells Canyon dam, the growing crisis in social services, the dreary, laissez-faire policies of the Republican administration in Boise. From afar, his insights made sense and lent thrust to our work. I found myself writing more and more with BJ and the *Tribune* in mind.

When I drove into Lewiston for my first visit in the summer of 1954, expecting to encounter an Idaho version of the *New York Times*, I found the managing editor hunched over his typewriter in an office barely larger than a broom closet, with room for just one visitor to squeeze in. In the adjacent newsroom, filled with the clatter of editors and reporters, someone had nailed down a sheet of plywood to cover a hole worn by a chair leg through the rotting floorboards. It was to these humble premises, in a town of less than 12,500, that BJ had drawn one of the most talented news staffs in the Pacific Northwest.

At thirty, well launched on a career pointing toward investigative reporting with a liberal political flavor, I was in search of kindred spirits. I was to find them in BJ and others at the *Tribune*.

BJ was more than a social critic and defender of the downtrodden. He was also a builder of projects he and others, including me, viewed as important to the welfare of the region his newspaper served. As a reporter and editor at the *Tribune*, I became a warrior in campaigns, orchestrated by BJ, for dams on the Snake River to give Lewiston merchants a route to the sea, for a highway over the Bitterroot Mountains into Montana to bring truckers and tourists into Lewiston, for a national park to celebrate the proud regional heritage of Chief Joseph and the Nez Perce Indians. BJ's insistence on full and fair reporting of these economic and political issues of regional importance won respect and credibility for the *Tribune* with power brokers in the U.S. Senate and elsewhere in Washington. It was part of the secret of his success.

"I have found that most of these people are very public spirited," he once wrote. "Through their contacts with newsmen they are likely to get the feeling that the press is inclined to grill. An aggressive press may be proper in Washington, D.C., but sometimes this attitude filters all the way down until the lowliest cub reporter feels it is his duty to make a United States Senator prove he isn't a son of a bitch.

"I have found that these people appreciate and reciprocate a show of genuine courtesy on the part of a reporter, a sincere attempt to get at the facts."

When I arrived in Lewiston at the end of 1956 to begin my seven-year stint I found that the beacon lit by Bill Johnston was not standing there all by itself. It rested on solid rock built by the editor and publisher, A.L. (Bud) Alford, whose father and uncle had founded the newspaper in 1892.

Great editorial writers like Johnston can't exist in a vacuum. The courage and enlightenment of an editor count for little unless they are matched by the courage and enlightenment of a publisher willing to risk the full resources of the newspaper when it becomes necessary. Alford never wavered from this responsibility, not even when, in the early 1960s, the local pulp and paper company, Potlatch Forests, Inc., with resources far in excess of those of the *Tribune*, levied huge economic reprisals against the newspaper because of its editorial positions. The *Tribune*'s editorial opinions, he said, were not for sale. Not only did he understand the need for independence and forthrightness on the part of those who wrote for the *Tribune*; he insisted upon it.

Alford amassed the biggest news staff of any newspaper in the state and drove it unmercifully in a daily search for what a proofreader, Phyllis Budweg, once described as Moby Dick, the great white whale: The Perfect Newspaper.

With the aid of a prodigious memory, a copious datebook, and clippings from other newspapers which he read far into the night, he would produce daily assignment lists so long and so detailed that veteran newsmen who occasionally wandered into the *Tribune* employ were rendered numb with shock.

A meticulous reader of his own newspaper and a critic who would tolerate no failing or excuse, Alford vented his feeling in a daily "gripe sheet" that was the terror of the *Tribune* newsroom. In its pure form, the gripe sheet consisted of a private memorandum to the managing editor couched in unrestrained invective:

"Pls fire whoever proof-read the John Jones obit. And pls get me the original copy, galley proof and page proof on this sty."

More often, though, the gripes contained enough corrective matter and constructive suggestions to permit the managing editor to draft an expurgated version for the benefit of the staff.

A shy man to whom the spoken word did not come easily, Alford used the gripe sheet as a release from the agony of his private passion. Some good staffers quit the *Tribune* because of those little yellow memo pages that bristled with the Alford prose. Others allowed such things to kill their initiative and stifle their sense of devotion to the ideals of self-reliance and resourcefulness which Alford himself respected above all others. The best of the *Tribune* reporters came to recognize the gripe sheet for what it was: a love song to a newspaper.

It was a love song that others shared. You heard it in the stories the staffers would tell about the old boy over their beer mugs at Bojack's after the paper had been put to bed for the night, or when Bud himself, two sheets to the wind, would roll home with his reporters from one of those frequent staff parties.

The *Tribune* attracted gifted and dedicated reporters from all over the country. Jack Wilkins gave up a lucrative job as a Revere Ware salesman in upstate New York to join the staff as a beginning reporter and stayed on to become the *Tribune*'s most sensitive writer on Indian affairs. Mel Snow quit in despair after his first day on the job, let BJ talk him into giving it one more day, and stayed twenty-five years. Hal Hollister, a convicted murderer, got a second chance from BJ and became an outstanding outdoors writer. We were a family. We celebrated our togetherness at late-night bull sessions in the M.E.'s office (reading Bud Alford's secret gripe sheet) after the paper had been put to bed, at all-night poker games with the typesetters and engravers in the back shop, and at good-by parties where, with BJ and Bud Alford in the chorus, we would sing farewell ditties to staff members departing for better paying jobs in the big cities:

> *There once was a guy named Al Booze,*
> *Whose language was rich and profuse:*
> *"Goddamit," he swore,*
> *"Sure I cuss like a whore,*
> *But Christ how it sweetens the news!"*

Al Booze was a crusty, colorful cuss from North Carolina who was sometimes relieved on days off by Ladd Hamilton, a gifted writer and editor who took the job less seriously. Ladd liked to sail through an eight-hour shift on the wire desk in half that time, using the extra hours to catch up on his reading. One day Al Booze returned to work to find that Ladd, in his carefree way, had put the wrong crossword puzzle in the paper the night before. Struggling, sweating, and cursing Ladd Hamilton under his breath, the wire editor composed an editor's note for the next day's paper that went something like this:

"The crossword puzzle that appeared in yesterday's *Tribune* was actually intended for today's newspaper. Today's puzzle was supposed to have appeared yesterday. The solution to today's puzzle is in yesterday's paper. Today's solution is for the crossword puzzle that will appear tomorrow...."

Al's tortured explanation continued for several sentences, piling confusion on confusion. The next day Ladd Hamilton clipped the editor's note, submitted it to the *New Yorker* as a humorous item, and received a check for $25.

I loved every aspect of the *Tribune*—the ink-stained walls and rotting floorboards of the decrepit building where we worked, the aroma of lead ingots melting in the pots of the Linotype machines, the hustle and bustle of the newsroom, the crisp finality of the page proofs coming off the ink-roller, the heft and solidness of the newspaper as it streamed off the press at 4 in the morning, the sense of community that came from the praises and complaints of readers. I was like the kid skidding his bicycle with his playmates on the gravel driveway in Johannesburg, the Boy Scout at camp in the Canadian woods, the private-first-class on bivouac with his buddies in a Bavarian pine forest.

Our years in Lewiston were an idyllic time for me and Kathleen, newly married and swept up in the excitement generated by a lively newspaper in a small town. The *Tribune* reporters and spouses accepted Kathleen immediately into their tight social circle. She also joined the local League of Women Voters and became its president. Both of us wanted children. The arrival of the first of our three sons, Philip, on February 4, 1958, brought me joy as his father and rekindled an empathy with my own father, then ten years into his retirement and free of the strictures and formalities of diplomatic life. He was baking his own bread, tending prune and apricot trees on his acreage in the Santa Clara Valley south of San Francisco, building cribs in his garage workshop for the growing numbers of his grandchildren. In Lewiston, we moved to a larger house to make room for our second son, Sam III, who arrived on January 30, 1961, and the third, Josh, born November 14, 1962.

I was never as close to the children as was Kathleen. The newspaper was still my universe. But on days off we explored the forests and mountains of the rugged Clearwater country in our Volkswagen bus, big enough to sleep two children simultaneously while the third perched on the seat next to the driver. We climbed the twisting gravel road to the rim of Hells Canyon, listened to the roar of white water on pebbles in the tumbling Clearwater, slept on the white sand beach of the Lochsa River in the awesome silence of the cathedral-like cedar grove preserved by the Forest Service in memory of Bernard DeVoto.

The interaction with my own three sons and concern for their future deepened and strengthened my empathy with children generally. This was soon to find expression in my newspaper work. I had already developed a reputation as an investigative reporter good at exposing problems in the public arena. I had also made friends and contacts in state government. One of them, Carl Moore, a state legislator, tipped me off one day in the spring of 1960 to a scandal at a state institution for the mentally retarded called the Nampa State School and Colony. The superintendent, a Syrian physician named Sheryl S. Humsey, had resigned, sending a lengthy bill of grievances to the state health director in Boise.

"You should see that place," Carl Moore told me, referring to the crowded and understaffed mental institution. "And you should get hold of Dr. Humsey's report. I hear it's dynamite." A week or so later, while in Boise with my family to visit Kathleen's mother, who still lived there, I introduced myself to Dr. Terrell O. Carver, a progressive young public health physician then beginning a distinguished career as state health director. I told him I'd like to read the Humsey report and visit the institution.

"Be my guest," he said.

My story took up more than a hundred column-inches in the Sunday section of the *Lewiston Morning Tribune* of May 1, 1960. It began:

> The doctor paused for a moment in the hallway, gazed through a wire screen at a row of iron beds in an otherwise empty room, and said:
>
> "Not a very pretty picture, is it?"
>
> It isn't.
>
> The boards of the bare floor creak and sag underfoot. Cracks line the ceiling. The walls are scarred by crevices and holes which expose the crumbling red brick beneath the plaster.
>
> Save for the beds and a few rough wooden benches, no furniture, no decorations grace these rooms. The stark outlines of the hallway are relieved only by a row of stone slabs with wooden handles—implements which are used for polishing floors.
>
> A dank smell pervades the building and a strange sound is present—a blend of cries, snorts and murmurs which one associates with the sound of animals, in a zoo.
>
> In a sense the noises are indeed the sounds of animals. They come from the throats and aimless shufflings of sixty men and boys—residents of the Nampa State School for the mentally retarded.

Until a few days ago, when they were moved to safer quarters downstairs, these ugly walls were the horizons of their world. Locked doors barred them then, and still bar them now, from an outside world in which they can play no part.

Nature has been cruel to these unfortunates, the most severely retarded of the school's 781 residents. Unable to speak, unable to bathe themselves, unable in many cases to wear clothes, unable to comprehend, they must be cared for like beasts.

But, unlike animals, they are defenseless. They must be protected from their fellow men, from each other and from themselves.

As the physician, Dr. F. O. Graeber, acting superintendent of the school, was touring these grim premises, a white-shirted attendant, Ira Pea, drew his attention to blood marks on the floor.

The blood had spilled a few moments earlier when a patient, eluding the watchful eyes of attendants who patrol the wards twenty-four hours a day, worked his fingers into a wall, pried loose a strip of metal reinforcement and thrust the metal up his nose....

The memory of that blood-stained floor at Nampa has stayed with me. My story about the state school went on to describe the shocking conditions—helpless children inhaling flies from the nearby school farm; near-normal children forced to remain in jam-packed, fire-trap dormitories for lack of social services outside the school; governors and legislators turning a deaf ear to the institution's repeated pleas for adequate funds. The story pointed a finger at Idaho's amply funded public welfare agency—the State Department of Public Assistance—for washing its hands of responsibility for Idaho's mentally retarded. The expose attracted the attention of social workers concerned about the lack of state services not only to the mentally retarded but to all neglected, abused, and dependent people in Idaho, particularly children.

From Nampa, the journalistic trail led to the state's two privately operated children's homes, both struggling unsuccessfully to do a job assigned by law to the publicly funded Department of Public Assistance. I wrote a five-part series about the plight of the children's homes. From the children's homes the path led to the juvenile courts, the state reform school, the county jails, and other agencies and institutions attempting to fill the void in child welfare services normally provided out of state welfare budgets.

As engineers and reclamationists and government insiders had come to BJ, feeding him and the *Tribune* staff the insights and information needed for editorial crusades for new dams and highways and national parks, so the social workers and clinical psychologists of Idaho came to me in 1960 and 1961 with the fodder for an editorial campaign to improve Idaho's child welfare services.

Always my investigations wound up at the door of the Department of Public Assistance, and in particular its long-time director, Bill Child, a fiscal conservative who believed it was better to spend no money at all than to risk spending it unwisely. My stories exposed the impact of the director's austerity policy on private and public social agencies overburdened with the problems of dependent children. Placed on the defensive, Bill Child came out swinging, accusing his detractors of trying to foist "Communist ideas" like foster care on Idaho's children. His futile counterattacks led to more exposures, including revelations that he had returned as unneeded $187,597 in federal funds (a large sum for a poor state) allocated to Idaho for child welfare services. "We see no point in squandering the money on senseless program activities," he said.

The upshot of the campaign was the establishment by the 1961 state legislature of an investigative commission which proposed sweeping reforms, subsequently enacted into law. For my part in helping bring about reform I received distinguished reporting awards from the Idaho Public Health Association and the American Political Science Association.

By the end of 1963—at the age of thirty-seven—I was ready to move on from Lewiston. The *Tribune* had given me seven years of training, experience, comradeship, community. I had tried out all the chairs—from police beat to sports to rewrite to Sunday section to city desk to occasional stand-ins for the managing editor—and found all to my liking. I had also tried my wings and learned to fly as a muck-raking journalist, liberal activist, and crusading editorialist. But this was a small family newspaper and there was no room at the top for me. I wanted to become an editor in my own right.

# 8

# Rocky Mountain Radical

The town of Salmon, Idaho (population about 2,500), is a cattle ranching center nestled between the Bitterroot and Lemhi mountains near the headwaters of the Salmon River, Idaho's famed "River of No Return." Almost a full day's drive from a city of any size (Boise to the south, Idaho Falls to the east, and Missoula to the north), it is as remote as any town of its size in the continental United States. The people there seem suspended in time and space, untainted by the outside world. That's one reason I found it satisfying as a newspaper town.

Accompanied by our three children, aged five, two, and one, Kathleen and I arrived in Salmon in our Volkswagen bus on a snowy afternoon in January 1964, following the path of the moving van that hauled our furniture the 500 miles from Lewiston. We were welcomed at the front door of our new home (a rental house not much bigger than a cracker box) by the manager of the country weekly I had been hired to edit.

Several months earlier I had decided to strike out on my own from the *Lewiston Morning Tribune*, where for seven years I had been a reporter and protege of William F. Johnston, the newspaper's dynamic managing editor. Casting around for a weekly newspaper where I could try my wings, I looked first at the *Hailey Times* in the Wood River Valley near fabled Sun Valley. It was a good newspaper in an attractive, even cosmopolitan region. The owner and publisher, a feisty country editor named

Berwyn Burke, was in declining health. I went to visit him, wrote him letters, hoped to talk him into taking me on as an assistant with an option to buy. Burke dickered with me for a while, then referred me to his brother Ronald, who owned a weekly newspaper to the north. Ronald Burke knew the printing business well and kept a sharp eye on the books, but he preferred to leave the editing to others. When a vacancy occurred toward the end of 1963 he hired me as editor of the *Salmon Recorder-Herald* and then drove off with his wife, Mae, to spend the winter in Arizona. I settled myself gingerly into the editor's chair. Taking my cue from a motto left on the wall by a former editor, "Be sure brain is in gear before putting mouth in motion," I promised in my first editorial to look and listen before sounding off on matters close to the citizens of Lemhi County. I also set forth some editorial principles distilled from my years with Bill Johnston and the *Lewiston Morning Tribune*:

1. It is the idea that counts, not the personality. There is a vital difference between the challenging of an idea and personal criticism of the one who espouses it. But often that distinction is blurred, both by the critic and the one criticized. The free-for-all of criticism is a necessary proving ground for ideas, particularly in the arena of public affairs. Inevitably, ideas will become intertwined with the egos of their authors and advocates. It is a poor and dishonorable critic who aims not at the high-flying idea but at the vulnerable ego astride it.

2. There is no substitute for accuracy. This is as true in editorials as in the reporting of news. Inaccuracies in news stories are usually the result of human frailty—perhaps the laziness or haste of the reporter or his inability to penetrate the barriers erected by a news source. But in an editorial the inaccuracy is more likely to be there on purpose. It arrives in the heat of argument, summoned in desperation to do a job that logic has failed to do. Lots of editorials, like lots of arguments, are full of lies.

3. Be fair to the other side. No good rule is more consistently violated than this one. No devious device is more frequently resorted to than that of the "straw man," in which the critic misrepresents an argument in order to demolish it. Any idea, especially an unpopular one, deserves to be set forth fairly, accurately and in its best dress. To fail to do this is to give in to a genteel form of mudslinging.

4. Be ready to change with the facts and with the times. Ideas are important, but they are not holy. None is written across the sky in letters of gold. Few are too precious to be abandoned for the sake of a better idea. An editorial writer, like anyone else, is entitled to a point of view. But beware of the writer who thinks too highly of his point of view. He is in danger of becoming transfixed, incapable of growing with experience, an interesting old fossil.

When the publisher hired me he said I could write the news and editorials without interference. But my first issue of the *Recorder-Herald* brought a constitutional crisis. It stemmed from a meeting of the parent-teacher association which turned into a shouting match over the issue of raising money for the municipal swimming pool. Observing me taking copious notes, a PTA bigwig asked to see my story before publication. When the business manager showed her a galley proof she asked that the story be toned down. I refused, and the manager telephoned the publishers in Arizona for advice. They backed me up. There were to be other such power plays, none successful, during the remainder of my tenure at the *Recorder-Herald*. But from then on I felt free to "tell it like it is" in Salmon. And the readers loved it.

Through the winter and into the spring of 1964 I covered the news of Salmon and the adjacent area. I sat through school board and city council meetings late into the night, dug through records in the county courthouse, interviewed the politicians and ranchers and merchants who ran the town, and, camera in hand, followed the volunteer fire department into the smoke-filled rooms of burning buildings. On Thursday mornings, when the paper went to bed, I helped the press crew by rolling, gluing, and addressing the "single-wraps" to be mailed to subscribers in distant places. In Lemhi County, *everyone* read the *Recorder-Herald*. Over the next day or two I would sit back and savor the reaction.

Editing the *Salmon Recorder-Herald* was a journalist's dream. I was virtually the only reporter in town—the only one in hundreds of miles. I had the newspaper entirely to myself, with a blank check from the absentee owners to edit the news as I saw fit. I waged frequent battles with bureaucrats of every stripe accustomed to thinking of the public's business as their private affair. The Salmon school board would put off some agenda items until after midnight in hopes that I would be gone by then, leaving the members free to conduct school business in private. ("Howcum we're spending $250 on a fancy typewriter?" I once heard a member ask the school superintendent. "The money comes out of the school library fund," the superintendent explained. "If we didn't spend it on the typewriter we'd have to spend it on books.")

The local funeral director often complained about my insistence on interviewing surviving family members in preparing obituary stories, claiming that this put needless stress on the bereaved relatives. (Later I learned that the real stress was to the funeral director himself, whose practice it was to include a charge for the newspaper write-up as part of his funeral bill.) Lawyers and court clerks tried to hide the records of divorces and other cases they wanted kept out of the newspaper. The local Idaho Power Company manager tried to have me fired for exposing the company's silent sponsorship of a local "grass-roots" petition campaign opposing public power in the region. But, with backing from Ron and Mae Burke, I brushed past those roadblocks.

In a face-lifting that brought the *Salmon Recorder-Herald* a shelf-full of press association awards the following year, I spruced up the musty old make-up of the paper and splashed the pages with photographs, feature stories, catchy headlines, and breath-taking coverage of the Salmon Savages, winners of the state's Class A high school basketball championship for 1964. I also filled the editorial pages with my pet notions— voting rights for blacks, recognition of the People's Republic of China, greater financial support for public education—soft-headed liberal views my readers were willing to tolerate so long as I continued to give them the news the way they liked it. For me, this mountain-locked country weekly provided a lively introduction to newspaper editing. But it soon became apparent to Kathleen and me that this was not the kind of place where we could sink our roots.

A poor town in an economically deprived area, Salmon had many social problems. None was more intractable or discouraging than the poor quality of education in the public schools. It forced the departure of many people—teachers as well as parents—who would have preferred to remain in Salmon to enjoy the area's peace and quiet. Some residents of the community dealt with the problem by denying it. But it became more difficult to sweep the matter under the rug after the school board president stunned the community by announcing that he, too, had decided to leave for the sake of his children.

In May of 1964 I covered a kindergarten graduation for fifteen Salmon children, including our son, Philip, six:

"I'm a little teapot
  Short and stout;
Here is my handle,
  Here is my spout.
When I get all steamed up
  Hear me shout:
'Just tip me over
  And pour me out.'"

The sound of little voices echoed through the Salmon Methodist Church Wednesday for the last time until fall as graduation came for Mrs. Bruce Raffety's kindergarten class.

A roomful of mothers and a sprinkling of fathers attended the graduation program. They heard the teapot song, Ten Little Fingers, The Billy Goat Gruff, Hickory Dickory Dock, Little Peter Rabbit and other selections.

Mrs. Raffety has conducted the private, five-day-a-week school since fall. Wednesday's class was the last for her, since she and her husband, a high school biology teacher, plan to leave Salmon this summer.


The following issue brought a news item that, along with the school board president, the kindergarten teacher, and unnumbered others for whom greener pastures beckoned, the newspaper editor and his family would soon be leaving the Lemhi Valley. I liked the town and I loved the sense of community that the newspaper gave me with its inhabitants, but the humdrum sameness of small town newspapering was not what I wanted for a career. After only eighteen weeks, still sounding a lot like William F. Johnston, I bade farewell to the readers of the *Salmon Recorder-Herald*:


A newspaper worthy of the name can be sure of a life of struggle. There is the battle against the self-appointed censors and managers of the news, against officialdom in and out of government which regards the public's business as its private business.

Of battles there are plenty, but the function of a newspaper is neither negative nor destructive. The newspaper which willingly takes on these battles can make a priceless contribution to the region it serves. It holds up a mirror to its community. If the newspaper has done its job well, the image will be one in which the community can recognize itself and take pride.

A few weeks after I first set foot in Idaho in the fall of 1953, a stranger, I happened by chance to attend the ceremonies surrounding the opening of the state's first television station—KBOI-TV in Boise. An aunt and uncle from Salt Lake City, good friends of the station manager, had been invited to the opening ceremonies as special guests. It was through them that I met H. Westerman Whillock, founder of KBOI, a hard-driving radio and television entrepreneur ambitious to make his mark in Idaho. A successful businessman, former mayor of Boise, and a Harry Truman Democrat, Whillock wanted to break the vise-like grip held on the region by old guard Republican business interests. He also saw his communications enterprise as an alternative to Boise's daily newspaper monopoly, the *Idaho Statesman*, which for years had dominated the politics of the city and state. During my years with the Associated Press at Boise and the *Lewiston Morning Tribune* in northern Idaho I developed a cordial relationship with Wes Whillock and his growing radio-TV news staff, which by the late 1950s exceeded that of the *Statesman* in size and quality.

As part of the expansion of his empire and sphere of influence, Whillock, with two associates, acquired a local weekly newspaper, the *Boise Bench Journal*, in hopes of developing it into a statewide political newspaper. For several years the *Boise Journal*, later rechristened the *Idaho Observer*, sputtered along from week to week, an odd mixture of local business listings (real estate transfers, bankruptcy filings, etc.), editorials of a liberal Democratic stripe, and investigative stories dug up by energetic KBOI reporters anxious to see their work in print. (Dwight Jensen, a TV reporter and prodigious writer who edited the *Journal* for a while, sometimes would write as many as three or four by-lined columns and stories for the same issue.) Even though heavily subsidized by the radio-TV station, the struggling weekly had failed to get off the ground by the spring of 1964, when Whillock decided to look for a new editor. That was when he called me at Salmon.

In May of 1964 our family of five packed up for the second time in five months and moved to Boise. I plunged into the job of running a newspaper, which meant not just the challenge of filling the news space but also the more difficult task of finding enough advertisers and subscribers to pay the bills. There was always the KBOI subsidy to fall back on, but my goal from the start was to make the *Observer* economically self-sufficient.

It wasn't easy. We were an unknown political rag struggling for identity and recognition in a big city controlled by media giants many times our size. The Boise merchants and advertising agencies scorned us because of our politics and our pitifully low circulation—barely 500 paid subscribers. An early circulation director, Nancy Bokich, managed to double the readership through energetic telephone promotion. But still we were too small. (One year, hoping to lure new readers, we folded a horse racing tip sheet into the newspaper and gave away thousands of copies at the track.) But nothing would be possible economically until the *Observer* could find its editorial voice.

In the first few years I practiced the lessons I had learned at the *Lewiston Morning Tribune* and modeled the paper on other political journals I found interesting. One was the liberal Democratic *Texas Observer*, published in Austin by Ronnie Dugger, which offered a yeasty mixture of social muckraking and political comment. Another model was a weekly political journal published in Pocatello, Idaho's second largest city, by a fellow journalist I greatly admired. The *Intermountain*, lively and irreverent, reflected the politics and personality of its owner and publisher, Perry Swisher, a gifted writer and speaker a few years my senior. Swisher, a man of many talents, operated a book store and served in the state legislature in addition to putting out the *Intermountain*. A Republican elected from a Democratic stronghold, he was to the left of me on some issues. (Under the leadership of Robert E. Smylie, serving his third term as governor at that time, the Idaho Republican Party was generally more liberal than the Democratic Party on state issues.)

Setting out to make the *Observer* a Democratic equivalent of Swisher's *Intermountain*, I and our other writers plugged the Great Society, Medicare, and other elements of President Lyndon Johnson's domestic agenda. We went after Barry Goldwater, the John Birch Society, and other right-wing causes that found favor in this conservative state. Picking up some old themes from the *Lewiston Morning Tribune*, we campaigned for a stronger tax base, a bigger state budget, and better social services for Idaho's poor, her unemployed, her neglected, her sick and disabled. Our team of political reporters and commentators began to jell during Idaho's tumultuous electoral year of 1966, when my boss, Wes Whillock, lost a bid for the Democratic nomination for governor; when Smylie was upset in the Republican primary by a little-known, arch-conservative state senator; when Perry Swisher jumped into the race as an independent, and when the Democratic gubernatorial nominee died in a plane crash, leaving the party badly divided on a successor. The resulting victory of right-wing Republican Don Samuelson plunged Idaho into four years of political chaos.

In the Samuelson era we fulfilled Wes Whillock's vision for the *Observer*. We were an up-and-coming liberal Democratic alternative to conservative Republican media domination in southern Idaho. Week after week we mined the Samuelson Administration for exposes (in higher education, in the mental hospitals, in the state penitentiary, everywhere) and for juicy political tidbits. Reporters from the daily newspapers tipped us on stories that they themselves weren't free to run; we assembled a galaxy of political columnists, including the governor's defeated predecessor, Robert Smylie. We treated art as hard news and gave it major attention.

In the fall of 1967 a merger with Perry Swisher's *Intermountain* gave us a new name, the *Intermountain Observer*, and greatly strengthened our circulation throughout the state. In the late 1960s the *Intermountain Observer* regularly swept the annual awards competition of the state's weekly newspaper association and came as close as it would ever come to achieving economic self-sufficiency. But the late 1960s also brought deep changes in American politics that left an indelible imprint on the newspaper.

Nowhere was this more evident than in the Idaho Democratic Party. In the spring of 1972 I wrote in the *Observer*:

> A white-haired, close-cropped Boise attorney, veteran of many a Democratic political gathering, turned toward a fellow delegate in Sun Valley's convention center last weekend with a look that lay somewhere between bemusement and despair. "You'd think this was an OB-gyn clinic," he said.
>
> The young woman at the microphone was deep in a discussion of the effect of birth control pills and other contraceptive devices on the female reproductive system. The crowd listened attentively, sipping its beer, as her argument moved from placenta to ovum and from physiology into public policy.
>
> And when she was done, and the thunderous voice vote recorded, the Idaho Democratic Party had added another plank to its 1972 platform, a platform as novel and breath-taking—and as upsetting to some—as any political document ever put together in this state.

Obstetrics and gynecology were only part of the action at this year's biennial gathering of the Idaho Democrats, a party which, like its Republican counterpart, is accustomed to talking the familiar language of tourist promotion, industrial development, farm price supports and other traditional political concerns of a small rural state.

In addition to calling for repeal of Idaho's anti-abortion statute, the Democrats of 1972 blew the trumpet of reform in virtually every area of government they could think of.

Abolition of the death penalty. Amnesty for those who have refused the draft. Revision of the Idaho constitution. Withdrawal from the Vietnam war in ninety days. Elimination of the federal highway trust. Help and support for bicycle riders. Conjugal visits for prisoners. Support for the farm workers' organizing efforts. No non-union lettuce at the convention banquet.

Long before the short-lived ascendancy of radicalism in Idaho's Democratic Party electoral process, the *Observer*'s attention had begun to drift away from the party and the process. To some Democratic politicians we continued to give unstinting coverage and support. One of them was Cecil Andrus, whom I had known and liked since his entry into politics in the late 1950s and who, as a state legislator from northern Idaho, had championed liberal reforms that interested me as a reporter and editorialist for the *Lewiston Morning Tribune*. (I assisted him in his first successful gubernatorial campaign in 1970; later he was to become Secretary of the Interior under President Jimmy Carter, then governor again in the 1980s.)

The other Idaho Democrat who received our unwavering support was Frank Church, first elected to the U.S. Senate in 1956. Church's early opposition to the war in Vietnam, beginning in 1965, had a profound effect on me. I read his first speeches on the war, studied them, printed them verbatim in the *Observer*, and let them guide me out of the Cold War liberalism that had framed my own political thinking since college days. My support for Church and other Vietnam "doves" put a strain on my relationship with Wes Whillock, an ex-Navy captain and ardent supporter of the policies of President Lyndon B. Johnson. (In a heated exchange with me one day on the sidewalk outside the KBOI building in Boise, the hot-tempered TV executive referred scathingly to Idaho's senior senator as "a god-damned yellow-bellied chicken.")

Through the 1960s the *Observer* remained liberal in its politics and reformist in its approach to social problems. We investigated and reported on injustice and oppression wherever we could find it. What separated us from other newspapers was our willingness to trust ordinary people caught up in the news (as distinguished from "objective" professional reporters) to tell the news in their own way. Lacking the money to employ trained reporters, we sought out the victims of injustice and oppression, gave them some guidance, and let them do their own thing in the pages of the *Observer*. Thus, students wrote about the problems in the schools, prisoners about the penitentiary, welfare mothers about welfare problems. In an award-winning feat that drew national attention, the *Observer*'s longtime assistant editor, Alice Dieter, organized a citizens' task force which roamed the classrooms, cafeterias, and playgrounds of the Boise school system, writing eyewitness reports that filled a special issue of the *Observer*. With the help of Ed Eline, editor of the prison newspaper at the state penitentiary, we organized and published, to the consternation of many sheriffs, an inmate survey of conditions in Idaho's forty-four county jails. Another nonprofessional reporter, Pete Henault (an Argonne National Laboratory scientist and avid naturalist), took his camera to an eastern Idaho church-sponsored "rabbit drive," in which hundreds of animals were herded into pens and clubbed to death by teen-agers swinging baseball bats. His story and photographs, published in the *Observer*, created a furor which deluged the legislature and governor's office with protests from around the world.

With Alice Dieter and other women a driving force in the life of the *Observer*, our newspaper developed an early sensitivity to feminist issues. When a group of women, all of them our friends, liberated a round table traditionally reserved for male lawyers and politicians in the main dining room of the Hotel Boise, the *Observer* leaped on it as a major story. Strong women made us an early voice for feminism in Idaho. We also sought out, interviewed, and raised the issues of gays and lesbians in Idaho at a time when few had yet come out of the closet.

No matter what the subject, we dug below the surface of the news, reveling in our reputation for "afflicting the comfortable and comforting the afflicted."

In March of 1969 there came an event that set the *Intermountain Observer* and its staff, including me, on a new course. We came to refer to it later as "the mother-fucker story." It arose from my coverage of a symposium at the University of Idaho in Moscow honoring the memory of "the Lion of Idaho," William E. Borah, who made international waves as chairman of the Senate Committee on Foreign Relations in the 1920s. The annual Borah Foundation conferences ordinarily were dry affairs where scholarly papers were presented and debated. But that musty tradition had been shattered in 1968 when, with the Vietnam war as its theme, the symposium was turned into a forum for bitter criticism of the war, a battleground for hawks and doves. Now, in 1969, with war protests again threatening to take center stage at the symposium, Governor Don Samuelson was putting heavy pressure on the Board of Regents to cancel the university's invitation to one of the more controversial speakers, Tom Hayden, a founder of the militant Students for a Democratic Society and soon to be indicted and tried with others of the "Chicago Seven" for conspiracy to disrupt the 1968 Democratic National Convention.

The governor's attempts and the regents' refusal to keep Hayden off the platform dominated the media's advance coverage of the symposium—to the exclusion of other issues and speakers. Hayden made note of the controversy in his opening remarks, calling the governor a fool and a clown and saying his efforts were part of a nationwide attempt to stifle dissent on university campuses. A similar situation had arisen earlier in Iowa, Hayden told the crowd. On that occasion, as he described it, a university dean who aspired to the university presidency lost favor with the state legislature for failing to put a stop to Hayden's speech at the university. At that point, I quoted Hayden's words in my account of the Borah symposium that appeared in the next issue of the *Intermountain Observer*:

> "I said mother-fucker this and mother-fucker that, and he didn't get up and grab the microphone and tear out the wiring. That killed his chance for the presidency."
>
> Hayden's language didn't seem to shake the University of Idaho audience of 1,200. As the day wore on, the question of four-letter words and their significance to the New Left became one of the minor themes of the symposium. Some of the speeches were liberally salted with shit, bullshit and fuck. All were broadcast live over KUID-TV to an audience estimated by Dr. Gordon Law, university communications director, at 20,000. He says he has received no complaints.
>
> Another speaker, Philip Luce, who is an arch-rival of Hayden, picked up the challenge.

"Pig! Pig! Pig!" he said. "Mother-fucker! Mother-fucker! Mother-fucker! That sure solves a lot of problems! They're just playing with you a little."

The New Left's four-letter words are like the New Left's political slogans—just a lot of talk to gain attention, said Luce. He denounced the movement as a fraud and said Hayden couldn't even lead a revolution against a public utility if his life depended on it.

The term scarcely raises an eyebrow nowadays, but the printing of "mother-fucker" and similar expressions (in lieu of some innocuous paraphrase) was a daring step in those times for a mainstream newspaper such as ours. Even though the naughty words were buried deep in a long story dealing seriously with the role of rhetoric in the youth rebellion, I knew there would be repercussions. And indeed there were. In the ensuing weeks a couple of dozen readers sent us letters of outrage, some cancelling their subscriptions. But we were unprepared for the full brunt of the storm.

A few days after the appearance of our March 22nd issue, Boise's flamboyant, right-wing sheriff, Paul Bright, long an antagonist of the *Observer*, asked the county prosecutor for a warrant for my arrest on charges of violating Idaho's obscenity laws. He was joined in this by the Boise police chief. The prosecutor refused to take action but said he might reconsider if the offensive words continued.

The sheriff's challenge, duly publicized by us and other newspapers, transformed an internal debate about propriety in the use of language into a highly public First Amendment controversy that gripped much of the state. The debate raged for weeks in the letters section of the *Observer* and in the editorial columns of other Idaho newspapers, almost all of which came to my defense. It also brought the *Observer* national attention and many more subscribers. The episode exposed me for the first time to the threat of prosecution as an editor and activist. For the *Observer* as well as for me, the printing of those unmentionable words was an important psychological step. It marked a sharp and deliberate break with the norms of our profession. It identified us with and helped make us a part of the social rebellion then sweeping the country. It also signaled my own impending departure from the world of established journalism, ending a journey that had begun two decades earlier in the copyboy pen of the *Washington Evening Star* and came to full stride at the side of Bill Johnston at the *Lewiston Morning Tribune*.

In Idaho, as elsewhere in the United States, the youth rebellion that had washed over the college and university campuses was seeping down into the high schools by the late 1960s. Students wearing arm bands, peace symbols, and long hair (in the case of boys) were testing the limits of their freedom and encountering ferocious opposition from those in authority. We at the *Observer* backed the students all the way.

Speaking of the unruly students under his charge at Borah High School in Boise, principal Richard Nelson told an audience in 1969: "It is dangerous to let them think they know more than we do, because even if they are smarter, and they aren't, they haven't had the experience." To which I replied in an editorial in the *Observer*:

One of the most remarkable things about the current crop of high school seniors is that they really are smarter than their elders. The fact that so many school administrators and teachers seem to sense it, but are afraid to acknowledge it, may account for much of the uneasiness which has characterized the current academic year.

Youth alone cannot confer wisdom on a child, any more than experience alone can confer wisdom on an adult. The youngsters of today can make no blanket claim to wisdom. But the performance of the present high school generation, taken as a whole, suggests a degree of mental awareness which exceeds the level of those who went before them and have now come to power.

Never before in Idaho have so many high school students asked so many questions and come up with the right answers, groping their way through issues with which the adult world seems largely unconcerned. Issues of personal freedom at Boise and Pocatello. Issues of free expression at Borah and Twin Falls. Issues of free inquiry at Idaho Falls. Never before have so many students asked so many pertinent questions about the quality of the education they are offered.

In challenging the system which surrounds them, the students have done it peacefully, openly and in a spirit of reason and good humor. All too often, the adult response has been one of evasiveness and hysteria, backed by the ultimate resort to force.

The confrontation of youthful reason with adult violence has become a hallmark of our times, mirroring the larger conflict on many of the nation's college campuses. A society beset by the questions of the younger generation responds with evasions, and, when pressed, falls back on force.

Evidence that the spirit of challenge has seeped down from the college to the high school level is the best assurance that reinforcements are on the way for those who have done so much to shake contemporary America out of its lethargy. It is the best assurance that the pressure which American society is just beginning to feel, through its colleges and universities, will continue, and, hopefully, increase.

Only through the continuation of the unremitting pressure of a newer and wiser generation, spurred on by the idealism of youth, can the world perhaps be saved from destruction at the dead hands of the old. The experience in Idaho suggests, in a small way, that young Americans do have that wisdom.

In Idaho's university and college towns and larger cities, do-it-yourself newspapers of every kind were springing up like desert flowers in the early 1970s, many of them inspired by and modeled on the *Intermountain Observer*. These publication efforts often sprang from social movements rebuffed by the established news media—the regular student newspapers, the small town weeklies, the daily papers, wire services, and radio and television stations. In the state's two university towns the alternative papers put the established student newspapers on the spot and helped open them up to what had become a substantial shift in student views and tastes. Even some small town weeklies began running into competition from the alternative papers.

Elsewhere, social movements transcending geographical limits spawned several alternative publications, all politically radical. *Helping Hand*, produced by dissident Air Force personnel, served to focus public attention and media attention on GI peace activism at Mountain Home Air Force Base in southern Idaho during the waning years of the Vietnam war. *Sisterwoman* (later the *Feminist*) gave voice to the women's movement in Idaho. The *Compass*, a libertarian periodical, launched the political career of one of its three editors, Steve Symms, elected to Congress and later to the U.S. Senate, replacing Frank Church.

"Such flowers are like wildflowers which spring up, bloom for a quick day, then wither away," I wrote in one of my last stories for the *Intermountain Observer*. "The sparsity and mobility of Idaho's population afford insufficient soil for this kind of flora to sink its roots deep enough to become long established. But institutional establishment never was the purpose of the alternative press. It is enough that some of them manage to live long enough to scatter a few seeds."

In writing about the wildflowers I was also writing about us. The radical winds sweeping Idaho in the early 1970s were also radicalizing us. In our looks and lifestyles, in our actions and interests, and in our search for new forms of expression and community, we became a part of our constituency, which was soon to scatter to the winds. In time, we, too, went the way of the desert flowers.

Relations between the *Observer* and its parent company, KBOI, grew increasingly frayed during the years of mounting social protest in Idaho. They reached the final breaking point in 1971.

First came the Amchitka affair—an incident that shocked our owners as much as it did the rest of the Boise business community. The presence of our full staff—office manager Donna Griggs and circulation director Milton Jordan, along with me—in the line of blockaders on Capitol Boulevard certified the *Observer*'s culpability. Then, a few weeks later, came the distribution of *Helping Hand*, wrapped inside the *Observer*, in solidarity with our Air Force brethren, resulting in my expulsion from Mountain Home Air Force Base.

It was now abundantly clear that the *Observer* and KBOI had reached a parting of the ways. The radio-TV station readily agreed to sell the newspaper for one dollar to a group of staff people and subscribers who were ready to go it alone. With enthusiastic promotion by Milton Jordan, the group raised $30,000 in shares. It seemed like a tidy sum at the time, but our nest egg lasted barely a year and a half.

Fully independent and financially on its own, the *Observer* continued to "tell it like it is" and to do its thing in Idaho. Circulation continued to grow, reaching a peak of 4,000 by the fall of 1973, but the newspaper failed to attract the advertising that was necessary for survival. Our cash reserves dwindled steadily. In late September of 1973 one of our faithful subscribers, Supreme Court Justice William O. Douglas, heeding our cry for help, flew to Boise to address a fund-raising rally. But it was too late. A few weeks later we decided to call it quits. Our farewell editorial appeared on October 20, 1973:

> The *Intermountain Observer* is suspending publication with this issue. We do so with regret but also with the satisfaction of knowing that we tried our best until the very end. We simply ran out of money.

It might have been possible to continue another month or even another year. But the newspaper's financial resources have dwindled to the point where the directors felt that to do so would be imprudent. Our efforts of the last few weeks to secure new financing for the paper went far toward insuring its continuation as a strong and vibrant voice in Idaho—but not quite far enough. Rather than jeopardize the credit, quality and integrity that so many have struggled so long to protect, we decided to call it quits.

By retiring now, rather than risking the financial pitfalls which lay ahead, we may at least have left the way clear for others with the courage—and the money—to take up where we left off. It will take plenty of both.

We will leave it to others to write the epitaph of the *Intermountain Observer* and its predecessor publications. Suffice it to say here that the work of many hands went into those 23 years of effort. The paper brought many people together. It defined and shaped some important issues. It influenced journalism. It was not commercially successful, but in a larger sense it yielded a profit.

The principles which guided the *Intermountain Observer* bear restating now for what insight they provide into why the spirit may live on after the body has died:

We seek:

1. To provide a fair, accurate and interesting account of the significant happenings of our time, as perceived by a diverse, ever-changing and occasionally fallible family of contributors.

2. To be outspoken in our opinions and to keep our biases in plain view.

3. To be honest with ourselves, to acknowledge error and to be open to dissenting views.

4. To be accessible to those who do not enjoy ready access to other communications media and to do all in our power to help them say it in their own way, within the bounds of fairness and accuracy....

Our thanks and best wishes to all of you who shared the journey.

In the privacy of my bathroom at home I sobbed on the day we folded the *Observer*, shedding tears for the first time since February 4, 1958, when I had cried with joy over the birth of our first child, Philip. The death of the newspaper brought sadness but it also brought release. The years of newspapering in Boise had brought a coherence to my life, an integration of work and play in the context of struggle and resistance—joyful struggle and resistance in the company of others. I had probed beyond the comfortable camaraderie of the Army and the *Lewiston Morning Tribune* to a more encompassing solidarity rooted in political commitment and personal risk. And it was a community I had been instrumental in creating. Some bonds were frayed along the way—with old colleagues like Bill Johnston and with friends and family, even Kathleen. But in the process, for better or worse, I had found the pattern that would characterize my work and life for the remaining years.

After the paper was put to bed for the last time I took down the collection of trophies and plaques that had accumulated on our office walls over the years. I wrapped each one. Then, over the course of several days, I distributed these last physical remains of the *Intermountain Observer* to people who had invested much in the enterprise. I reserved the biggest and most important of the pieces for Wes Whillock, thinking he might appreciate it as a memorial to the newspaper of his dreams that had flowered for a brief period and then died in the street on the day of Amchitka.

I kept just one small piece for myself, knowing in my heart that in the years to come there would be other things to hang on the wall.

# 9

# Discovering Doomsday

**P**hysically preoccupied and emotionally drained by the myriad details of putting the *Intermountain Observer* to rest, I paid little attention to my own future until after the newspaper was buried. But friends looked out for my interests. One of them was Bryce Nelson, who had worked with me at the *Lewiston Morning Tribune* before moving on to the *Washington Post*, *Science* magazine, and the Washington office of Senator Frank Church. Now he was chief of the Chicago bureau of the *Los Angeles Times*. A man of many connections in journalism, he made inquiries in my behalf. One was to a friend and neighbor, Ruth Adams, who had long been associated with the *Bulletin of the Atomic Scientists*, a monthly magazine with offices in a chemistry laboratory at the University of Chicago. On a November morning in 1973 the telephone rang at my home in Boise. The caller was Victor Rabinowitch, a director of the *Bulletin*. Had I heard of the *Bulletin of the Atomic Scientists*, Rabinowitch asked, introducing himself, and was I interested in applying for the editorship?

The question took me aback. I explained to Rabinowitch that I was not a scientist and knew nothing about atomic physics. He was unfazed. In a long conversation he went on to tell me that the *Bulletin* was looking for a journalist, not a scientist. The magazine had been adrift since the death six months earlier of his father, Eugene Rabinowitch, who had been its guiding spirit since its inception in 1945. Now the managing editor,

Richard E. Lewis, had submitted his resignation and the magazine was in dire need of a replacement.

Giving Victor Rabinowitch a noncommittal response, I went to the Boise public library to take a look at the magazine. My first impression was discouraging. I found a dull academic journal laden with footnotes, impenetrable prose, and forbidding titles like "The Role of Antimatter in Big Bang Cosmology" and "International High Level Nuclear Waste Management." Groaning, I put the magazine back on the shelf, but then an earlier issue caught my attention. It carried a series of tributes to the late founder. One story in particular, by Ralph Lapp, a frequent contributor, sketched a sympathetic picture of Eugene Rabinowitch and his driving ambition to warn the world of the danger and consequences of nuclear war. I decided I liked Eugene's vision for the magazine. By mid-December I had visited Chicago for interviews with the staff and directors and had signed a six-month contract. (It turned out I was the only applicant for the job.) On a bitter cold January morning I set out with my family in our Volkswagen van and a rented truck on the 1,800-mile drive to our new home in Chicago.

The *Bulletin of the Atomic Scientists*, I soon discovered, was on the verge of financial collapse. The first thing I did as editor, out of necessity, was to lay off a third of the staff and cut my own salary by twenty per cent. The next thing I did was restore the name of the *Bulletin of the Atomic Scientists*, which a few months earlier had been subordinated to a new title, *Science and Public Affairs*, in the apparent belief that the nuclear threat was no longer salable to the public. I felt instinctively that the *Bulletin*'s link to its unique origin was its most important asset.

My first year at the *Bulletin* was a frenzy of desperate efforts to raise enough money to keep the door open, to initiate promotion programs that would arrest the ominous decline in circulation, to learn my way around the arcane world of arms control and nuclear energy, to find readable authors, and to package their material in a way that would interest a wider readership.

For all the frenzy, there was still time for me and others at the *Bulletin* to reflect and act on the fundamental purpose for which the magazine was founded by the scientists who built the first atomic bomb. In our first issue of the fall we reset the *Bulletin*'s famed "doomsday clock" that warns of the danger of nuclear holocaust.

For twenty-seven years the clock of the *Bulletin of the Atomic Scientists* has symbolized the threat of nuclear doomsday hovering over mankind. The minute hand, never far from midnight, has advanced and retreated with the ebb and flow of international power politics, registering basic changes in the level of the continuing danger in which people have lived since the dawn of the nuclear age.

Two years ago the minute hand was pulled back to 12 minutes to midnight as a consequence of the signing of the first arms control agreements which emerged from the Strategic Arms Limitation Talks between the United States and Soviet Union. This was an event which seemed to usher in a new era of sanity in superpower nuclear arms policies. In recognition that our hopes for an awakening of sanity were premature and that the danger of nuclear doomsday is measurably greater today than it was in 1972, we now move the clock forward to 9 minutes to midnight.

We do not thereby venture a prediction as to when, or even whether, a nuclear holocaust may come, or to imply that the likelihood of its occurrence can somehow be closely calibrated. We offer instead an assessment and a warning. Our assessment is that in these past two years, and in particular these past few months, the international nuclear arms race has gathered momentum and is now more than ever beyond control. Our warning is that so long as control continues to elude us civilization faces a growing risk of catastrophe....

The editorial went on to explain our reasons for concluding that the world had moved measurably closer to nuclear doomsday. The 1972 Strategic Arms Limitation Treaty (SALT), signed with much fanfare by Richard Nixon and Leonid Brezhnev in Moscow, had proved to be more cosmetic than substantive. Far from restraining the forces it was meant to curb, SALT had sustained and nourished them, providing acceptable channels for business as usual. New generations of nuclear weapons were coming off the drawing boards and going into production. Further, with the detonation of a nuclear explosive under the north Indian desert the previous spring, a sixth nation had joined the "nuclear weapons club." The willingness and ability of a poor Third World nation to cross this fateful threshold underlined the growing danger of worldwide nuclear proliferation. We also viewed with misgivings the decision of the United States, announced in June, to introduce nuclear reactors into the volatile

Middle East. Finally, we warned of dangers inherent in the industrialized world's increasing reliance on nuclear power without adequate safeguards against diversion of nuclear fuels for use as weapons.

The *Bulletin*'s deep concern about the nuclear arms race was something with which I felt comfortable from the outset. I knew about the issue of nuclear weapons and for years—going back to my days at the *Lewiston Morning Tribune*—had editorialized against each new monster weapon that rolled out of the military-industrial complex. I needed no persuading about the seriousness of the nuclear threat. I was, if anything, to the *left* of the *Bulletin* on this. I favored total nuclear disarmament over the more moderate "arms control" approach of the *Bulletin* and its allies in the liberal scientific community. I felt much less secure, however, on the touchier question of nuclear power, which was then surfacing as a contentious issue in the pages of the magazine.

From the beginning, the *Bulletin* had shared the hope of most atomic scientists that nuclear power would prove to be the silver lining of the dark cloud cast by the atomic bomb. Through the 1950s and '60s and into the '70s its authors—many of them veterans of the wartime weapons labs—beat the drums for "atoms for peace." But in recent times the magazine had come to be a forum for occasional dissenting views on the health and safety aspects of nuclear power development. Some of the magazine's directors and editorial advisors found such articles disconcerting, especially when they came from lesser known authors of uncertain academic reputation. I was frequently reminded that the *Bulletin* was not a "political" magazine.

As a reporter with long experience covering political news I had had enough contact with the atomic energy bureaucracy to recognize that nuclear power was an issue steeped in politics. The Atomic Energy Commission operated a vast nuclear reactor testing station in the eastern Idaho desert, and I knew of scientists and other workers there whose concerns about nuclear safety had systematically been stifled. A year before coming to the *Bulletin* I had read and reported on a series of illuminating articles in *Science,* by reporter Robert Gillette, about the Atomic Energy Commission's suppression of scientists' doubts about the adequacy of the emergency core cooling systems of nuclear reactors then going into production. I felt instinctively that the nuclear power safety issue was one to which the *Bulletin* should give primacy. But, unschooled in science and technology, I felt unsure of myself.

Help and encouragement came, however, from public-spirited scientists who shared my concern. One of these was Frank von Hippel of Princeton University, grandson of James Franck, a Nobel laureate who helped build the wartime atomic bomb and was one of the first to challenge its use as a conventional weapon of war. (With Rabinowitch and other scientists in the World War II Manhattan Project, Franck felt it would have been better to detonate the first bomb on an uninhabited Pacific atoll as a way of demonstrating to the Japanese that further resistance would be futile, rather than dropping it on a defenseless city. Their inability to advance this view in the councils of government was a principal reason for the founding of the *Bulletin*.)

With von Hippel and other scientists running interference, I plunged ahead on the nuclear power issue.

In the fall of 1974 the *Bulletin* editorialized against a mammoth Atomic Energy Commission reactor safety study—the "Rasmussen report"—intended to allay public concern about the risks and consequences of nuclear accidents. The AEC had concluded that a reactor accident more devastating than a flood or earthquake was unlikely to happen in a million years. We criticized the study as shoddy and self-serving. With help from young scientists at Princeton, M.I.T., and the University of California we launched a reactor safety study of our own and published a special report calling the policies of the Atomic Energy Commission into question. *Bulletin* writers joined voices with consumer advocates, environmentalists, physicists, and biologists in a rising chorus of doubts over the risks and benefits of this vaunted yet untried new technology. Friends in the scientific community helped me find science activists willing to challenge the official line of government and industry on nuclear power. The pages of the magazine began to bristle with their questions: How were future generations to be protected from the effects of radioactive nuclear wastes, some of which will remain dangerous for tens of thousands of years? How can the world live safely with nuclear power's deadly by-product, plutonium, a few pounds of which is enough to illuminate a huge city for a year or blow it up in an instant? When would society begin to make effective use of the nuclear reactor which already puts out more than enough energy from the safe distance of the sun, ninety-three million miles away?

At the end of 1976 I sought to console the *Bulletin*'s diminishing number of nuclear power enthusiasts with a tongue-in-cheek editorial column that looked on the brighter side:

91

To General Electric and Westinghouse, to Commonwealth Edison and Pacific Gas & Electric, to Exxon, to Kerr-McGee, Atlantic Richfield and other pillars of the nuclear establishment this must seem like an increasingly lonely world.

But all is not lost. Some may doubt and others may shrink, but there remains one place where support for the cause is undiminished. And it isn't just another corporate boardroom. It happens to be the headquarters of the international communist conspiracy.

When it comes to nuclear power, the Union of Soviet Socialist Republics is anything but revolutionary or conspiratorial....

The column went on to quote a long list of Soviet experts and officials extolling the benefits and safety of nuclear power.

Among those who were not amused, and who worried about the *Bulletin*'s growing skepticism toward nuclear power, was Hans Bethe, a Nobel laureate at Cornell University who chaired our blue-ribbon Board of Sponsors. Bethe, a colossus in his field of theoretical physics and a heavy-weight in science policy circles, had launched a crusade to drum up scientific support for nuclear power. Another nuclear power crusader in the *Bulletin*'s inner circle was Alvin Weinberg, director of the Oak Ridge National Laboratory and author of the notion that a "nuclear priesthood" was needed to manage the nation's nuclear power program. Bethe and Weinberg let it be known that they'd like to see a more responsible hand at the helm of the *Bulletin*. But I was only a symptom of their problem. The changing voice of the *Bulletin* reflected a sea change in public confidence in the safety and practicality of nuclear power as a major energy source. It was a tide that was to become irreversible, even in the Soviet Union, after the accidents at Three Mile Island in 1979 and Chernobyl in 1986.

Nevertheless I felt increasingly hemmed in by the conservatism of the *Bulletin*'s board of directors, especially after the all-consuming battle for survival was won in the summer of 1975 through the development of effective fundraising and circulation-building techniques. The directors were an assortment of scientists, professors, and business entrepreneurs, most of them attracted by the magazine's illustrious name and history. At the personal level they were supportive of me, for the most part, but collectively they seemed obsessed by the fear of being dragged into controversy. They wanted to keep the *Bulletin* above the fray, an Olympian dispenser of moral truths based on unassailable research and respectable scientific opinion. They were also plainly uncomfortable with editorials, articles, and actions that might cast the magazine in a political light.

On one occasion a majority of the board signed a letter to the *Bulletin* disavowing my criticism of the 1976 Israeli raid to free hostages at Entebbe—an action I cited as contravening the principles of nonviolence for which the *Bulletin* stood. On another occasion the board concurred in the magazine attorney's opinion that we should not join in subpoenaing surveillance records of a Chicago Police Department agency that had spied on us and other liberal organizations. The attorney said this might rock the boat, jeopardizing our federal tax-exempt status.

Sometimes, of course, I was in the wrong. Following our delivery from the financial shoals in 1975, and anxious to be rid of the day-to-day fiscal headaches that had plagued my life at the *Observer* as well as at the *Bulletin*, I hired an experienced publisher and gave him full authority in that field. What I didn't make explicitly clear to the board was that I had agreed to an incentive plan in which the publisher could earn a salary considerably higher than my own. When the board learned of this arrangement it caused me no end of grief.

In 1977, at the beginning of my fourth year as editor of the *Bulletin*, I asked myself a question: Should I remain at the helm of this world-renowned international journal that called itself "the conscience of the scientific community"? It was a good life in many ways. The magazine was growing and prospering. Its future seemed secure in a world that plainly needed to be reminded of the ticking of the doomsday clock. Our financial worries were over because we had learned how to tap the purses of our readers and the liberal grant-giving foundations. My own salary had become more than adequate. The job gave me entry to scientific gatherings and retreats all over the world, with the time and budget to attend them. I was in a position to follow the example of my predecessor, Dick Lewis, who had traveled the world and written several books while editing the magazine in his spare time. Day-to-day affairs were now in the hands of two competent lieutenants, managing editor Sue Cullen and publisher Jim Cahill, both of whom I liked and trusted.

I could afford to relax. I loved the hustle and bustle of Chicago, as did Kathleen and our three sons, then in their teens and attending public schools in Hyde Park, the upscale neighborhood that surrounds the University of Chicago. Our third-floor condominium apartment commanded a view of Lake Michigan. I was only a short walk from my office on the leafy, grassy university campus, where I was accorded faculty perks and privileges. At fifty, I could look forward to a prestigious conclusion of my career in journalism as an editor, writer, speaker, and recognized authority in the field of arms control—and to a comfortable retirement.

Had I chosen to be cooperative, the door was open for me to take that course. Kathleen would have preferred it. She enjoyed Chicago and Hyde Park even more than I. As administrative director of a Montessori school in the neighborhood, she had her own career to think about. We had a growing circle of friends in Chicago. Neither of us relished the idea of pulling up stakes for the second time in four years, for the fourth time in our married life.

Despite the amenities of the job, or perhaps because of them, I felt increasingly out of place at the *Bulletin*. I sensed a contradiction between the magazine's public image and its private character. Outwardly, to my mind, we were a voice of conscience calling on the world to put aside business as usual; we were the embodiment of Einstein's warning that, with the unleashing of the power of the atom, everything had changed except our way of thinking—and so we drifted toward unparalleled catastrophe. That was the *Bulletin* I wanted to portray to the world. But privately we were different. We were the embodiment of business as usual, leading pampered lives. As an institution we took no risks, we crossed no lines, we played it safe. We had made our peace with the Bomb. It bothered me that some of our directors and sponsors had lucrative ties—as corporate officers, advisers, researchers—with the military-industrial complex; that to them the women on our staff were errand girls; that the university which gave us a prestigious address was, like the *Bulletin* itself, a bastion of white male supremacy. I found myself suffocating in the intellectual elitism and social conservatism of the university and the magazine.

A nonscientist, uncredentialed, a hick from the sticks of Idaho, I remained ill at ease among the academics who ran the *Bulletin of the Atomic Scientists*. We had differing notions of the role and purpose of the magazine. And they outnumbered me. Midway through my term as editor the board of directors accepted my suggestion that we appoint a successor to Eugene Rabinowitch as editor-in-chief. He was Bernard T. Feld, a physicist at the Massachusetts Institute of Technology who as a young man had helped build the bomb that destroyed Nagasaki. Then in his sixties and still tortured with guilt over his role in the Manhattan Project, Feld had devoted his life to redemptive works, including long service on the *Bulletin*'s board of directors. With help from Bernard Feld and younger public interest scientists then coming into power in the *Bulletin* family, I could fend off editorial interference from other members of the board. But that support evaporated when a majority on the board challenged and overrode the terms under which I had hired the new publisher. Faced with an ultimatum to surrender business management of the magazine to the Chicago faction that controlled the board, I decided that this would effectively undermine my authority, reducing me to a mere functionary living off the reputation of the famous doomsday clock. So I turned in my resignation.

Like the *Observer* and the *Tribune* before it, the *Bulletin of the Atomic Scientists* was not to be my life's work. The magazine had given me a crash course in the scientific and technological issues underlying what is doubtless the most urgent problem of our time. I was grateful for that. But I had had enough of science and technology and academia. I wanted the freedom to dig deeply into the political roots of the problem. That led me to *The Progressive*, a preeminently political magazine published 140 miles away in Madison, Wisconsin. By the middle of 1977 I had made an agreement with the editor, Erwin Knoll, to join the staff of *The Progressive* the following year.

In December, in a farewell to readers of the *Bulletin*, I poured out my feelings about Eugene Rabinowitch's magazine and its unique role in the world:

> Thirty-two years ago this month the Atomic Scientists of Chicago, taking note of the anniversary of the nation's entry into World War II, issued an appeal to the American people to work for the establishment of international control of atomic weapons as a first step toward permanent peace.
>
> "Let us realize," they said, "that all we can gain in wealth, economic security or improved health will be useless if our nation is to live in continuous dread of sudden annihilation."
>
> The appeal served as the introductory editorial when the organization's magazine, the *Bulletin of the Atomic Scientists*, made its first appearance three days later. It has been repeated often in these pages. I recall it now, on the occasion of my own departure as editor of the *Bulletin*, because, for all its repetition, it remains a fitting farewell text.
>
> Elimination of the specter of nuclear war is still the most urgent business of mankind—no less necessary today than it was in 1945.

Indeed, the threat which seemed so overwhelming then has grown immeasurably greater.

The tiny collection of crude atomic bombs built with such great effort in the 1940s has become a vast, multinational arsenal of tens of thousands, some of them many hundreds of times more powerful than the weapon which obliterated Hiroshima. The lumbering, propeller-driven plane which took hours to deliver the first atomic bomb to its target has given way to intercontinental rocket systems that can do the job in minutes.

In 1945 there was only one nuclear weapons state; today there are six; tomorrow there may be 20. In those days, nuclear war-waging capability was little more than an abstraction; in these times it is a reality—imbedded in the political and military doctrines of the world's most powerful states.

The manufacture and delivery of nuclear weapons could once be accomplished only by mobilizing vast scientific and industrial resources and diverting them out of the economic mainstream. Now, three decades later, those resources are very much a part of an economic mainstream which steadily enhances the world's nuclear war-waging capability.

There is one danger which exceeds even the threats of the growing stockpile, the improved delivery systems, the increasing numbers of nuclear weapons states, the acceptance and refinement of nuclear war doctrines, the growing dependence on energy systems that lend themselves to nuclear violence. And that is society's fading perception of the danger.

The "continuous dread of sudden annihilation" foreseen by the atomic scientists in 1945 turned out instead to be an obliviousness which has increased in direct proportion to the increase of the danger. The passage of time dulled the memories of Hiroshima and Nagasaki. A whole generation grew up knowing no other world than one which has lived with the possibility of annihilation. It is as though the world, unable to find a cure, took a pain-killer.

The reawakening of society to its peril has become the primary challenge facing those who share the vision of the Atomic Scientists of Chicago. Until the fear and dread can be rekindled, it is unlikely that international control or any other social mechanism will put the danger to rest.

Nuclear war itself, of course, will rekindle the spirit. But it would be at a fearful price. Short of a holocaust, what can be done to bring the world to its senses?

It is my hope that the *Bulletin of the Atomic Scientists* will continue to play its part by finding imaginative, forceful and persuasive ways of scaring the hell out of people. It must retrieve the concept of nuclear violence from those who would sanitize it; it must continue to clothe the concept in its real garments of unimaginable death and destruction.

# 10

# Unfolding of the H-Bomb Case

At the end of 1977, as I was preparing to leave the *Bulletin of the Atomic Scientists,* I received an invitation to speak the following April at a meeting of a local peace organization in Crawfordsville, Indiana. I had no way of knowing it at the time, but the letter from Crawfordsville—and the encounter it produced—were the seeds of an epic First Amendment battle that was to dominate my brief career at *The Progressive.*

Fulfilling the Indiana engagement as managing editor of *The Progressive,* I arrived in Crawfordsville to discover that I had been pitted in a debate about the nuclear arms race with a high-ranking Department of Energy official from Washington. Charles K. Gilbert, deputy administrator of the Department's nuclear weapons program, proved to be a congenial antagonist. We treated each other graciously in our debate. After the meeting our hosts took us to a local tavern. We hit it off. Over a beer Gilbert readily agreed to my request for a tour of nuclear weapons factories.

As editor of the *Bulletin of the Atomic Scientists* I had visited and reported extensively on the Department's nuclear weapons laboratories at Los Alamos, New Mexico, and Livermore, California. I concluded that the rival labs, competing for contracts for new weapons designs, were a driving force behind the nuclear arms race. Now I wanted to take a look at other parts of the Department of Energy's vast industrial infrastructure—the nuclear weapons production complex—a maze of factories stretching from coast to coast. I had encouragement in this from Editor Erwin Knoll and others at *The Progressive* equally interested in raising nuclear weapons issues. From the beginning of the nuclear age the magazine had opposed each new step into the nuclear arms race. The year before my arrival in Madison the senior contributing editor, Sidney Lens, had written a landmark article, "The Day Before Doomsday," that helped re-energize and mobilize public sentiment against nuclear weapons and led to the creation of Mobilization for Survival, a leading advocacy group in the 1980s. In the spring of 1978 Knoll had begun work with Theodore A. Postol, an Argonne National Laboratory scientist to whom I had introduced him, on an article depicting the consequences of a hydrogen bomb burst over downtown Chicago. We were gearing up for a journalistic assault on the nuclear weapons establishment.

Preparing for my tour of the nuclear weapons production complex, I checked with several friends in Washington, one of whom directed me to an antinuclear activist in New Hampshire who he said had put together an interesting slide show on nuclear weapons. Starting my tour, I arranged to stop off on my way from Madison to Washington, D.C., at Logan International Airport in Boston for a short interview with the activist. That was my first meeting with Howard Morland, the free-lance writer whose story about the "H-bomb secret" was to lead to a legal test of our First Amendment rights.

Over coffee at an airport cafeteria, Morland showed me some sketches. I was impressed by his brief but earnest presentation of his ideas about how the design of a nuclear warhead could help illuminate such policy questions as cost, safety, and environmental impact. I also concluded that a penetrating investigation of nuclear weapons design and manufacture would require more time (and probably more skill) than was available to me.

From my first encounter with Howard Morland and our follow-up letters and meetings came the concept of a story that would deal with the issue of nuclear secrecy by challenging it frontally. I asked him whether, working as a reporter rather than as a spy, he could come up with a simple explanation, intelligible to the lay reader, of what might be the Government's deepest, darkest secret, such as, for example, the making of a hydrogen bomb. I saw the exercise as a dramatic way of exploding the secrecy mystique that intimidates the public, including the news media, from serious scrutiny of nuclear weapons policies and issues. Howard said he would try.

I continued my tour, visiting nuclear weapons production plants in Colorado, New Mexico, and Texas, and writing an article commenting ironically on the liberalism that characterizes the weapons program. We titled it, "The Nicest People Make the Bomb." Meanwhile, Howard went his own way, traveling the country by bus and car, visiting bomb factories, and occasionally submitting memos and reports, most of them laden with impenetrable technical detail. After several attempts, an acceptable manuscript about H-bomb secrecy began slowly to emerge.

From the very beginning, the notion that the Government of the United States might go to court to prevent publication of Howard Morland's H-bomb article had struck us at *The Progressive* as preposterous. It was our hope and intention that the article would have an impact. We savored the thought that the Department of Energy might help draw attention to the article by making a fuss of some kind. But we never imagined that the article would plunge our magazine into a crisis of historic dimensions.

Initially, our fears and expectations ran in quite the opposite direction: We worried that the article might be a dud, ignored by *The Progressive*'s own subscribers, let alone by the public. That had been our problem with Morland from the outset. He articulated his thoughts well, but the manuscript he submitted to us in September—his first attempt at consolidating his ideas in article form—had been a disappointment and an embarrassment. I still wince at the memory of that schoolboy recitation of nuclear arms race history, with its impenetrable admixture of atomic bomb technology. Now, in January 1979, with a revised draft and his diagrams before us, the story at last showed promise. But as a piece of writing, it was only barely digestible.

In my first rewriting of Morland's manuscript, I focused on the politics of the Government's nuclear secrecy policy, knitting the politics into the H-bomb technology, and thinning out the technical material. But even these efforts left us far from satisfied. Despite the deliberate provocativeness of an editor's note conceived to entice reader interest—"The following report contains 'secret/restricted data'..."—no manuscript reviewer at *The Progressive* could summon enthusiasm for the first redraft.

"From what I'd been told I thought I'd be seeing skyrockets going off," said Ron Carbon, *The Progressive*'s publisher. "But there were no skyrockets. The story left me cold." Associate Editor John McGrath, whose forty years as a science buff made him the closest approximation to a science editor at *The Progressive*, took an interest in the scientific details; but even for him the article was "much too dull and technical." John Buell, the magazine's other associate editor, whose background was in political economy, clipped this memo to the redrafted Morland article: "I am afraid that some of the significance of this piece is lost on me. He has dug up information on how the hydrogen bomb is put together. In the process he illustrates the thesis that there can be no real long-term atomic secrets. But the piece gets so bogged down in technical detail that its major thrust is lost. By the time he gets back to his major theme, most readers will have lost the thread...."

Clearly, the manuscript did not yet have the impact we wished it to have. Another rewriting would be necessary. Meanwhile, however, troubles of another sort were developing.

During Morland's investigations in the fall of 1978, word had filtered back to me in Madison that his inquiries were making waves at the Department of Energy. On one occasion, Morland upset one of the Department's public relations officers by visiting the Rocky Flats plutonium-trigger factory in Colorado as a tourist after having been denied admittance as a reporter. On another, he displeased the Department by persuading a member of Congress from California—Representative Ron Dellums—to submit a list of highly sensitive questions about plutonium production. The complaints about Morland's activities would come to me from James Cannon, the Department's director of public affairs in Washington, with whom I had conducted frequent and cordial dealings since the previous spring. "I don't know what he's up to, but he's no ordinary reporter," Cannon once told me. *"Even the questions he's asking are classified."* But there was nothing in such warnings to prepare us for the confrontation to come. Regardless of what the Department of Energy might say to reporters who asked piercing questions or strayed into forbidden territory, we knew it was the Department's invariable policy, inherited from the old Atomic Energy Commission, never to confirm or deny the accuracy of stories dealing with nuclear weapons information the Government regarded as "classified." The policy had stood like a rock since World War II. We had no reason to suspect that it was about to change.

When the first signal of our impending crisis came at the end of January, therefore, I did not take it seriously. The signal was a telephone call to me from Randall Forsberg, a graduate student at the Massachusetts Institute of Technology, whom I had met about ten days earlier in Santa Cruz, California. She and I had been there, along with Morland and several dozen others, for a workshop of the Nuclear Weapons Facilities Task Force, an antinuclear project sponsored by the American Friends Service Committee and the Fellowship of Reconciliation. Randy Forsberg, later to gain fame as a founder of the Nuclear Weapons Freeze movement, was one of those to whom Morland—always probing for reactions that might prove helpful—had passed out copies of his manuscript and diagrams.

Forsberg was obviously troubled. "I know what Howard's trying to do, and I really support his idea of demystifying the H-bomb program," she told me. "But I hope you won't print the article in this form." She explained that while she had found a great deal of merit in the manuscript when she had first read it in Santa Cruz, she now had second thoughts, especially after showing it to friends at M.I.T. Forsberg said she had been persuaded that the article might contribute to the danger of nuclear proliferation—that it might help another country build an H-bomb. She asked me to get in touch with one of the friends who had persuaded her, another graduate student named Ron Siegel.

Until that time I had accepted Morland's technical thermonuclear descriptions purely on faith. I was relieved to receive confirmation from a fairly knowledgeable quarter that Morland seemed to know what he was talking about. Eager to receive further confirmation, and highly skeptical of Forsberg's fears that the article might somehow help a foreign government build an H-bomb more rapidly, I readily agreed to her request.

When the first rewriting of Morland's manuscript was finished early in February, I mailed copies to Forsberg and Siegel—and to four nuclear scientists at the Argonne National Laboratory who had helped me with earlier material from Morland: Ted Postol, Alex DeVolpi, Gerald Marsh, and George Stanford. These six became the "technical advisers" who— some willingly, some not—helped shape the article into final form.

By mid-February, both Forsberg and Siegel had responded at length and in detail to my first redraft of the Morland manuscript—the same redraft that had left our own staff so cold. Their recommendation: Eliminate the technical details describing how the fission and fusion systems are coupled in an H-bomb. Why risk giving "a broad hint," as Siegel put it, that might help India or Israel or South Africa build the H-bomb more quickly? Forsberg even supplied a "sanitized" version in which those portions of Morland's text and diagrams that troubled her had been blanked out. "I urge you in the strongest possible way not to publish the unedited version,

and to get further, competent (physicists') views on the potential useful-
ness of what you are publishing to countries that might otherwise not get
H-bombs," she wrote.

We were more intrigued than concerned by these warnings, and still
incredulous at the notion that anything in the pages of *The Progressive*
could be of practical value in the weapons laboratories of Israel, India, or
South Africa. But I relayed the messages to Morland while I busied myself
with remedying what for me was the more worrisome problem: the
dullness of his article. As a close-up portrait of the H-bomb and the
H-bomb program, it had what we wanted. But it needed more political
substance to justify the devotion of so much space to technical specifics
and to explain the relevance of the detail. We were not looking for ways
to take material out; we were looking for ways to keep it in.

And then, on the morning of February 15, came the first telephone call
from George Rathjens.


George William Rathjens did not need to identify himself. His name was
a household word in the "arms control community." The author of many
books and articles on military policy, weapons limitation, nuclear nonproliferation, and related topics, Rathjens was a political science professor
at M.I.T., which, with neighboring Harvard University, is the academic
heart of the arms control movement. Rathjens had been a director of the
Council for a Livable World and was then the outgoing chairman of the
Federation of American Scientists—organizations that have done pioneer
work in resisting the development of nuclear weapons. Among the many
who had studied under him, I was to learn later, were Randy Forsberg and
Ron Siegel.

Rathjens opened the telephone conversation almost apologetically. He
spoke casually, but with the precision of an academician. He had just seen
a copy of the Morland article, he said, and he had ambivalent feelings
about it. On the one hand, its publication would help expose the pernicious
effects of secrecy, and that would be all to the good. But on the other hand
there were some arguments against publication: "I have the impression
that the information could be used very mischievously, with possibly
catastrophic effect." Furthermore, "if perceived as a major expose, the
article could lead to punitive action on the Hill"—it could worsen the
political climate in Washington and provoke enactment of an American
version of Britain's Official Secrets Act.

Rathjens paused, then went on: He had talked to "the security people" about the article on a hypothetical basis. "They were very curious. They wanted to know who was doing it. I didn't tell them, but I asked them, 'What would you do about such an article?' They said that if it were as damaging as I suggested, they would try to persuade the editor not to publish it, and if they were unsuccessful they would get a restraining order."

Rathjens said he believed the article could make a difference of a substantial period of time in the efforts of a near-nuclear country to develop the H-bomb. When I challenged that assertion, Rathjens seemed to waver: "I may be all wrong. Perhaps this is all in the public domain. I have had no access to weapons designs in fifteen years. I'm not in a position to comment on the accuracy. But I do have apprehensions."

This warning was not one to be taken lightly. Rathjens had important connections both in the Government and in academia. In the 1960s, he had held high positions in the Arms Control and Disarmament Agency and the Institute for Defense Analysis. Recently he had signed on with the Department of State as a consultant on nuclear nonproliferation matters—a job that took him to Washington once a week. He moved easily in and out of official circles. He had the reputation of a heavyweight, a careful pragmatist.

Nevertheless, I was struck by the ambivalence of his tone—and by the way he seemed to back off at the end of the conversation. The same impression came through the following morning when my old colleague at the *Bulletin*, Bernard Feld, telephoned me from M.I.T.

"Ron Siegel asked me to call you," Feld began, somewhat hesitantly. "He told me about this article you have. I haven't seen it, but I know about it in a general way. He is disturbed. He thinks it has information that would be useful in construction of an H-bomb. I don't think it's a terribly good idea to publish this sort of thing. My own instinct would be not to do it."

Feld launched into the arguments I had already heard from Forsberg, Siegel, and Rathjens. But, like Rathjens, he seemed to be only half-persuaded. I construed it as a duty call; the young graduate students were obviously bringing out their big guns, but the guns seemed strangely muted. Within an hour, however, another telephone call conveyed an entirely different signal.

"This is Dr. Rathjens's secretary," said the voice at the other end of the line. "Dr. Rathjens is in a meeting, but he asked me to notify you that he is turning over the story to the Department of Energy." I was dumb-founded:

"He doesn't have our permission to do that."

"But the messenger is here now."

"Tell Dr. Rathjens to call back. He is not authorized to turn our manuscript over to anyone."

Early that afternoon—Friday, February 16—George Rathjens called back. I was away, so Erwin Knoll took the call. It was a brief conversation. Rathjens told Knoll that he had, "as a matter of conscience," turned the Morland article over to the Department of Energy. For the first time, it seemed we might be in serious trouble.

If the Morland article had become a problem for me and Knoll, it would soon become an even thornier one for Gordon Sinykin, *The Progressive*'s principal business adviser, legal counsel, and chairman of its board of directors. A protege and one-time legal partner of Wisconsin Governor Philip LaFollette, son of the famed U.S. Senator Robert M. ("Fighting Bob") LaFollette Sr., who founded *The Progressive* in 1909, Sinykin embodied the LaFollette tradition both in the magazine and in the law firm, one of Wisconsin's most prestigious, of which he had become the senior partner. Now, as seldom before, *The Progressive* needed a lawyer, and it was natural to turn to him.

Some time earlier, I had scheduled a luncheon meeting with Sinykin for the following Thursday, February 22, to get help with a fund-raising program for the perpetually impoverished magazine. On the Monday following Rathjens's telephone call I contacted Sinykin, just home from a meeting of the American Bar Association, and asked him to have our conference moved up a day—to Wednesday. In the meantime, I completed my second and final rewriting of the Morland article and prepared to move it into production. We were satisfied with it, at last. It was to be the lead and cover story for *The Progressive*'s April issue, scheduled to go to press on Monday, March 5, then barely two weeks away.

Despite the anxieties it evoked, Rathjens's decision to turn over Morland's article to the Government resolved whatever doubts we had that the article was worth publishing. His action seemed to underscore one of Morland's essential points—in the name of "national security," the heavy presence of the Government could stifle public awareness of the reality of the H-bomb program. I read and reread the earlier drafts, assured myself that Morland's scientific concepts could not conceivably be of more than fleeting value to a nation bent on developing H-bombs, and stressed that point in my final redraft.

"What you are about to learn," I began, writing under Howard's by-line, "is a secret—a secret that the United States and four other nations, the makers of hydrogen weapons, have gone to extraordinary lengths to protect.

"The secret is in the coupling mechanism that enables an ordinary fission bomb—the kind that destroyed Hiroshima—to trigger the far deadlier energy of hydrogen fusion.

"The physical pressure and heat generated by X- and gamma radiation, moving outward from the trigger at the speed of light, bounces against the weapon's inner wall and is reflected with enormous force into the sides of a carrot-shaped 'pencil' which contains the fusion fuel..."

The new conclusion of the article read:

The secret of how a hydrogen bomb is made protects a more fundamental "secret": the mechanism by which the resources of the most powerful nation on Earth have been marshaled for global catastrophe. Knowing how may be the key to asking why.

Is it dangerous to tell how a hydrogen bomb is made? No. For one thing, the information falls short of providing a blueprint for nuclear weapon construction. The general features of nuclear fission bombs became available long ago in the Smyth Report. Subsequent Atomic Energy Commission declassifications and the accumulation of mountains of data and experience with the growth of the worldwide nuclear enterprise have eliminated the secret of fission bomb construction. Credible designs and instructions for these have been prepared by college-level physics students.

The building of a hydrogen bomb, which can be ignited only by a fission weapon, is a different matter. It would take millions of dollars worth of specialized equipment and hundreds of trained technicians to build a hydrogen bomb—a feat beyond the capability of all but the most industrially sophisticated nations.

Whatever insights these descriptions may provide to nations seeking to perfect their thermonuclear capability—Israel and South Africa, for example—they are at best a trifling addition to the information already available. No government intent upon joining the nuclear terror club need long be at a loss to know how to proceed. Nothing you or I could learn would long elude the nuclear physicists and engineers whose participation would be essential to such an enterprise.

The risks of proliferation of hydrogen weapons, such as they are, must be weighed against the public gain that may come from greater awareness of how and why they are already being produced.

Whether it be the details of a multi-million dollar plutonium production expansion program or the principles and procedures by which nature's most explosive force is being packaged in our midst, we have less to fear from knowing than from not knowing. What we do with the knowledge may be the key to our survival.*

Was there any chance that we were wrong and Rathjens was right, that the article might indeed contribute to H-bomb proliferation, I asked Ted Postol. Not a chance, Postol replied. "Any well-grounded physicist, with sufficient effort, could have come up with what Morland did. The information is available to any nation-state that really wants it."

Did that mean that we could breathe easily? Not at all, said Postol. "The drawings are *very damaging* to classification, although not to national security. There is not much doubt at all that classification has been penetrated. I think the shit may hit the fan."

But three days had passed since the Department of Energy had received the article from Rathjens—and, so far as we knew, nothing had hit the fan. All through the weekend we had expected to hear something from the Government, but there had been no word. After Monday passed, then Tuesday, we concluded—falsely, as it turned out—that the Government did not, after all, agree with Rathjens and Postol that the Morland article constituted a breach of its classification program. And once again we wondered whether our blockbuster might be a dud. Erwin and I decided to put it to a further test. On Wednesday, February 21, I mailed Morland's diagrams and captions to James Cannon:

"I enclose a copy of some material—entitled "How a Hydrogen Bomb Works"—which has been submitted for publication in *The Progressive*. Since this is a subject on which the Department of Energy has authoritative information, we would appreciate your verifying the accuracy of the material.

* © 1979 by Howard Morland, reprinted by permission.

"Please drop me a note at your earliest convenience. Mail delivery uncertainties being what they are these days, I am taking the precaution of sending you this by certified mail."

The description, "How a Hydrogen Bomb Works," a phrase that would later return to haunt us, was a "slug" typed over the diagram captions for identification purposes. It was never intended for publication. The Morland article itself, not included in the letter to Cannon, had no title yet. The letter, sent with some misgivings, was intended to smoke out whatever response the Government planned as a result of the Rathjens leak. We assumed that the response, if any, would be swift. We hoped, naively, that the Government might grumble just loudly enough to give us a few additional quotes and add a little weight to our story. What we didn't know was that the letter, mailed just when Washington had experienced its worst snowstorm in twenty-two years, would take a full eight days to reach its destination.

That same afternoon, Knoll and I called on Gordon Sinykin to discuss the magazine's perennial financial crisis and to talk to him for the first time about Howard Morland's article—a topic raised almost casually toward the end of the conference. There was a reason for this. Editorial matters at *The Progressive* were, by long tradition, the exclusive responsibility of the editor. Knoll did not want to seem to be soliciting editorial guidance. He wanted the chairman of the magazine's board to be aware of the possible legal and financial implications. We told Sinykin about the call from Rathjens and indicated that we "might have a problem." Sinykin did not seem to take it very seriously. We emphasized that Morland had seen no classified documents and had received no information on a "confidential" or "background only" basis. Sinykin asked to see the article, and he took it home with him that night.

"The whole thing hit me like a bolt out of the blue," Sinykin recalled later. As a former military officer (he supervised press arrangements on the *U.S.S. Missouri* at the Japanese surrender in Tokyo Bay in 1945) Sinykin worried about the scientific and technical detail in Morland's article, just as the rest of us had. Was it a hoax, he wondered, that would make *The Progressive* look ridiculous? Or was this a real secret? Who was the author? It troubled him that he knew nothing at all about Morland, and that the editors themselves knew not much more. And it troubled him even more when he reached for his copy of the *U.S. Code* and looked up the Atomic Energy Act of 1954.

At about 9:30 that night, the telephone rang at Erwin Knoll's home.

"Do you know what's in that law?" Sinykin asked, and he proceeded to tell the editor about the notion that *all* nuclear weapons data—regardless of source—were automatically "restricted." He added wryly: "You'll be glad to know that the death penalty no longer applies." (It had, in fact, been reduced to ten years in prison for those who violate the act "with intent to injure the United States.")

Sinykin said he hoped we could persuade the Government that Morland's article was innocuous and thus head off the possibility that a whole issue of the magazine might be seized. He asked whether the manuscript we intended to publish—the one we had given him earlier that day—was identical to the one that Rathjens had transmitted to the Department of Energy. Knoll told him it was not; that the piece had been extensively rewritten. Sinykin suggested that we send a copy of the revised manuscript to the Department.

Knoll said he had strong reservations about doing that, and wanted time to think about it some more and discuss it with me. To submit an article to the Government, or to anyone else, was unheard of at *The Progressive*. Sinykin pressed the point, saying we could avoid a "misunderstanding" and confrontation with the Government without compromising our right to publish Morland's article.

"I had considerable difficulty with the editors on that point," Sinykin recalled later. "I felt strongly that the first thing we should do was find the answers. Was the article accurate, or was it just silly? Was there a real secret? If there was going to be a lawsuit, I would much prefer restraint to criminal sanctions."

Knoll and I kept stalling for time, hoping that a response from Cannon or some other Department official might obviate the need for sending the full article, an act which could be construed as an invitation for governmental review. To send the diagrams and captions was one thing; they were, after all, highly technical material, and it seemed at least plausible to check them for technical accuracy. But to give the Government an opportunity to review the entire article before publication seemed to be a violation of journalistic ethics—and we would later be severely criticized for it by some of our colleagues in the press.

We stalled until we could wait no longer. On the morning of Monday, February 26, I put in a telephone call to Jim Cannon. No, Cannon had received no letter. He knew nothing about any diagrams, captions, or article about the H-bomb. That afternoon, I mailed the finished article through an air express service guaranteeing twenty-four-hour delivery, and enclosed the following letter:

"Following up my letter of February 21 and our telephone conversation of this morning, I enclose a second copy of some material—entitled 'How a Hydrogen Bomb Works'—which has been submitted for publication in *The Progressive*.

"Also enclosed is a copy of an article written to accompany the material.

"As you will note, the material and article contain technical information pertaining to hydrogen weapon design and manufacture. We would appreciate your verifying the technical accuracy of the enclosures.

"Since our publication deadline is fast approaching we are sending this via Federal Express direct to your office in Germantown. Please give me a telephone call when you have received it."

The press deadline for our H-bomb issue was one week away.

Jim Cannon—slim, white-haired, and close to retirement at that time— was a veteran journalist trusted and liked by his bosses in the Department of Energy and by the reporters with whom he dealt as the Department's director of public affairs. As a former Associated Press writer, he understood the needs and limitations of the media; as a bureaucrat wise in the ways of one of Washington's most labyrinthine bureaucracies, he could be helpful to the agency and to those who occasionally ran up against it. In the last days of February 1979, he was helpful both to the Department of Energy and to *The Progressive*.

At about 3:30 p.m. on Tuesday, February 27, Cannon returned a telephone call from me. Yes, he said, the letter had arrived just a few hours earlier. He had glanced at the subject matter of the enclosed article and sent it on to "our technical people."

"I try to keep out of stuff that's over my head," Cannon said.

I asked when *The Progressive* might expect a response, and Cannon said he didn't know. He noted that the manuscript was a "thick document." Cannon asked if we were in a hurry. I told him that *The Progressive* was working against a deadline and would like to hear by the next day. Cannon said that might be impossible, but that he would do what he could by the following day, Thursday. We chatted for a while, and then Cannon asked if he could speak as a friend rather than as a spokesman for the Department of Energy.

Cannon said he worried about articles that "get into areas that are classified," as this one appeared to. He told a story about a television

111

reporter who had begun asking questions about a sensitive subject in the Department's weapons program and then "backed off right away" when he told him that the information was classified.

"Now I know you're not dumb, and you seem to know what you're doing," Cannon said, "but I hope you're familiar with the Atomic Energy Act and its penalties. This is just Jim Cannon speaking, not as an official but as an old newsman." I thanked him for his candor.

Cannon added that when the Department did get back to us on this matter, it might be through some other representative. But if the response came through him, he said, we should remember that "I'm just a little cog in a big wheel." The implication was that his tone might be less friendly and informal.

Cannon's gentle warning was unmistakable. It appeared we were headed for a showdown of some kind with the Department of Energy, but just when and how we did not know. By this time, the Morland article had been set in type and our artist was at work on the cover and illustrations. The rest of the April issue was ready to go. As a precaution, Knoll had spent much of the preceding weekend writing an alternative article, based on a trip to Israel he had made in January. It was not until 3 a.m. Monday that, bleary-eyed, he pulled the last page out of his typewriter. "O Promised Land!," originally scheduled for this issue but then deferred in favor of the Morland article, would now be our alternative lead and cover in case something happened to the Morland piece. For the time being, we were keeping both options open.

On Thursday, March 1, at about 10:30 a.m., I telephoned Cannon again to get another reading. No, said Cannon, he had not yet heard from his "technical people" about the manuscript. I reminded him of *The Progressive*'s deadline problem and asked when we might be hearing.

"How long can you wait?"

"Until noon tomorrow."

"Thanks. That will help me spur them a little."

Reminding him of our conversation two days earlier, when he had brought up the Atomic Energy Act and its penalties, I told Cannon we were working on the assumption that there was no "security problem," since the Department had expressed no official concern.

"I wouldn't necessarily read it that way," Cannon replied. He said the Department would be in touch with us if there were a security problem, but he couldn't say when.

In the absence of further word from the Department, I said, *The Progressive* would go to press with the Morland article at noon the following day. (Our April issue already was in serious danger of delay.)

Cannon said he would relay the Friday noon deadline information to the appropriate authorities. He indicated, but did not promise, there would be a reply by then.

For two weeks we had been receiving mixed signals. We were concerned about the growing possibility of postponement of a major article. If it were delayed a month, we feared it might be leaked to another publication— possibly even by the Department itself. Having found no evidence of Governmental concern over the Morland article, despite the various private warnings, we had no inkling of the vast commotion it had actually caused. For almost a fortnight a small army of bureaucrats, unbeknownst to us, had been furiously busy.

I put down the telephone and notified *The Progressive*'s paste-up crew that we appeared to be losing the H-bomb article for the April issue and should prepare for a possible switch to the Israeli piece; then I called the printers to negotiate a delay in the press start. I was told that *The Progressive* would have to decide by noon the next day whether to order a one-week delay.

As it turned out, we didn't need that much time to make up our minds. Within the next half hour—at ten minutes past noon on Thursday, March 1—the Department of Energy made up our minds for us.

# 11

# The Government Strikes

The voice on the telephone sounded faintly Southern and distinctly formal. It asked for Samuel H. Day, Jr., managing editor of *The Progressive*. When the caller, Lynn R. Coleman, identified himself as general counsel of the United States Department of Energy, I asked Erwin Knoll to come on the line.

Coleman said he was calling in reference to an article which, he understood, it was our intention to print and distribute. The article had been read by several assistant secretaries in the Department of Energy, by Secretary James Schlesinger, by the Department's attorneys, and by Coleman himself. He said it was their conclusion that the article contained "restricted data" as defined in the Atomic Energy Act. Publication of the article would injure the United States, give a decided advantage to a foreign country interested in building a thermonuclear device, and be contrary to the Carter Administration's interest in preventing the proliferation of thermonuclear devices.

"We have to ask you to refrain from publishing the article in its present form," Coleman said. He noted that our deadline was noon the next day. Then Coleman paused and observed that in his opinion an article could be written to make the same points without violating the law. He offered to discuss this with us, saying the Department was reluctant to interfere with free speech.

"Is the Department prepared to tell us which portions of the article contain 'restricted data'?" Knoll asked.

"No, but our people could sit down with you to work out an article."

If *The Progressive* intended to proceed with publication, Coleman said, he would have "no alternative" but to state that the Department would seek to enjoin us from publishing. Consultations on this point had already been conducted with the Department of Justice, the Department of State, the Department of Defense, and the Arms Control and Disarmament Agency. He said the Government was prepared to proceed with dispatch.

We told Coleman we would consult with our own counsel and get back to him that afternoon.

By now, the atmosphere at *The Progressive* was electric. Tensions that had been steadily building week to week seemed finally to be resolved—or close to resolution. The Government of the United States had made its move—decisively and massively. Whatever happened from this point on, whenever and however it was published, the Morland article would serve its principal purpose—to draw public attention to the problem of nuclear secrecy and its impact on public policy. I felt a surge of excitement, Knoll an immense sense of relief.

In rapid succession the telephone calls went out—to Gordon Sinykin's office to schedule an emergency meeting that afternoon, and to the printers to begin work on "O Promised Land!" and to delay the press run for a week. We knew now that, whatever the outcome of our difficulties with the Department of Energy, there was no way we could publish the Morland article on time.

At two o'clock on that Thursday afternoon, Knoll and I and Publisher Ron Carbon were ascending an elevator to the third-floor law offices of LaFollette, Sinykin, Anderson, and Munson. We were in high spirits. The issue was joined, and we were in a fight we intended to win.

"I love it!" Knoll said.

At the lawyers' office, we decided it would be prudent to let the Department of Energy state its case in full. It was agreed that Knoll and I should fly to Washington that night and offer to listen to the Department the next morning. A call was put in to Coleman's office; in his absence I located Eric Fygi, one of his deputies.

"Are you familiar with this matter?" I asked, by way of introduction.

"Unfortunately, I am familiar with it up to my eyeballs," the deputy replied. I began to outline *The Progressive*'s offer to fly its editors to Washington. Fygi interrupted to tell us not to bother; arrangements were already being made, he said, to fly a party of Energy and Justice Department officials to Madison. They would arrive the next morning.

Late that afternoon, on the five-block walk back to *The Progressive*'s office, Knoll, Carbon, and I were accosted by two reporters for the *Madison Press Connection*, a local morning newspaper. Was it true, they asked, that *The Progressive* was about to publish a sensational story about the H-bomb, that the Justice Department was upset, and that the FBI had been in touch with us about it?

Knoll took the reporters into his office and told them that something big was afoot, but their information was partially incorrect. He said he could tell them nothing about the matter for the time being, but when the story broke they would be the first to know. They wrote down their home telephone numbers, and Knoll carried the piece of paper in his pocket for a week.

The H-bomb story had acquired a life of its own.

The Government had proposed that its representatives meet with us at about 10 that Friday morning at *The Progressive*. But the circumstances ill-suited our cramped, cluttered office. For one thing, the Government would be sending a party of six. With an equal number attending from *The Progressive*, there simply would be no room. We had no conference table, not even enough chairs for everyone. Furthermore, if this were to be a confrontation, a test of power, we did not want the arena to be one that would so tellingly proclaim the poverty of *The Progressive*'s worldly resources. The law office, with its thick rugs and paneled walls, provided a far more imposing setting. We had one additional reason for not meeting at the magazine's office: We were reluctant to play host to our would-be censors. So the meeting place was changed to the more neutral ground of LaFollette, Sinykin.

Delayed by fog at Chicago's O'Hare International Airport, the visitors from Washington trooped into our lawyers' spacious conference room a little before 2:00. The delegation was headed by Duane Sewell, the Assistant Secretary of Energy in charge of the Department's military programs—the top administrator of the nation's nuclear weapons establishment. With him came a deputy, two legal officers, and two lawyers from the civil division of the Justice Department.

Sewell, a tall, self-assured scientist-turned-administrator (he had been a senior weapons designer himself before taking the job in Washington), came quickly to the point: Howard Morland's article contained data that could save another country two to five years in developing an H-bomb.

Sinykin asked Sewell to what data he was making reference, but the scientist turned the question aside: "By picking out specific pieces, we are identifying restricted data," he said. To do that would be to violate security. But he said all the illustrations and captions, as well as about twenty per cent of the text, involved "restricted data."

Then Brady Williamson, one of our lawyers, bored in. Were there any inaccuracies in the article? Yes, said Sewell, but "in the overall context they are not substantial."

That answer astonished us: Sewell had confirmed that Morland was right. His casual phrase, uttered almost as if in parlor conversation, had changed a third of a century of public policy on confirmation of nuclear weapons data. (When told, a few hours later, of Sewell's confirmatory statement, Morland exclaimed, "My God! I didn't really know until now!")

And there was more: Sewell said this was the most comprehensive unclassified report he had ever seen on the subject; it included material that had never been published in the open literature.

The discussion turned to the mechanics of how the Department might go about rewriting the article. Sewell said this could be done in Washington in a few days. The Department would confine itself to the technical descriptions, replacing specifics with general statements. No meanings would be changed. The politics would be left untouched. There would be no quibbling over literary style.

Then, a return to legal questions. Asked what would happen if there were no agreement, Sewell said the Department would take whatever legal steps it could to prevent publication. "Our first goal," said Ronald Olson, one of his legal officers, "is to avoid going to court. But as a last resort we are prepared to ask the Department of Justice to go forward to restrain publication."

"As a matter of fact," said David Anderson, one of the two Justice Department lawyers present, "the Department of Energy has already sent in a referral. We are ready to act if necessary." This meant the delegation was ready to walk the four blocks to the Federal courthouse and file for an immediate injunction.

Anderson and Brady Williamson, almost seeming to relish the prospect, agreed that it would be "a novel suit."

Then Erwin Knoll spoke up for the first time, referring to the Morland article and the Government's reasons for wanting to censor it. "Frankly," he said, "I am incredulous that a writer of Morland's limited background and a magazine of *The Progressive*'s pathetic resources could so readily penetrate what you are describing as perhaps the most important secret possessed by the United States. If this were really the case, it would constitute a national security scandal of horrendous dimensions." Sewell replied that he, too, was at a loss to explain it.

"Was it a quirk? A fluke? A particular ability of this writer? I don't know. We are going to investigate it. We are concerned that there may be a fault in our system."

In what appeared to be a final statement, Sewell stressed the eagerness of the Department of Energy to tell the public as much as possible about its programs without violating security. He urged *The Progressive*'s editors and lawyers to see the question as a moral one—the morality of turning over to other nations valuable information on nuclear and thermonuclear weapons.

About an hour had passed, and the visitors were clearly anxious for our decision. *The Progressive* contingent retired for a conference in Sinykin's private office while the Government people finished sandwiches ordered for them by the firm. In Sinykin's office, there was an early consensus: Whatever we might think of the Government's proposal, we shouldn't reject it out of hand. We did not want to act in haste—or to give the appearance of doing so. We needed more time for our response. Reconvening the meeting, Gordon Sinykin spoke for *The Progressive*: "Our editor finds your offer to rewrite the article more than objectionable," he said. "However, we have taken note of your concern, and we feel we need the weekend to mull things over." The Government would have *The Progressive*'s answer by 6 p.m. on Tuesday, March 6, he promised. In the meantime, it had the magazine's assurance that the article would not be published before then.

For Knoll and me, at least, the overriding significance of the meeting was that it provided confirmation of Morland's thesis: In attesting to the accuracy of Morland's diagrams and text, Sewell had underscored his larger point—that there are no "secrets," except from those who do not choose to know them.

Our author had had only a modicum of scientific training; he had drawn on few resources other than his own wits; he had operated entirely in the open; he had strewn his writings and his drawings far and wide; his findings consisted of nothing more than general ideas and concepts; the Government even up to that moment had made no move to recover the material itself.

Thousands of persons in the five thermonuclear nations (the United States, the Soviet Union, Britain, France, and China) already knew the "secret" of the H-bomb—we all knew that. Thousands of others who wished to know it could readily duplicate what Morland had done—that was implicit in what Duane Sewell had just told us. It seemed to us that we were being asked to protect nothing more than a secrecy mystique—and yet the shattering of that mystique had been the central (and successful) purpose of the article.

The policy of secrecy was a fraud. Now we were being asked to help perpetuate fraud. And we were being threatened with the direst consequences if we failed to do so. To have bargained away so much as a single comma in order to save the story would have been worse than suppressing it in its entirety.

Suddenly, it was no longer a question of whether and how to enhance what we had come to recognize as an important story about H-bomb secrecy. The issue now was censorship. Those were our thoughts as editors that Friday afternoon as the teams of attorneys put away their papers and congratulated each other on the "lawyerlike" conduct of their meeting.

On that same day, U.S. Attorney General Griffin B. Bell signed a memorandum to President Jimmy Carter ominously entitled "Possible Litigation to Enjoin the Publication of an Article Containing Previously Undisclosed Details of the Construction of a Thermonuclear Bomb."

Most of the letter, released years later in response to a Freedom of Information Act request, has been blacked out by Justice Department censors, but a fragment of the concluding sentence read, "...the potentially grave consequences to the security of the U.S. and the world itself resulting from disclosure of the data are obvious and frightening."

On the face of the memorandum the President had penned a brief, handwritten notation: "Good move; proceed. —J."

There was an additional reason for asking the Government to wait until Tuesday for a response. Two of the four members of *The Progressive*'s board of directors had been out of the country for ten days and were not due home until Monday evening. It was unthinkable that a decision of this magnitude could be made without Morris Rubin, who had been the magazine's editor for thirty-three years, and his wife, Mary Sheridan, its longtime managing editor.

In 1940, the Rubins, talented young journalists fresh out of the University of Wisconsin, had stepped into the breach at *The Progressive* at a critical time when the LaFollette family, which had owned the magazine since its founding in 1909, was looking for fresh editorial blood. The Rubins had run the magazine, then a weekly tabloid, almost alone during the war years. Then, with Gordon Sinykin's help, they had nursed it through recurring crises in the postwar years, including a financial squeeze that forced suspension of publication for two months in 1947. Morris Rubin turned over the editorship in 1973 to Erwin Knoll, the magazine's Washington correspondent, but continued to serve as publisher for three more years before retiring in 1976. He remained an influential presence in the life of the magazine until his death in 1980. Mary Sheridan stepped down as managing editor when I joined the magazine in 1978 but continued to serve as part-time editor of the book review section. No others had invested more deeply in *The Progressive* or were more entitled to have a say about its future.

The Rubins had had no inkling of the problem when they left on the morning of February 20 for a two-week winter vacation at Puerto Villarta on the west coast of Mexico. Nor did they know about it when, long after the crisis had hit, they drove home from the Madison airport on the evening of Monday, March 5. A telephone call from Gordon Sinykin about 9:30 the next morning alerted them to the trouble. "We have an article that might involve litigation. How soon can you get down to the office?"

The next few hours were a nightmare for the returning vacationers. Arriving at Sinykin's office without even having fully unpacked, they tried to absorb the import of the events of the preceding days, listened to the complex explanations of the lawyers and the sometimes conflicting interpretations of the editors, and leafed despairingly through the forbidding manuscript, with its pages and pages of thermonuclear minutiae. It was too much. They pleaded for an extra day to read the article quietly and think about the implications.

While the lawyers rescheduled the promised response to the Government from 6 p.m. Tuesday to 3:30 p.m. Wednesday, Morris Rubin and Mary Sheridan went home to rest, to read, and to make up their minds.

Meanwhile, at *The Progressive*, a mood of anxiety had been building through the afternoon. Erwin Knoll and I had arrived back at the office from our meeting with the Rubins and the lawyers. It seemed to us that the unanimity and determination that had prevailed the previous day between lawyers and editors was in danger of disintegrating. Morris Rubin had indicated serious doubts on some major points—the risk to *The Progressive*, and the propriety of publishing information the Government called "secret." Sinykin seemed to have become tense and uncommunicative. A third lawyer, Earl Munson, had just joined *The Progressive*'s legal team and had a lot of catching up to do, with little time to do it. We wondered whether *The Progressive*'s governing body would be able to hang together under the growing pressure of a situation that might jeopardize the magazine's survival.

In midafternoon, Knoll, Publisher Ron Carbon, and I were joined in Knoll's office by the two associate editors, John McGrath and John Buell. There was unanimous agreement that *The Progressive* should inform the Government the next day that it would publish the Morland article in full. We felt it was a matter of principle involving the editorial integrity of the magazine.

These somber ruminations were interrupted by a telephone call from Brady Williamson. The lawyers, he said, were going ahead with legal preparations and needed material for affidavits. By the next morning he would have to have complete information about *The Progressive* and its editors, and a copy of Howard Morland's travel schedule.

"When can Morland get to Madison?" Williamson asked.

"He could leave Hawaii tonight."

"Get him on that plane!"

Morris Rubin dropped off Mary Sheridan at *The Progressive* early Wednesday morning, March 7, on his way to the offices of LaFollette, Sinykin. Knoll arrived at the magazine a short while later, and I a few minutes after that. There were the usual early morning greetings, but everyone sensed the tension in the air. A meeting at the lawyers' office was scheduled for 10 a.m.

I poked my head into Knoll's office and asked if Mary Sheridan had said anything to him about the Morland article. Erwin shook his head. I talked with Mary, hoping to detect some tell-tale sign, but she volunteered nothing on the subject.

At 9:45 a.m. it was time for the three of us to climb into Knoll's car for the short drive to the lawyers' office. When we were all seated, I decided to break the ice.

"Mary, have you thought any more about the article?"

She began with a few noncommittal remarks, and then: "...I think the First Amendment is pretty important." There was an audible sigh, then a torrent of words from the vastly relieved editor. Knoll's words poured out as if to smother any "but" or "however" that might be lurking in her next breath.

There was a "but": Mary Sheridan said Morland's article was dull, long, and technical. Erwin and I agreed volubly, but carefully steered the subject back to the First Amendment. The three of us were chatting cheerfully when we reached the lawyers' office.

We felt we knew now what the response of the Rubins would be at the meeting that was shortly to convene. We got an additional hint when, greeting us in the lobby of the lawyers' office, Morris Rubin announced with a chuckle, "Here comes the bomb squad!"

We went into Sinykin's office. The time had come, finally, for *The Progressive* to decide what it would tell the Government of the United States about its intentions with regard to the Morland article. Knoll made some small talk. There was a long silence, and then Brady Williamson looked at Morris Rubin and asked him to begin.

Rubin made the most of his moment. Bringing out some paper on which he had jotted some notes, he launched into a vigorous critique of the Morland article, as if this were a manuscript selection conference. The article was too technical. It was not political enough. It was definitely not the sort of thing *he* would have accepted as editor, said Rubin, looking pointedly at Knoll. The former editor made a reference to the potential disaster *The Progressive* faced, then paused for effect, ready to deliver the punch line we all knew was coming. Despite all that, Rubin announced, with finality, there was an inescapable First Amendment issue. Now that the Government had made its move, we were stuck with the story—the full story.

It was all downhill from there. The conference call was placed one minute before the appointed hour. Gordon Sinykin opened the conversation.

"I can now report that the editors have carefully considered what you've said," he began. "We have concluded that the Department's position against publication is untenable. We decline your request not to publish the article, and we do not believe it is proper to permit the Department to rewrite it."

Sinykin said any collaboration between the magazine's editors and the Government would "violate the constitutional guarantees of a free and independent press."

Lynn Coleman, general counsel of the Department of Energy, seemed resigned to the news. There was a discussion of legal logistics, an exchange of information, and then the lawyers put down their telephones. The call lasted eight minutes.

Moments later, the three lawyers for *The Progressive* were together in a conference room with Knoll, Carbon, and me, who had been waiting impatiently outside. Now, we all knew, the battle would be joined. Gordon Sinykin, senior partner in the law firm and senior person on the magazine, looked around the room and said, "If we're going to have a lawsuit, let's have a lawsuit—and a good one."

Just then there was a telephone call from Teri Terry of *The Progressive*'s business-circulation staff. Howard Morland was at the Madison airport—and she was on her way to get him.

Howard Morland had spent a busy two weeks in Hawaii, where he had gone to testify at a trial involving the environmental impact of a Navy nuclear weapons storage depot. Since his arrival there on February 19, three days after the Rathjens leak, he had been simultaneously juggling his two antinuclear causes. The legal and publicity buildup was under way for the Navy nuclear weapons trial, due to start March 5, and his H-bomb story was heading for a showdown in Madison. One minute he would be preparing his testimony as an expert witness in the forthcoming Honolulu trial; the next minute he would be on the telephone with Ted Postol, checking out some aspect of the H-bomb article. He kept in almost daily telephone contact with *The Progressive* in Madison. He liked to stay close to the University of Hawaii where pay phones and copying machines were readily available. Because of the three- to six-hour time differential between Hawaii and the mainland, he had to crowd much of his activity into the morning hours.

Corrections, revisions, and additions to the H-bomb article, straightening out the technical problems in the manuscript, were still coming in from Morland as late as March 1—the day that Lynn Coleman of the Department of Energy was calling to advise *The Progressive* not to publish.

On March 2, realizing the need to gather ammunition for the approaching legal battle over nuclear secrecy, he had put in a series of calls to Dr. Edward Teller, "father of the H-bomb," at his Stanford, California, office, and come up with a useful quotation: "Any aspect of technology which can be communicated in simple language should be declassified. This includes the technology of nuclear weapons and thermonuclear weapons."

As the confrontation with the Government approached, Morland made plans, at *The Progressive*'s request, first to fly to Washington for a press conference on March 9, and then, as the outline of the legal struggle took shape, to fly to Madison sooner.

His departure was finally scheduled, on a few hours' notice, for Tuesday, March 6, the day after he had stepped down from the witness stand in Hawaii. That afternoon, carrying two backpacks and five spiral-bound notebooks, he boarded a plane at Honolulu International Airport.

Now it was about 4 p.m. on Wednesday, March 7, in the Midwest, and Teri Terry was looking for him in the Madison airport terminal.

"Hi! I'm Howard!"

Teri Terry whirled around and found a tall, dark-eyed man in a down jacket, green work pants, and tennis shoes.

"I expected to see an older man," she recalled later. "I should have known him by the big grin on his face."

Morland chattered excitedly all the way into town. When Teri dropped him off at *The Progressive*, he bounced into the office and introduced himself to Kathryn Juderjahn and Nancy Denholtz, the only two staff members remaining on duty late in the afternoon. They offered him some cookies they had saved from lunch.

Returning to *The Progressive* from our long session at the lawyers' office, Knoll, Carbon, and I found the H-bomb whiz kid holding court. He was in high spirits. Knoll took him into his office and began to fill him in on the day's dramatic events. But Morland had some things to show us first. He pulled out a piece of paper and read us the newly minted quote from Edward Teller. Then he reached into a backpack and brought out a t-shirt he had illustrated in Hawaii. Emblazoned on the front was his diagram of the H-bomb secret.

I took Morland home, gave him dinner, and debriefed him far into the night. Howard stayed up until 4 a.m., putting the H-bomb secret into verse.

At about 8 the next night the telephone rang in the home of Joe Skupniewitz, clerk of the Federal Court in Madison. It was the U.S. Attorney's office, requesting an immediate meeting with District Judge James E. Doyle. The clerk telephoned the judge, and then drove the few blocks to Doyle's home on Madison's West Side. He waited in the driveway.

By then the telephone had rung at LaFollette, Sinykin, where the three lawyers were at work. It was Frank Tuerkheimer, the U.S. Attorney. He was on his way over to serve papers on *The Progressive* and its editors. Would someone meet him at the front door of the lawyers' office building? Minutes later, his car pulled up, dropped off a sheaf of legal papers, and drove on.

At about 8:30, Joe Skupniewitz saw a car stop at the curb in front of Judge Doyle's residence. Four men alighted, and he quickly recognized two of them—Frank Tuerkheimer and his assistant, Fred Erhardt. The clerk and the visitors greeted each other at the judge's front door and went in. The judge ushered them into his living room, and Tuerkheimer got right to the point.

"Frank said it was a matter of considerable urgency, and that was why they had sought me out at home," Judge Doyle recalled later. "They were seeking something immediately." The U.S. Attorney told the judge he was there to file a complaint, with motions for a temporary restraining order and a special court order that would protect other legal filings, some of which would be highly secret. He said they had to do with "secret information on atomic weapons." He handed the papers to the judge. The top sheet bore the title, *"United States of America, Plaintiff, v. The Progressive, Inc...."*

"I didn't read anything beyond that title," Judge Doyle said later. "As soon as I saw who the defendants were I laid the papers down." He told the visitors it was quite clear to him he could not sit in the case. Pausing another moment to give it final reflection, he mentioned his close association with Morris Rubin, Mary Sheridan, and Gordon Sinykin.

Few people were closer to Jim Doyle than those three. He had known and worked with Sinykin for more than thirty years, and his friendship with the Rubins was just as strong. For a quarter of a century the judge had met for lunch every Friday with Rubin and another close newspaper friend, Miles McMillin, former editor and publisher of the Madison *Capital Times*. Doyle and his wife, Ruth, were regular bridge partners of the Rubins. Further, he was not only a subscriber but also a financial contributor to *The Progressive*.

It was clear to Judge Doyle that he would have to "recuse" himself—the legal term for self-disqualification by a judge who is too close to one of the parties in a legal case. Doyle did not need to pursue the point, and

Tuerkheimer did not try to dissuade him. The visitors, still in their overcoats, took their leave. The meeting in the judge's home had lasted only three minutes.

Word of Judge Doyle's recusal was quickly relayed to Earl Munson by Frank Tuerkheimer, who asked for renewed assurance that *The Progressive* would continue to hold the press while the Government tried to get its case into court. It was an academic matter, because by this time the Morland article was under lock and key, and the April issue, bearing a substitute article, was a week away from its delayed press deadline— though the Government was unaware of these facts. Munson, determined to keep the pressure on while relieving the Government of any immediate anxiety, told Tuerkheimer *The Progressive* would wait if the Government would move quickly to find another judge.

At the Federal Building in Madison, Joe Skupniewitz had returned from Judge Doyle's home with the Federal attorneys and had attempted without success to help them get in touch with one of the three Federal judges of the Eastern District of Wisconsin in Milwaukee. Early the next morning— on Friday, March 9—he called Ruth LaFave, the clerk of that court, to alert her that a "high-visibility case" was on the way.

# 12

# Free Press vs. Nuclear Secrecy

On the morning of March 9, 1979, the United States Department of Justice found a federal judge willing to stay publication of Howard Morland's article for reasons of national security. He was Robert W. Warren, a conservative Republican and Nixon appointee who had served as Wisconsin attorney general during the Vietnam war, when Governor Warren Knowles had called out the National Guard to quell student demonstrations on the university campus in Madison. Before a packed gallery in his ornate courtroom in the Federal Building in Milwaukee, Judge Warren listened to the Government's impassioned claim that publication of the article could put thermonuclear weapons in the hands of terrorists. Declaring that he would think a long time before allowing the H-bomb to fall into the possession of Idi Amin, the Ugandan dictator, Judge Warren issued an order—good for one week—restraining us from publishing the article or revealing its contents.

Stepping out onto the sidewalk after the brief court hearing, facing a battery of radio microphones and television cameras, and legally gagged from speaking about the substance of the story, Erwin Knoll and I found ourselves at a disadvantage in countering the Government's media barrage. The Department of Justice had jumped out in front the night before with a press release depicting our story as a blueprint for construction of a thermonuclear weapon. Unbeknownst to us then, Secretary of Energy

James Schlesinger had already put in calls to editorial offices of the *New York Times*, the *Washington Post*, the *Washington Evening Star*, and the *Los Angeles Times*, cautioning them against rushing to our defense. Alone among these four, the *New York Times* suspended judgment for the time being and later came to our editorial defense, but already the liberal press and the liberal scientific community were lining up solidly against us.

Typical of the editorial reaction was this early pace-setter from the *Washington Post*: "As a press-vs-Government First Amendment contest, this, as far as we can tell, is John Mitchell's dream case—the one the Nixon administration was never lucky enough to get: a real First Amendment loser."

Typical of the early public reaction was this letter we were to receive from one of our own outraged readers: "What in the name of God ever possessed you to print information on how to manufacture a thermonuclear bomb? I hope the Government wins its case, as the First Amendment was surely never meant to cover irresponsibility of this kind."

A few minutes before six in the evening after Judge Warren's ruling, above the clatter of our crowded editorial office in Madison, I heard the voice of John Buell, an associate editor:

"It's Henry Kendall," Buell cried out. "He's just made a statement on the news."

"Tremendous!" I shouted back. It came as no surprise to me to learn that Henry Kendall, the M.I.T. physicist whose battle against official secrecy in atomic energy was legendary, had been the first scientist to spring publicly to our defense.

As founder and chairman of the Cambridge-based Union of Concerned Scientists, Kendall had been the first to challenge the old Atomic Energy Commission in its cover-up of negligence in its nuclear reactor safety program. He had worked for years, with towering success, to bring the hazards of nuclear power and nuclear weapons into the open.

I couldn't help smiling with pleasure.

"But you don't understand," Buell said. "Kendall has come out *against* us. He says this was an irresponsible act. He has just been on television about it."

I felt I had been hit on the head. But it was only the first of many blows I and others at *The Progressive* took during the long, grueling, and disheartening weekend of March 10-11, when we learned that many of the nation's most distinguished public-interest scientists—some of them our close friends—had rushed to judgment on the basis of the Government's allegations.

It was with utter disbelief that I read a telegram the next day from three long-time colleagues who formed the directorship of the Federation of American Scientists:

"Your effort to publish an article whose draft title was 'How a Hydrogen Bomb Works' is not in the interest of nonproliferation but quite the reverse. And your effort to invite and induce a temporary restraining order on publication is not in the interest of freedom of the press but quite the reverse again.

"A great deal of the damage may now be irreversible since there is a possibility that some other press organ will secure and reprint any deletions you might make. And the unfortunate precedent of Government restraints of freedom of the press is in the process of being made. But we urge you in the name of the atomic scientists of conscience who founded our organization to do whatever you can to mitigate the damage this action has caused."

All through the weekend and into the next week I called scientists on the telephone. I spoke to Jeremy Stone and Frank von Hippel of the Federation of American Scientists and to Henry Kendall of the Union of Concerned Scientists and to many more in the liberal scientific establishment.

Did they really think *The Progressive* had gone mad and was intent on publishing a how-to-do-it manual for the H-bomb?

"Of course not," they would say. "But what in the world are you up to, anyway?"

"Would you like to judge the story for yourself?" I would ask. "It can be done through special arrangement with the Justice Department. We will need your date of birth and Social Security number so that we can receive special clearance for you to read the article."

There was a score of different responses to that offer:

"I'd really like to, but under the circumstances I'd better not. I can't get involved."

"I'm with you, but I really can't get into a fight over this."

"It's the wrong issue. You should drop the case. It can only lead to a bad precedent."

"I can read it only if invited to do so by the court. I must remain neutral."

"As a matter of principle, I will not submit to security clearance." (I had no argument with that answer.)

"I am already cleared for top secret. I don't see how I can properly read the article without running the risk of revealing secrets myself." (This from a former weapons designer turned arms-control advocate who had labeled us irresponsible on network television.)

"I can't do it, but why don't you try so-and-so?"

The answers were friendly, sometimes plaintive, sometimes embarrassed, almost always sympathetic. They all amounted to "no." Only once did I slam down the telephone.

All through the weekend John Buell and Publisher Ron Carbon and Associate Editor John McGrath and Ted Postol (the Argonne Laboratory scientist) and I put telephone calls through to the scientific community. We found no one.

So we turned to those we should have thought of first. In short order physics professor Charles Schwartz of Berkeley, long a burr under the saddle of the University of California (contractor for the two nuclear weapons labs at Los Alamos and Livermore), put us in touch with his friends.

Ron Carbon caught a plane late that Sunday and came back thirty-six hours later with half a dozen affidavits from scientists in Colorado and California. They were not able to read the article, but like Postol they agreed that the basic scientific concepts are already in the public domain.

Saturday, March 17. The hearing on our preliminary injunction had been postponed ten days (to March 26) and I was off on a plane to see seven scientists—all I could find in the short time allotted us—who had agreed to read the Morland article to see if the Government had made its case that publication would irreparably harm the United States. I was armed with the article itself, with Ted Postol's supporting affidavits, and with a court protective order that permitted me to show those secret documents to the scientists if the Government would clear them in time.

My first stop was Cambridge, where I received my first welcome in the liberal scientific establishment. Kosta Tsipis, a stubborn Greek in the M.I.T. physics department, had agreed to take a look.

"I give you fair warning," he had said. "If I don't agree with you I'll come out against you."

I spent five hours that Saturday afternoon in Tsipis's office, pacing back and forth as he retired to his private room, slowly read the article, laboriously composed his affidavit, summoned a typist, then signed the paper in the presence of the notary public I had hired for the purpose.

I read the affidavit hurriedly, puzzling over its elaborate but carefully constructed logic (Kosta Tsipis was not one of our more lucid contributing authors at the *Bulletin of the Atomic Scientists*), thanked him cordially, and left posthaste for the airport.

Sunday, March 18. It was 2 a.m. and I was in a bungalow somewhere in Los Angeles. I was with two other scientists—physicists Roger Dittmann and Edward Cooperman of California State University at Fullerton. I called one of our attorneys, Earl Munson Jr., in Madison; the Justice Department had not yet granted clearance to these two—even though we had asked thirty-six hours earlier and the Department had promised to provide clearances in about twenty four hours. I could not legally proceed to take their affidavits. So I flew on to Oakland, California.

By noon that day I was in the Oakland living room of Martin Brown, a University of California agricultural economist (formerly a physicist) and friend of Charles Schwartz. He had agreed to read the Morland article, as had others in the room—Schwartz and Henry Pierre Noyes, a former nuclear weapons designer who then worked in physics at the Stanford Linear Accelerator Center.

But there was a problem: Schwartz and Brown had decided, upon reconsideration, that they could not on principle submit to security clearance. And Noyes, who was willing, had not yet received his clearance—even though forty-eight hours by then had elapsed since submission of his name, date of birth, and Social Security number to the Department of Justice.

I was stalemated. The only remaining candidate was Hugh E. DeWitt, a physicist (also a friend of Charles Schwartz) who had volunteered only at the last moment on Friday. There had been no problem getting security clearance for him—and for a simple reason. As a staff member of the Lawrence Livermore nuclear weapons laboratory, he was already cleared for top secret data.

A career scientist at the Livermore lab, DeWitt was no ordinary nuclear weapons researcher. For years he had played a maverick's role at Livermore, challenging management on a wide assortment of policy issues ranging from working conditions at the lab to the merits of various weapons concepts that rolled off Livermore's drawing boards. As editor of the *Bulletin of the Atomic Scientists* I had met and interviewed him three years earlier for a story about a citizens' group seeking conversion of the University of California nuclear weapons labs (Livermore and Los Alamos) to peaceful purposes. He had been helpful to the group.

The others departed, leaving me alone with DeWitt and the Browns. I read him the "security rites" from the package provided me by the Justice Department, then gave him the Morland article. He went into Martin and Janet Brown's sunroom and closed the door behind him.

DeWitt emerged three hours later. His face was ashen. "No wonder they're trying to stop you," he told me. "The manuscript and diagrams are loaded with secret/restricted data. There's nothing I can do to help you."

I persuaded him to reserve judgment until he had read Ted Postol's paper about thermonuclear design information in the open literature. He took the Postol affidavit and disappeared once more into the sunroom. Re-emerging an hour later, he borrowed Janet Brown's typewriter and began to type, slowly and grimly, alone with his thoughts.

Another two hours passed before DeWitt was ready to show me his statement. It was incredibly powerful.

Everything was there—his acknowledgment that, after having examined the open literature, he had found that the H-bomb secret "is not so secret anymore." Watching his reaction, it became clear to me for the first time why the Government had reacted so violently to the Morland article. Could it be that the Department of Energy was so immersed in secret/restricted data that no one there was aware of the contents of public libraries across the country?

DeWitt handed his statement to me and I gave it back to him. "Think it over and we'll meet tomorrow," I said.

The next day, Monday, we met at the Berkeley home of a notary public, Rebecca Boone. She typed the statement, notarized his signature, and handed the paper to me. We walked out to the street, and then DeWitt asked for it back. He was troubled by the fact that the laboratory might misinterpret what he was doing, and he wanted me to meet first with a friend of his who held a senior post at the Livermore lab and was willing to see me at his home that evening. I returned the affidavit to DeWitt and made ready to meet that night with Ray E. Kidder.

All through Monday I badgered our attorney, Earl Munson, in Madison, who in turn badgered the U.S. Attorney for the Western District of Wisconsin, Frank Tuerkheimer, about security clearances for our California three—Dittmann, Cooperman, and Noyes. The answer was that there were no clearances yet—even though more than seventy-two hours had now passed.

Then an inspiration: Frustrated by the Government's roadblock on security clearances, I called the Livermore laboratory and asked for

The Samuel H. Day family on the porch of their Pallinghurst Road home in Johannesburg, South Africa. Left to right: Samuel H. Day, Margery Day, the author, Chris, Mayflower, and Aunt Anne, Margery's sister from Salt Lake City.

As a twelve-year-old boy in Washington, D.C.

A member (bottom right) of the 43rd Infantry Division Public Information Office bowling team at Augsburg, Germany, in 1952.

With family in Boise, Idaho, in the late 1960s. Left to right: Kathleen, Sam III, Joshua, and Philip.

Celebrating *The Progressive*'s victory in the H-bomb case, September 1979. Left to right: Teri Terry, Kate Juderjahn, John Buell, Erwin Knoll, Margot Olmstead, Ron Carbon, Laura McClure, and the author.

Brent Nicastro

H-bomb truck watchers hold a press conference at the Benedictine Peace Center in Oklahoma City to publicize passage of unmarked nuclear weapons convoys. Left to right, facing camera: the author, Nathaniel Batchelder, Tom Faudree, Bert Zipperer.

Official photograph of an unmarked tractor-semitrailer of the type used to transport nuclear warheads and their parts and ingredients. Nukewatch has distributed thousands of copies to peace activists.

John Stennes

A peace school at the fence of Missile Silo E46 near Starkweather, North Dakota, in 1987. Air Force trucks stand guard inside the fence.

The author at an anti-MX rally in Cheyenne, Wyoming.

Delivering a "notice of seizure" to Falcon Air Force Base, a Star Wars facility near Colorado Springs, Colorado.

Travis Spradling

With Nukewatch co-directors Sue Nelson (left) and Bonnie Urfer, padlocking main door of the Federal Center in Madison, Wisconsin, to protest U.S. troop buildup in the Middle East in 1990.

Joseph Blough

John La Forge

Emerging from six months in prison on September 22, 1989, with a flower brought by well-wishers.

permission to interview scientists there for the purpose of collecting affidavits. There was a long pause—a three-hour pause—and then the laboratory acquiesced. Like any solicitor, I could use the facilities at the West Pass Office, which is open to the public. I told them I would be there the next morning.

I called DeWitt, and he agreed to spread the word at Livermore. I called Kidder and he agreed to see me at the lab the next day. I called Rebecca Boone, the notary public, and she agreed to go with me to Livermore.

By now the tide seemed ready to turn. Postol told me that his three Argonne colleagues, Alexander DeVolpi, George Stanford, and Gerald Marsh, who had read the Morland article in its early stages but had been reluctant to side publicly with us, were now preparing affidavits in our behalf and would file them through the American Civil Liberties Union, which would soon enter the case as counsel for Knoll and me.

Tuesday, March 20—the first battle of Livermore. Postol, Boone, and I arrived at Livermore and set up shop in the West Pass Office, where the laboratory had set aside a small private room for our use. A guard, Richard Perkins, was stationed outside the room to make sure there were no breaches of security. The acting laboratory director, Chester Frankhauser, and his security chief, Kenneth Sebrell, were polite but correct.

First came Hugh DeWitt. We reviewed the material again, then he returned to his office to retrieve the affidavit he had already signed.

Next came Ray Kidder. He took a long time to read the Morland article and the supporting material. We discussed the subject at length, then he asked for more time to consider it. I turned to DeWitt and asked if he was ready to turn over his own affidavit to me. The affidavit, it turned out, was still in his office. He disappeared.

There were two more interviews to go. The first was Calvin G. Andre, a close friend of DeWitt. He read the Morland article, then the Postol affidavits, taking his time. He flashed a wry smile, shrugged, and said, "Looks to me like it's all out there in the open."

"Will you give me an affidavit to that effect?" I asked.

"Why, sure!"

It was all downhill from there. Within half an hour I had the first Livermore affidavit, Andre's, in my briefcase. By 7 p.m., DeWitt and a third scientist, Ralph Hager, had followed.

We had the backing of scientists, first at Argonne and now at Livermore, who did not necessarily agree with our politics (some were decidedly opposed), or even with our attitude toward secrecy, but who were willing to stake their reputations and even their careers on affirming publicly what their eyes and their minds told them.

On Wednesday, March 21, I flew to Los Angeles, then took an airport bus to Disneyland, the closest stop to Fullerton, only to find that Dittmann and Cooperman still had not received security clearance (now more than five days after the request had been submitted). I returned by bus to Los Angeles late that night, found a motel room in Santa Monica, and decided to wait there until the Justice Department had decided to clear our three Californians. By mid-afternoon the next day I got the word from our attorney: It would be six to eight weeks before Dittmann, Cooperman, and Noyes could be cleared. I decided to return to Madison, but first, on a hunch, I called DeWitt to see if there were further prospects at Livermore. DeWitt was out of his office—gone to the dentist. I called Kidder to find out the name of DeWitt's dentist. Kidder told me he was ready to sign an affidavit.

I called Frankhauser at the Livermore director's office and told him I was returning to Livermore the next day. He explained there had been a change in policy: There would be no more interviews. I asked for permission to complete the interview that had been begun on Tuesday— Kidder's. He reluctantly agreed.

Friday, March 23—the second battle of Livermore. I arrived with Rebecca Boone at the West Pass Office shortly before noon, the appointed hour for completion of the Kidder interview. Perkins, the security guard, was waiting. Kidder poked his head in the door, said he would be back with his affidavit already typed, then pedaled up ten minutes later on his bicycle.

He strode to a front desk in the West Pass Office with two affidavits in hand, put them face up with just the signature lines showing, and explained in a loud voice he was doing this because one of the two documents contained classified information. He offered to sign them and then seal them in an envelope.

I asked him to step first into the private room so he could read aloud from the unclassified parts and give me the general drift. I wanted to know what I would be taking back to Madison. We went into the private room, and then Perkins, the guard, sprang to a telephone and called the security office.

"That's it," he cried. "He's turning over classified information!"

Inside the private room, Kidder read me his unclassified affidavit, later to be known as Kidder No. I. It was our most powerful instrument to date. I summoned Rebecca Boone, and she notarized both papers. Kidder sealed the affidavits and handed them to me. Then we were interrupted by a knock on the door. It was Kenneth Sebrell, the security chief, and Jeff Garberson, the public information officer.

"Is it not a fact," asked Sebrell, looking at Kidder, "that you are turning over classified information?" Kidder nodded.

"In that case, I must advise you that Mr. Day is not authorized to carry classified information."

I put Kidder I in my briefcase and asked for time to call our lawyer in Madison, giving Kidder II to Perkins to hold until the dispute could be resolved. There followed a twenty-four-hour standoff (first at Livermore, then at Berkeley) while the lawyers in Madison and Washington argued how Kidder II could be transmitted to the Federal courthouse in Milwaukee before Monday morning's hearing without violating Livermore's security rules.

The dispute was resolved when a high Energy Department official agreed to release of the document if a courier with security clearance could be found to take it to Madison by hand. That evening the secret affidavit turned up in the suitcase of a volunteer courier who had decided to accompany me on the weekend's last available plane to Wisconsin. The volunteer was Hugh DeWitt.

The last of the affidavits went into the court record a few hours before Judge Warren read his historic decision in Milwaukee on March 26—a decision which hardened his temporary restraining order of March 9 into a permanent injunction against us. Nevertheless, with help from Ted Postol, Hugh DeWitt, Ray Kidder, and a few other "scientists of conscience," we were prepared to meet the Government on our own scientific turf.

# 13

# Unraveling of the Case

The H-bomb case continued for six months. It was a bizarre legal battle in which none of the three defendants—Erwin Knoll, Howard Morland, and I—lacking security clearance, was privy to affidavits and motions filed and argued in secret by lawyers from the two sides. The Government's case attracted enormous attention from the news media and from others curious about the phenomenon of nuclear secrecy. It was this that brought the unraveling of the case.

In the winter of 1979, as it was preparing to take *The Progressive* to court, the Department of Energy overlooked or ignored the fact that, by coincidence, the same material had just appeared in much greater detail in a political magazine written for a technical readership interested in the science that underlies the design of thermonuclear weapons. The painstaking efforts of a small group of "weapons buffs" to bring this curious double standard to light eventually forced abandonment of the case.

The secrecy rules laid down by Judge Warren, at the insistence of the Government, made it impossible for participants in the case to draw public attention to "The Secret of Laser Fusion," an unsigned article in the March issue of\*Fusion* magazine, published and distributed unbeknownst to us before publication of Howard Morland's article for *The Progressive* was blocked on March 9.

The editors of *Fusion*, oblivious to our plan to publish Morland's article in our April issue and to the Government's plan to prevent it, had drawn provocative attention to their own article in an editorial "Note to the Reader":

"We fully expect that with the appearance of this issue of *Fusion* magazine, Energy Secretary James Schlesinger and his staff will begin circulating the story—if not attempting legal prosecution—that the information in 'The Secret of Laser Fusion' is classified. Therefore, we want to make it clear that this article is based on information made public by the Soviet Union and readily available in Soviet and other international scientific circles, as well as upon information contained in a scientific paper published by Bernhard Riemann in 1859."

Rather than prosecute *Fusion*, Schlesinger chose to suppress *The Progressive*, whose author, by coincidence, had selected some of the same "secret/restricted" material to make the same point that information of this sort is readily available to people who know how to look for it.

The scientific concepts specified by the Department of Energy as "secret" were set forth by Morland in layman's terms and by *Fusion* in more technical language.

Although there was no way for others to know what the Department of Energy found objectionable in the Morland article, the relevance of the *Fusion* article to the case gradually became apparent to a few outsiders.

The first to make the connection was a *Milwaukee Sentinel* reporter, Joe Manning. Hoping to duplicate Morland's feat, he wrote an explanation of the workings of the hydrogen bomb after spending a week reading library sources, one of which was the *Fusion* article. Manning's condensation of "The Secret of Laser Fusion" was remarkably close to the pertinent Morland descriptions. His speculative linking of the two gave a helpful clue to other amateurs in pursuit of the H-bomb "secret."

Another hint came with the filing of a "friend-of-the-court" brief by the Fusion Energy Society, publishers of *Fusion*. In arguing that the principles of thermonuclear weaponry are already well known (though classified in the United States), the brief repeated the substance of the *Fusion* article and thereby spread on the open court record a virtual paraphrase of what the court was holding in secret.

By this time, the Department of Energy was putting out unintentional hints of its own.

In the earliest days of the case, three Argonne National Laboratory physicists, Alex DeVolpi, Gerald Marsh, and George Stanford (our scientific advisers for the Morland article), filed a "friends-of-the-court" affidavit documenting public sources from which design principles for the H-bomb could be learned. A fourth Argonne scientist, Theodore Postol, also an adviser, submitted two defense affidavits in the same vein.

Under the secrecy rules of the case, the Department of Energy had an opportunity to censor all materials. In the case of the Argonne scientists, the Department let several helpful references slip through, the most valuable of which was a ten-year-old Encyclopedia Americana article by Edward Teller, father of the hydrogen bomb. Diagrams accompanying the Teller article explicitly detail the H-bomb's unusual configuration.

At about the same time, the Government submitted an affidavit by a nuclear weapons design consultant, Jack Rosengren, depicting Morland's design as not just an ordinary H-bomb (as the author had described it) but as a representation of the most efficient weapon in the U.S. stockpile. This affidavit, too, escaped censorship.

The Argonne scientists reasoned that a careful investigator could conclude from this that the Government had accidentally identified Teller's encyclopedia diagrams (which themselves had never been cleared for security) as the key to the design of the most efficient H-bomb.

Incensed by what they regarded as security breaches by the Government itself, the Argonne scientists spelled this all out in a letter to Senator John Glenn of Ohio, chairman of a Senate subcommittee that oversees national security matters. The scientists asked the Senator to investigate the Department of Energy. The Department responded, a month later, by classifying their letter.

Glenn and another subcommittee member, Senator Charles Percy of Illinois, had already tangled with the Department of Energy on another matter involving *The Progressive* case. Seeking evidence to bolster the magazine's contention that the H-bomb design information is readily available, an investigator for the American Civil Liberties Union, Dmitri Rotow (himself an amateur nuclear weapons designer), visited the Los Alamos Scientific Laboratory public library and pulled from the open shelf a highly sensitive and highly technical H-bomb report, UCRL-4725. The Department promptly closed the library and reclassified the report and an equally sensitive companion document, UCRL-5280.

Glenn and Percy both expressed amazement. The Government later admitted in court that the two documents would have been as valuable to an H-bomb designer as anything in the Morland article.

Among those who followed these developments with an eagle eye was Charles Hansen, a California nuclear weapons hobbyist. Hansen, a Palo Alto computer programmer, had spent five years writing a book about nuclear weapons. Fascinated by the case and enthusiastic in his support of the magazine's cause, he quickly became a sidewalk superintendent, orchestrating his own campaign of harassment against the Department of Energy.

Enlisting the support of his congressman, Representative Pete McCloskey, Hansen bombarded Department of Energy officialdom with letters challenging their conduct of the case. Throughout the spring he drove the Department's chief classification officer, John Griffin, to distraction by organizing an "H-bomb design contest." The first entry to be classified by Griffin would be the automatic winner. (The Department threatened to refer the matter to the FBI.) But Hansen's heaviest ammunition was still to come.

Before the Department of Energy declared the Argonne scientists' letter to Senator Glenn to be "secret/restricted data," Hansen already had moved into higher gear.He had secured a copy from one of the half-dozen sources to whom the scientists had sent copies, made copies of his own, and mailed them around the country. One of the recipients, the student-run *Daily Californian* at Berkeley, defied a Department of Energy warning and printed the text of the letter. Six other college newspapers later followed suit.

Proliferation of the forbidden Argonne letter reignited Senator Percy's interest in the case. Toward the end of the summer an aide contacted Hansen and asked to be kept informed. That was all the encouragement Hansen needed.

Within days, eighteen pages of single-spaced type were on their way to Senator Percy. For openers, Hansen drew up a bill of particulars against three Government weapons experts—Edward Teller, George Rathjens of the Massachusetts Institute of Technology, and Theodore Taylor of Princeton—saying they, not *The Progressive*, should be charged with spilling nuclear secrets. But the meat of the letter was in what Hansen called "a brief history...of some of the theoretical ideas which led to the concepts now at issue in The *Progressive* case."

The "brief history" consisted of a puzzle into which Hansen had carefully fitted pieces from *Fusion* magazine, the "amicus curiae" brief of the Fusion Energy Society, the Teller diagram, and the Rosengren affidavit. For good measure, he included a diagram drawn with the aid of a tuna fish can and some jar lids.

Hansen thoughtfully mailed copies to a half-dozen newspapers—and to the Department of Energy.

On August 30, his hometown newspaper, the *Peninsula Times-Tribune* of Palo Alto, printed a story about his charges, reproducing the crude diagram he had provided but making no effort to decipher his physics. Other newspapers—the *Oakland Tribune*, the *San Jose Mercury News*, the *Milwaukee Sentinel*, and the *Wall Street Journal*—sat back and wondered whether they had a story.

At the *Daily Californian*, editor Tom Abate and his staff also wondered. They had their answer a few days later when, on September 12, word came that the Hansen letter—like the one they printed three months earlier—had just been classified "secret/restricted data."

On the same day, a Milwaukee nuclear weapons hobbyist, Jerry Fass, interviewed by the *Sentinel*'s Joe Manning, checked in with another successful description of the H-bomb "secret," but already the fat was in the fire.

For a few hectic days the Department of Energy scurried from newspaper to newspaper, attempting to retrieve its "secret." But by then it was too late. Already the Hansen letter was multiplying—as were the consequences. Unsure of the *Daily Californian*'s intentions, the Department rushed into Federal court in San Francisco on Saturday evening, September 15, to secure an injunction against the student newspaper. Before the ink was even dry the presses were preparing to roll 2,000 miles away.

Publication of Hansen's letter by the *Press Connection* in Madison, Wisconsin, the following day, coupled with a threat by the *Chicago Tribune* to do the same unless taken to court, ensured the final triumph of the H-bomb amateurs.

On Monday, September 17, the Justice Department announced it was abandoning its case against *The Progressive*. Three weeks later the article and diagrams appeared, without so much as a comma changed, in our issue of November 1979. Indeed, so intent were we on publishing the article in its original form that we let stand an embarrassing error—the placement of the Livermore Laboratory in Ron Dellums's congressional district—that ordinarily would have been corrected.

Morland's purpose in writing the article, and The *Progressive*'s purpose in publishing it, was to dispel the secrecy mystique that protects and nourishes the nuclear weapons program. The weapons, not the "secrets," were the prime target. Demonstrating that hydrogen bomb design information could be readily obtained from public sources, and then revealing and commenting on it, was for us a means to an end. We wanted to raise the level of public consciousness about America's continuing preparations for nuclear war.

Few of the H-bomb amateurs shared all those assumptions, but their collective efforts helped make our point about the H-bomb secret.

The contribution of the Fusion Energy Society toward cracking the Government's case was rich in irony. There could be few groups more ideologically distant from *The Progressive* or more fundamentally at home with Pentagon notions of "national security."

To the society and to the editors of *Fusion* magazine, the problem was not with the H-bombs themselves but with secrecy as a mechanism for protecting and strengthening the nation's technological lead in H-bombs and other forms of modern weaponry. Not only is secrecy self-defeating in this regard, they argued, but it also retards the nation's general scientific-industrial progress, notably in fusion energy, which is the society's pet project.

Thus, by spilling "The Secret of Laser Fusion" in an article spiced with thermonuclear fusion concepts they knew to be "secret/restricted data," the *Fusion* editors hoped to challenge the Department of Energy's classification program. The article, drawn mainly from the international literature (some of it 120 years old), focused tantalizingly and explicitly on the same supposed secrets that were to be at issue in the Morland article.

When the Government ignored *Fusion*'s published report and concentrated instead on suppression of Morland's unpublished article, the magazine concluded there was a conspiracy between *The Progressive* and the Department of Energy to set up an easy test case that would establish the Government's right to suppress scientific research and industrial development in the field of fusion energy. (In the Fusion Energy Society's view, we and Energy Secretary Schlesinger were in the same despised environmentalist, antitechnology camp.)

Denied a test case of its own, the Fusion Energy Society jumped into the *Progressive* case in hopes of upsetting the "conspiracy" by ensuring a victory for *The Progressive*, not the Government. The society's unsolicited "friend-of-the-court" brief, filed in the open record and loaded with "secret/restricted data" culled from scientific journals, was a loaded cannon pointed at the Government's case.

For all their paranoid overtones, the Fusion Energy Society's article and brief were persuasive indictments of the irrationality of the Government's classification program and of the Government's heavy-handed influence on freedom of the press.

None of the four Argonne scientists shared *The Progressive*'s conviction that publication of the Morland article would serve a useful purpose. (Most of them counseled vigorously against publication because they thought Morland's science was sloppy and his political point dubious.) But the Government's act of suppression made them defenders of our right to publish it.

For scientists at Argonne and at the Lawrence Livermore Laboratory who had read the Morland article and knew its publication would be harmless to the national interest, it was easy to support publication on First Amendment grounds. And they did so with dedicated energy. Their prestige as nuclear weapons experts blunted the Government's allegations that national security had been endangered and made the First Amendment fight a safer one for others who were unwilling to take *The Progressive*'s claims on faith.

The blunders of the Department of Energy—the closing of a public library and the attempted suppression of citizens' letters to their Senators to cover its own mistakes—vastly weakened the Government's case. Such mistakes demonstrated the absurdities of the classification program and lent credibility to our argument that the Morland material was already in the public domain. There is evidence that the Government welcomed the opportunity to drop the case. From time to time through the summer of 1979 we heard rumors of discontent among some Justice Department lawyers. The bizarre behavior of the Department of Energy was a growing embarrassment to them.

After the early rulings by Judge Warren granting an injunction against publication of the Morland article, the Government also seemed to be losing headway in the courts. In arguments before the Seventh Circuit Court of Appeals in Chicago in September a three-judge panel peppered the Justice Department with skeptical questions.

We looked forward with growing confidence to vindication in the courts, perhaps even by the United States Supreme Court in Washington. But then, with the tide running clearly against it, the Government backed off.

Like after-shocks following an earthquake, tremors from the H-bomb case continued to be felt long after the Government abandoned its lawsuit

145

against us. It took Hugh DeWitt more than a year to shake off efforts by the Livermore Laboratory to penalize him by revoking his security clearance. Erwin Knoll, Ron Carbon, and I traveled extensively on speaking tours to publicize the issues of the case and to raise money to pay the magazine's substantial legal bills. It was not until the spring or summer of 1980 that the publishing rhythm had returned sufficiently to normal for me to appraise fully my future at the magazine. By then I was well into the process of deciding to move on.

Three years earlier, during the last months of my editorship of the *Bulletin of the Atomic Scientists* in Chicago, Erwin Knoll and I both sensed a potential pitfall in my impending move to Madison. I was a few years older than he, and I had been an editor in my own right for more than a dozen years. I had provided the voice and set the tone for publications of my own in Idaho and Chicago. I was also accustomed to a participatory form of journalism in which editing blended with other forms of activism and the work of volunteers went hand in hand with that of the paid staff. Would my experience and style fit comfortably into the more rigid and hierarchical structure of *The Progressive*, a magazine reflecting the style, personality, and authority of a single individual, the editor?

Knoll and I were extraordinarily alike in some ways. Our political views were almost identical. Our thought patterns were sometimes uncannily alike. Once, during an editorial conference, after I had uttered some chance remark, he looked at me in amazement and exclaimed, "My God, I was about to use exactly the same words!" Both of us hugely enjoyed the craft of writing, editing, and magazine production. Both of us tended to be single-mindedly devoted to our joint enterprise. Our differences in managerial style presented no insuperable problem. The difficulty that stood in the way of my long tenure at *The Progressive* was that Erwin and I were too much alike. We were two editors with only one magazine.

The crisis of the H-bomb case suppressed the rivalry for many months. There was plenty of work and plenty of glory to go around. But when the case was over our internal problems began to surface. At the end of 1979 I burned my bridges with Gordon Sinykin and others on the board of directors by leading a fundraising campaign in support of the *Madison Press Connection*, then on its last legs. This was difficult for them because the *Press Connection* had been born as a strike organ against the local newspaper monopoly, including the *Capital Times*, with which Sinykin and the board had close ties. I also disagreed openly with Knoll and Ron

Carbon, the publisher, over inequitable pay and working conditions for lower ranking members of *The Progressive* staff.

"For all the high-sounding rhetoric about workers' rights and 'workplace democracy' that regularly filled its editorial pages, this bastion of progressivism operated essentially like a cotton plantation," I once wrote. "The editor was its 'massah' and the rest of the editorial and business staff its house niggers, some with privileges but few with any real power."

Those words were penned years later, in a column in *Isthmus*, a Madison weekly newspaper, complimenting *The Progressive*'s management and workers on signing a union contract that addressed many of the inequities. But in 1980 I had no desire to make trouble for Erwin or Gordon Sinykin or others who had the heavy responsibility of keeping this struggling enterprise alive. I had come to Madison to help them, not to add to their burden.

Other factors were pulling me away from the magazine, and from journalism itself. The ending of the H-bomb case left me with a sense of unfulfillment with regard to the issues we had raised. We had won a First Amendment victory by blocking the Government's heavy-handed attempt at censorship. But we still had a long way to go in achieving our original objective in publishing the H-bomb story, which was to encourage public defiance of nuclear secrecy, thereby strengthening opposition to the nuclear weapons enterprise. As one who had come through the fire of that historic confrontation, I felt drawn both as a writer and political activist to further battle against the demon of nuclear secrecy. It seemed that new ground was opening up before me.

In the fall of 1980, two-and-a-half years after joining *The Progressive*, I told Erwin I would soon be embarking on a new career as an independent peace activist working with others to raise public consciousness about the threat of nuclear weapons. There was little need for us to talk about what had led me to leave the magazine staff.

"There can't be two bosses," I said.

"I know," he replied.

# 14

# Going It Alone

The scene was the cozy living room of a family therapist in Kensington, a suburb beyond the Berkeley hills east of San Francisco. Seated in a semicircle of chairs and couches facing the psychologist were the members of my family: Mayflower and Chris, Mother and Dad, and me. The year was 1978. My father, still mentally alert, had reached his early nineties; Mother was twelve years younger. We had gathered there at the request of my younger sister, who, then approaching fifty, had become a family therapist in Oakland and, as was common in that profession, was herself in continuing therapy. The family session—the first we had ever undertaken or even contemplated—was desirable as part of her own therapy, Mayflower explained. Dad agreed to pay the bill, and I took on the responsibility of persuading a suspicious Chris to take part.

The two-day session, two hours each day, had been timed to coincide with one of Chris's infrequent visits to the West Coast from his home in New Jersey. "It's no big deal," I reassured him. "Dad thought this might be a way of helping Mayflower with her problems." He agreed to come along.

Now we were near the end of the final session. All through the first session and halfway into the second, four of us had listened impassively to a dialogue between Mayflower and her therapist, occasionally interjecting a word or two. We nodded sympathetically as Mayflower told of the loneliness and isolation of her childhood, of resentments in her later years, of the difficulty of rearing three young children in an unhappy marriage.

There came a pause. Then the therapist glanced at her watch and turned to the rest of us. "We've heard a lot about Mayflower's problems," she said. "Now time's almost up. Before we leave, do any of you have a problem you'd like to share with us?" She looked first at Chris.

My brother shifted in his seat and waved off the question. "No, nothing at all," he replied, "but I'm glad to do what I can to help Mayflower."

My father shook his head and my mother replied with a polite no, thanking the therapist for her interest. Then it was my turn.

"What about you, Sass?" the psychologist asked, looking at me. "Do you have anything you'd like to tell us?"

This was the moment of truth. I paused for reflection, wondering whether to duck, as the others had, closing ranks in the interest of family unity. If ever an occasion demanded the speaking of the truth, if ever there was a time to support Mayflower in her courageous effort to puncture our family's conspiracy of silence, I decided, this was it.

"Yes," I replied, "I do have a problem. It's a marital problem."

There was a stunned silence, then a chorus of exclamations.

"Patch it up, patch it up," said Chris, insistently. "You can patch it up."

"I don't want to hear a word about it—not a word," added my father, clamping his hands over his ears.

My mother fixed me with a "naughty boy" look of mixed amusement and disapproval. "Now, Sassie," she said, "stop teasing us."

Nothing more was said about the subject in the remaining minutes of the session—or afterward. But I had made my point about our family's stultifying lack of communication. For a brief time after we had left the therapist's office my bombshell managed to loosen a few skeletons in the family closet. At breakfast the next morning my mother found the heart to tell Chris for the first time how alienated she had felt since his marriage thirty years earlier. Drawing me aside later, my father bared his soul to me about such things as the frustration of sexual impotence in old age. The weekend unloosed a veritable chain reaction of revelations and confessions that had never been spoken of before within the family. It was the last time all of us were together.

The differences with Kathleen to which I referred in the therapist's office had been a long time in the making. They were to widen during my two-and-a-half years at *The Progressive* and again at the end of 1980, when I struck out on my own as a free-lance peace activist. The H-bomb case rekindled the anxieties Kathleen had first felt when I incurred the risk of prosecution in Boise for my unorthodoxies as a newspaper editor. On one level, reflecting her own visceral fear of prosecution and jail, she worried about my physical safety. At another level, while agreeing with me in principle, she found it difficult to accept the tactic of disobeying the law, whatever the reason or the consequences. This ingrained disapproval was shared by many close to her, including her sisters and brothers. It was a disagreement in which we could find no satisfactory compromise. Kathleen would have preferred that I follow a more traditional way of taking my stands, leaving the personal risk-taking to others.

To these anxieties were added the new economic uncertainties occasioned by my forsaking a regular paycheck at *The Progressive*, meager as it was, in order to test the untried waters of independent peace work; my income would depend entirely on my own fund-raising efforts. By this time Kathleen was well launched on a new career of her own, as director of the Wisconsin Legislative Hotline in Madison, and would soon be exceeding my modest contribution to the family income.

"You should have married someone your own style," she would say, with a sigh.

Nevertheless, our marriage continued and grew stronger despite—or perhaps because of—our differences in style. Beneath the flamboyant exterior of the crusading editor turned antinuclear activist she could still find qualities that had drawn her to me. I remained at heart the diplomat, the reporter, the dutiful son. Despite occasional lapses that in later years were to land me in jail and prison for political offenses, Kathleen still sensed in me the innate respectability and conservatism that were so evident in my father. "He'll come around eventually," she seemed to be saying to herself.

As for me, I valued in Kathleen the qualities that permitted me my eccentricities. Despite her deep misgivings, she provided the emotional support I needed to sustain the balance of confrontation and conformity that was necessary in my life. Her strength and understanding came to be an essential ingredient of my work, even while she was not a part of it. Her warmth and affection toward me and others whose style she disapproved of nourished my own hope that she, too, would come around eventually.

The emotional tether Kathleen provided—and continues to provide—could not have come from someone my own style.

From time to time we talked, even argued, about these and other stresses and strains, including our joint worry that our oldest son, Philip, showing early signs of emotional difficulties, had dropped out of college and drifted some place out West. We had not heard from him in more than a year.

My initial venture into independent antinuclear activism was with two associates whom I had met while covering nuclear weapons issues for *The Progressive*. Pam Solo, a Sister of Loretto, worked for the American Friends Service Committee in Denver, Colorado. Mike Jendrzejczyk was disarmament director for the Fellowship of Reconciliation in Nyack, New York. Together they had organized a joint AFSC-FOR campaign called the Nuclear Weapons Facilities Project, a loosely knit network of about a dozen local citizens' groups focusing on nuclear weapons laboratories, factories, and military bases. I joined them in the fall of 1980 as Midwestern organizer for the project, a job that took me all over the Midwest and Great Plains and put me in touch with peace activists trying to raise public awareness of nuclear weapons and their danger.

One day my travels for the Nuclear Weapons Facilities Project took me to Omaha to address a meeting of the Nebraska Civil Liberties Union. A woman approached the speakers' table and introduced herself to me as Jenna, the daughter of Virginia and George Spriggel, old friends in Idaho. George Spriggel had been the advertising director of the *Intermountain Observer*, the newspaper I had edited in Idaho in the 1960s and early '70s. A good salesman but also an arch-conservative, George enjoyed reminding me in those days of his daughter whose husband was an officer in the Strategic Air Command, knowing of my occasional tangles with the U.S. Air Force at Mountain Home Air Force Base in Idaho. But by 1981, long after my departure from Idaho, the story of Jenna and Ronald Coleman had taken an unforeseen turn.

Following our initial encounter in Omaha I got to know the Colemans well. Later, in the pages of *The Progressive*, I told the story of how Coleman, a computer expert, had progressed from command of a Titan missile in Arizona to a seat on the nuclear targeting team of Strategic Air Command (SAC) while nursing doubts that he could ever turn the key launching a nuclear missile toward its target.

The fact that Coleman and his colleagues worked behind vaulted doors, seldom disturbed by generals or other high-ranking officials, permitted the venting of their feelings through raucous humor. Coleman's branch chief took delight in a grim addendum to SAC's official motto, "Peace is our profession." He added, "Mass murder is our specialty." Coleman himself displayed in his office a popular Vietnam-era poster that ridiculed nuclear civil defense practices by listing mock safety rules, ending with the instruction to "bend down and kiss your ass goodbye."

For most of his friends, humor helped dispel the inevitable misgivings. But for Ronald Coleman it only worked for a while.

Coleman had always been able to cling to the rationalization that, whatever its other evils, the nuclear weapons program at least deterred nuclear war. But finally, after Biblical study and intensive prayer, he could no longer believe even that. "First of all, to be credible, you've got to be ready and willing to use the weapons. You have to have the intention of using them. In a number of places in the Sermon on the Mount, Christ makes quite clear that what our intentions are is just as important as what we actually do. So I came to the conclusion that the threat of their use—just the mere possession—was wrong."

In the end, the systems analyst solved the ethical equation with a simple finding of faith: "For a Christian it is totally incompatible to take part in the mass murder of millions of innocent people. It is simply wrong."

When Ronald Coleman's resignation became effective on September 11, 1977, after fifteen-and-one-half years in the Air Force, his annual income dropped from $25,000 to $12,500—the salary he was to receive later as a mathematics instructor at the University of Nebraska at Omaha. He estimated the value of the pension and other benefits he would have received had he stayed the normal minimum of twenty years at about a quarter of a million dollars.

In his first months out of uniform the former nuclear targeter would occasionally join the Pax Christi vigils at the gates of Offutt Air Force Base. His former colleagues failed to recognize him, or pretended not to know him. To them—and to others—he was just another bearded protester.

On April 25, 1981, Coleman appeared for the first time in public, at an Omaha Pax Christi teach-in on the worldwide dangers presented by SAC's nuclear targeting system at nearby Offutt Air Force Base. Two days later he gave a similar talk to a busload of Iowa ministers brought to

Omaha by an ecumenical task force. In May he spoke to a Presbyterian study group in Omaha.

"Oh gee, is he good," a woman told Joyce Glenn, who worked with Omaha Pax Christi. It wasn't the former SAC officer's information or his arguments that impressed the woman. It was the simple fact that a man stood up and told her that he had once been part of something that was wrong, and that he could no longer do it.

"In Ron Coleman's personal salvation we may well find the surest path to our salvation as a nation," I wrote in *The Progressive*. "When political, economic, intellectual, and even strategic arguments are exhausted, the ultimate collective decision may well be taken on simple faith that, as a people, we cannot turn the key."

$M$y debut as a free-lance political activist coincided with the arrival of the Reagan Administration, which, with its bellicose rhetoric, inspired the rebirth of the peace movement in the United States. Suddenly, it seemed, the whole country worried again about nuclear war. The Nuclear Weapons Freeze Campaign arose out of nowhere, piling up impressive majorities in several state referenda, including Wisconsin, in the fall of 1982. The Freeze swallowed up some of the older campaigns, including the Nuclear Weapons Facilities Project, and spawned many others, some of dubious merit.

Fund-raising letters from organizations promising a quick fix to the problem of nuclear Armageddon flooded the nation's mail boxes. "New Age" organizations peddled such panaceas as thinking new thoughts, staying nonpolitical, and sending in membership contributions. I wrote in *The Progressive*:

> For some individuals, such overtures—in a living room or through the mail—may be the threshold to action. But it is at least as likely that they will serve as substitutes—as the thermonuclear equivalent of the mouthwashes, pills, and deodorants used to lull the innumerable lesser anxieties of everyday life.
>
> Before putting your money down on any program to save the world from nuclear extinction, ask yourself these questions:
>
> Does the program affix responsibility for the nuclear arms race and other forms of militarism to insttutions here at home, some of them uncomfortably close to home?

Does it call for far-reaching and perhaps painful structural change in those institutions?

Does it deal with injustice in the same manner that it confronts the threat to peace?

And after the talking and meeting and voting are over, does it do anything?

If the answers are no, you are being offered a placebo.

Early in my independent career, after months on the road watching small and isolated citizens' organizations nibbling away at the military-industrial complex, like ants on a dragon, I decided to refocus my efforts. Returning to Madison, I threw in my lot with a group that had evolved from *The Progressive*'s H-bomb case in 1979. The Progressive Foundation had been created by the magazine in the heat of the case in order to counter the Government's propaganda and to rally public support for the magazine's right to publish nuclear secrets. After the case was over the foundation took on the name of Nukewatch and broadened its agenda to include general resistance to all forms of nuclear secrecy.

I liked the name and the mission, so in the spring of 1981 I moved in with Bill Christofferson, the executive director and sole employee, who had been trying to keep the organization afloat and on course in the financial doldrums that followed settlement of the H-bomb case.

From Nukewatch's tiny office off State Street in downtown Madison we churned out fund-raising appeals and sought to fashion an image that would perk the interest of our dwindling list of supporters while establishing a suitable niche for ourselves amidst the host of organizations offering a dizzy array of peace and justice programs.

We started a campaign against campus military research, coordinating the efforts of a dozen Midwestern student groups. We spearheaded the early organizing work of the Wisconsin Nuclear Weapons Freeze Campaign. From the Freeze, we moved on to a Nuclear Free Zone campaign, in which innumerable people, homes, automobiles, dog kennels, dormitories, campuses, and whole communities, including Madison, declared themselves free of nuclear weapons and free of the right to be defended by nuclear weapons. From Nuclear Free Zones we developed an "invest in peace" program to help the buyers of stocks and bonds screen out investments in corporations engaged in substantial military work.

In time, after Bill Christofferson's departure for a career in electoral politics (he was to become a political king-maker in Wisconsin in the late

1980s), Nukewatch evolved new forms of internal management and decision-making and found its distinctive niche outside of conventional politics. We eschewed elections, lobbying, and other efforts to influence the actions of elected officials. Instead, we adopted the concept of "direct action"—on the highways, in missile fields, and elsewhere—to raise public consciousness about the Government's continuing preparations for nuclear war. By mid-decade Nukewatch had found a useful role for itself, but through the end of 1981 and into 1982 our organization was still groping, as was I.

On February 17, 1982, my father died, at the age of ninety-five, in the arms of my sister, Mayflower. He had hoped to share vicariously in a sentimental journey I had been planning, with his active interest, for the following spring—a return to South Africa.

# 15

# Return to South Africa

In the fall of 1981, about a year after my departure from day-to-day journalism, I decided to take some time off from anti-nuclear organizing. I applied for a visa to travel in South Africa.

I had two reasons for wanting to return to the land of my youth. One reason was purely nostalgic—to visit the homes and schools and neighborhoods of my childhood, to recover the long-forgotten sights and sounds and smells, to look up old friends. Except for a brief stopover in the summer of 1945, when I went there and back as a merchant seaman, I had not set foot in the country since the age of eleven. I wanted to go back for a while. The other reason was political and professional. As a journalist covering the nuclear beat, I wanted to investigate an important question: Had South Africa built her own atomic bomb?

I was not the only one who wondered about that. Earlier events had pointed ominously to the possibility that the *apartheid* state had reached and perhaps crossed the threshold of the exclusive "nuclear weapons club." There was world-wide speculation and apprehension on this point.

One event was the discovery by Soviet and American photo reconnaissance satellites of evidence of South African preparations for a nuclear weapons test in the Kalahari Desert in August 1977. The other event was the recording of a tell-tale nuclear blast by a U.S. surveillance satellite off the South African coast in September 1979. Coupled with the existence of a South African uranium enrichment plant capable of producing weapons grade fuel, these occurrences had aroused widespread international concern.

I myself had reported on these developments in *The Progressive*. But the response of the South African government to the international furor had been evasive and ambivalent. What was lacking was evidence from the scene tending to confirm or discount the existence of an "Afrikaner Bomb."

I met with a South African consul in Chicago and told him of my desire to return to the scenes of my boyhood and of my interest in learning about South African nuclear energy and nuclear power, hoping he would not learn of what I had written on the subject of nuclear weapons. *The Progressive* agreed to pay for the trip, with help from the Fund for Investigative Journalism in Washington. For months I read up on the subject and sought advice from friends in the nuclear weapons and intelligence fields. And then, to my surprise and joy, the visa was granted.

On May 20 I landed at Johannesburg's Jan Smuts Airport aboard a South African Airways jumbo jet from Brussels. Two months later, following my return to Madison, I filed my report with *The Progressive*.

One of the experts I consulted before setting out on my trip to South Africa was Theodore Taylor, a Princeton physicist who designed some of the early warheads at the U.S. nuclear weapons laboratory at Los Alamos, New Mexico, and in later years had become an apostle of tough anti-proliferation measures.

"It will be like looking for a needle in a thousand haystacks," Taylor told me. "Why don't you just ask them the question point blank—and then look at the expression in their eyes?"

His advice came to be my operating guide in South Africa: I probed openly and repeatedly into a subject seldom mentioned above a whisper in that country, eliciting responses sometimes more interesting for what they omitted than what they touched on.

In the office of Wynand de Villiers, president of the Atomic Energy Board, I watched his muscles tighten visibly when I asked about the Kalahari bomb test, then relax when we moved to other topics.

My questions about a South African atomic bomb produced empty looks from otherwise well-informed people in and out of government; they indicated they had made it their business not to know about such things. Most whites with whom I discussed the subject reacted enthusiastically to the idea of an *Afrikaner Bomb*.

Openness served me well as a fact-finding tool and may also have helped protect me from South African laws which treat unauthorized activity in the nuclear field as akin to espionage. (A South African academic, Dr. Renfrew Christie, was sentenced to a lengthy prison term for disseminating Atomic Energy Board seismological data and floor plans for the new Koeberg nuclear power plant, both of which are readily obtainable from public sources.)

But fortuitous circumstances helped me get into South Africa in the first place, enabling me to start digging into a highly sensitive subject without attracting undue suspicion from the authorities. My background as an American who had spent his childhood in South Africa opened doors that might have remained closed to other foreign journalists. And by frankly specifying my interest in the energy field, I fashioned a safe base for focusing my inquiries progressively from energy to nuclear energy to nuclear weaponry.

The South African Department of Foreign Affairs and Information became my early ally, arranging initial appointments for me, including entry to the Atomic Energy Board's nuclear research center at Pelindaba, a mountaintop retreat not far from Pretoria. There soon proved to be limits to this cooperation, but the government's "seal of approval" helped get me going and may ultimately have proved to be the insurance for my safe return.

Journalists and others in South Africa to whom I confided my mission were astounded that I had attracted no notice from the police. They were mistaken, I am convinced, in their predictions that my mail would be opened and my telephone tapped. Tight-lipped as is the country's nuclear elite and Orwellian as is its political surveillance system, I operated no less freely as a foreign prowler through South Africa's shadowy nuclear weapons world than I had in a decade of investigation into the labyrinthine nuclear weapons empire of my own country.

International suspicion about South Africa's actual entry into the nuclear weapons club was aroused by the news, which leaked out more than a month after the event, of the sighting of a mysterious flash by a U.S. satellite over the Southern Hemisphere.

The satellite, built specifically to detect nuclear weapons tests in the atmosphere, had never given a false report in its many years of successful operation and was believed to be in good working order. The double light pulse it recorded at 3 a.m. South African time on September 22, 1979, was uniquely characteristic of a nuclear detonation, in which the initial burst of light is momentarily dimmed by a blast wave.

The Los Alamos Scientific Laboratory, which designed the Vela satellite, and the Office of Naval Research, which operated it, were convinced of the validity of the sighting. But the satellite could not pinpoint the occurrence in the vast stretch of ocean encompassed by its lens, and no hard, undisputed corroboratory evidence had ever come to public light.

There were the usual indignant South African denials and the floating of conflicting theories. Others outside South Africa speculated about an Israeli nuclear weapon test, undertaken either in cooperation with South Africa or independently and in such a way as to divert suspicion to the South Africans. Eventually, a special investigating committee appointed by President Carter's science adviser concluded that what the satellite saw was most likely the product of a collision with a tiny meteorite no bigger than a grain of sand. That conclusion remains in dispute.

I went to South Africa with no expectation that I would be able to settle the arcane Vela satellite argument. Thus, it was a surprise to me, while poring over old newspaper files in the basement of the Johannesburg public library, to come upon an item from the Vela satellite period I had not previously encountered in the Western press. Buried at the bottom of Page 2 of the *Rand Daily Mail* of September 26, 1979, was a story headlined, SA COULD HAVE SECRET WEAPON, HINTS PW.

Fascinated, I read on:

"The Prime Minister, Mr. P.W. Botha, yesterday prompted renewed speculation about South Africa's nuclear capability by stating that the country might possess a secret weapon.

"He told the Cape National Party congress that South Africa had, and could produce, sufficient arms to counter terrorism effectively insofar as this could be done militarily.

"'If there are people who are thinking of doing something else, I suggest they think twice about it. They might find out we have military weapons they do not know about.'

"Mr. Botha said he did not want to say anything more about the subject."

What gave the news account its significance were, of course, the timing and the circumstances.

The allusion to a new secret weapon, noticed and recorded by only one of the many reporters at Cape Town's packed City Hall Auditorium on the night of September 25, was all but lost in a torrent of what seemed at the time far weightier fare: Botha's triumphant return to his home base at

Cape Town on the first anniversary of his accession to power, following the downfall of John Vorster in the sensational Information Department scandal of 1978; his throwing down the gauntlet to Afrikaner conservatives within his own party; his epochal announcement that night that the government was prepared to consider changes in one of *apartheid*'s most inviolable strictures—the Mixed Marriage and Immorality Acts, which proscribed sex or marriage across the color line.

Botha was at the height of his political power that night, well on the way to moving the country toward racial reform of sorts, unchallenged on the Left or Right, untroubled for the moment by serious pressure from inside or outside South Africa. He had no apparent reason then to be sending the world a message about new South African weaponry. If that had been his intention, why was the matter dropped so quickly and never raised again?

A more plausible explanation, it seemed to me, was that in his exuberance over the news that South Africa's entry into the nuclear weapons club had finally been accomplished three days earlier, he indiscreetly let slip a hint.

In Cape Town, I looked up Michael Acott, political correspondent for the *Cape Times* and *Rand Daily Mail*, who had written the story for both papers.

"Why didn't you follow up on the story?" I asked—especially after the Vela satellite sighting came to light on October 25, just a month later.

Acott shrugged: "Of course I thought of the connection, but what would have been the point? I couldn't have used the information anyway."

The same point was made to me in a different way by Robert Molloy, science correspondent for the *Cape Times*, who had spearheaded opposition to construction of the nearby Koeberg nuclear power plant. Nuclear power is a growing issue in Cape Town, he explained to me, "but I steer clear of the bomb stuff. I'm too intelligent to get into that."

If you were going to a foreign country to find out if a peaceful nuclear research effort harbored a secret nuclear weapons program, what signs would you look for? I put that question to a Lawrence Livermore Laboratory nuclear weapons expert whom I consulted before traveling to South Africa.

"High explosives," he replied, almost immediately. "Look for evidence of regular and sustained conventional explosives testing."

My consultant explained that the essence of atomic bomb manufacture, once the fuel is in hand, is the arranging of the surrounding explosive charges in such a way that they compress the fuel with perfect symmetry, creating a critical mass. That requires a great deal of expertise and much testing with conventional high explosives.

If I should find signs of frequent high explosives testing at South Africa's nuclear research center, as there is at the U.S. nuclear weapons labs, that would be reasonable grounds for suspicion, the scientist told me. If not, I should look for another place where lots of blasting goes on, such as a mine, which might mask a high-explosives testing program for nuclear weapons.

In South Africa, I found no evidence of high explosives work at the nuclear research center at Pelindaba or at the adjacent uranium enrichment plant at Valindaba. But even before my arrival, my attention had been drawn to another quarter.

In preparing for the trip I had asked for a list of *The Progressive*'s current and recent subscribers in South Africa, of whom there turned out to be only four. One was in Cape Town and two were in the Johannesburg area, but it was the fourth that caught my eye. The subscription label read:

The Librarian AECI Ltd
Somerset West Factory
Dynamite Factory 7120
So Africa

AECI, I soon discovered, stood for African Explosives & Chemical Industries—the world's largest manufacturer of explosives. The company had entered a subscription to *The Progressive* at the beginning of 1981 and allowed it to lapse a year later.

What was this American monthly political magazine doing in the research library of an explosives factory ten thousand miles away? I resolved to find out when I reached South Africa. Meanwhile, I wondered whether the explanation might have something to do with the worldwide publicity which attended the Federal Government's suppression of Howard Morland's 1979 article in *The Progressive* about hydrogen bomb secrecy.

Could it be that an AECI researcher, like others for whom the H-bomb case served as introduction to *The Progressive*, had ordered the magazine under the mistaken impression that it was a technical journal dealing with nuclear weapons design?

One of my first visits in Johannesburg was to the headquarters of AECI in the fifty-story Carlton Center, the tallest office building south of the Equator, where entry to the company offices is through guarded doors with electronic control devices, and where signs in the elevator advise that "visitors to AECI Ltd. must report to security control on the fourteenth floor." Such precautions struck me as unusual, even in security-conscious South Africa, but they were only a mild foreshadowing of the fortress mentality I was to encounter at AECI.

How was I to check out the Somerset West dynamite factory without arousing suspicion? Explosives did not fit logically into the subject—energy policy—I had specified to the South African tourist authorities as my area of reportorial interest. Hence, I could not readily ask for an official introduction to the factory. But the fact that AECI is a conglomerate spilling over into many fields gave me a chance to get my foot in the corporate door. Within a few weeks after my arrival in Johannesburg I found myself in an office at the company's plant at nearby Modderfontein, chatting with Collin Schlesinger and Lincoln J. Partridge, who were in charge of a project to make methanol, a liquid fuel, out of coal.

The two scientists, both genial, third-generation South Africans of English descent, could soon tell that my interest in methanol was limited. At the first opportunity I steered the conversation to explosives. Where did AECI do its explosives research and testing?

At Modderfontein, they replied. Also, of course, at Somerset West. They mentioned that the two plants—one near Johannesburg and the other outside of Cape Town—were traditional rivals.

I started to dig more deeply into the goings-on at Somerset West but was afraid of arousing undue suspicion, so I backed off. Later in the interview I mentioned as off-handedly as I could that I would be traveling to Cape Town later in the month and might like to drop by Somerset West.

They expressed surprise and said they doubted the visit would be worth my time. But I persisted, explaining with a laugh that I wanted to meet the company librarian because he was one of our subscribers. Schlesinger gave me the name of the Somerset West manager—J.P. van Leeuwen—and wished me luck.

Two weeks later in Cape Town, after much mulling of strategy, I decided to take the direct approach to AECI. Telephoning the Somerset West manager's office, I identified myself as an American journalist and said I'd like to visit the explosives operation. The secretary told me Mr. van Leeuwen was out for the day, but she could assure me no tour was possible. It was against company policy.

Taking another tack, I asked her if I could visit the company library and meet the librarian, who was one of our subscribers. The secretary, sounding increasingly suspicious, asked me why I wanted to do that and went on to inquire about *The Progressive*. I pleaded some more, and she told me to call back two days later, when the manager would be in.

My prospects in Somerset West did not look good. The next day I gave it another stab, trying to bypass the manager and his secretary by going directly to the librarian. My strategy was to find out who had placed the order for *The Progressive* subscription, make contact, and see what developed.

I telephoned the AECI operator, got through to the library, and spoke with a woman who identified herself as the librarian. So far so good.

I identified myself and asked to speak with the person who had ordered our magazine at the end of 1980. She told me this was before her time, so I asked her to guess who the person might have been.

"I'll put you through to the chief chemist, Mr. Rousseau."

Now we were getting somewhere, I thought. But then, to my dismay, the familiar voice of the manager's secretary came on the line. She was angry and insistent, demanding to know if I were the same person who had called the day before. I had to admit that I was.

She announced with finality that there was no way I could get into the Somerset West plant and that it would be fruitless to call the company manager the next day, as we had agreed earlier.

Taking full command, she concluded the conversation: "I'm sorry, Mr. Day, we don't allow anyone into our nuclear—I mean our manufacturing—areas."

Her slip was as close as I could come to establishing the AECI connection.

If Somerset West was indeed the Pantex of South Africa's nuclear weapons program, mirroring in miniature the Texas Panhandle final assembly plant that services America's far larger effort, what route would the prototype *Afrikaner Bomb* have taken on its journey to the sea in 1979?

I asked myself that question as I explored South Africa's Cape Peninsula for a week in June of 1982. The most obvious port of embarkation was Simonstown, site of the country's principal naval base, less than thirty miles south of Somerset West. But my attention had been drawn to a smaller, less conspicuous port a somewhat greater distance away.

Browsing one morning among the periodicals in the Cape Town public library, in search of signs of unusual naval activity in September 1979, I came upon a "notice to mariners" in the *South African Shipping News and*

*Fishing Industry Review*, a monthly journal. The notice, promulgated by the South African navy shortly before the September 1979 Vela sighting, established a "prohibited area" along the northwest coast of the Cape Peninsula about 100 miles north of Cape Town.

Curious, I checked other issues of *Shipping News* and found that this was the only prohibition of its kind declared anywhere in South Africa during 1979. Clearly, such an order was not an everyday thing. I bought a nautical map, plotted the coordinates given in the notice to mariners, and located the "prohibited area" on a peninsula jutting into Saldanha Bay, a deep-water harbor which South Africa had been developing for iron ore exports. The map also showed a "military practice area" just offshore. I decided to have a look.

Setting out one morning in a rented car on my last full day in Cape Town, I drove around the flank of Table Mountain to the city of Somerset West and parked outside the front gate of AECI's sprawling dynamite factory, from which I had been unceremoniously excluded. The gate was a thicket of guards and barricades. Surveying the scene for a moment, I turned around and headed north toward Saldanha, following a route that took me past the lush vineyards of the Eerste River Valley, the gabled buildings and oak-lined avenues of the 300-year-old university town of Stellenbosch, the glistening mountaintop *Taalmonument* built by Afrikaners as a tribute to their Afrikaans language, and into the dry rangelands that lead eventually to the barren and windswept Atlantic coast.

At Saldanha I found an ore dock leading into the bay, a busy fishing port and dockside cannery, a sleepy little tourist town, and a small naval base with an adjacent military training center. From across the bay I peered at the peninsula from which the South African navy had barred the public three years earlier. It commanded a fine view of the harbor, I noticed, but there was nothing much to see now except a flock of grazing sheep and the graceful swooping of the sea gulls.

In the nearby town of Vredenburg, I dropped by the office of the region's weekly newspaper, *Die Weslander*, and chatted with a printer I found working over an old press, his arms up to his elbows in ink.

Is there ever much excitement around here, I asked? No, he said, but the fishing was great. He gave me some back copies of *Die Weslander*. Soon it was time to go. As I was leaving, I turned to him and said:

"By the way, I happened to notice in a magazine the other day that around three years ago the navy declared a prohibited area around here. Do you know what that was all about?"

The printer scratched his chin for a moment and then replied:

"Oh, yes, I remember. It was down there near Langeban," pointing in the direction from which I had come. "They used it for machine-gun firing practice. It's very dangerous. I wouldn't go near there if I were you."

W as Saldanha the port from which South Africa embarked on its nuclear weapons test, somewhere far to the south? My investigation established no hard evidence that it was. But it did uncover an unusual pattern of naval interest and activity in that out-of-the-way spot at a crucial time three years earlier.

Was Somerset West the place where the bomb came together? Once again, I had found no proof that would stand up in a court of law. But a web of circumstances suggested that this key installation clearly had the capability and was the most likely candidate for the job.

Was there, in fact, a successful nuclear weapons test on September 22, 1979, and was South Africa responsible for it? I found no one in South Africa who would admit to witnessing it. But, notwithstanding the conclusion reached by President Carter's special commission, the evidence of a South African test has always been substantial; my discovery of Prime Minister Botha's hint of a new secret weapon, three days after the event, added to the plausibility of the case.

Was South Africa preparing for a nuclear weapons test in the Kalahari Desert in August 1977 when the outside world discovered it and blew the whistle? Again, I found no eye-witnesses, but no other interpretation of that bizarre episode made sense.

Blacks, who constitute four-fifths of South Africa's population, seemed in no doubt about whether there was an *Afrikaner Bomb*. Not one of the dozen or so with whom I discussed the subject doubted the existence of the weapon or the readiness of the government to use it. Said Bishop Desmond Tutu, secretary-general of the South African Council of Churches:

"I have no doubt there are some here who would use the bomb as a form of scorched earth policy. Their raids into Angola are evidence that they will stop at nothing."

What of the Afrikaners themselves? Most of those with whom I raised the topic said they assume the government was at work on a bomb. With few exceptions, such work had their firm support.

I concluded my article in this way:

> The defiant righteousness of [those] for whom the nuclear button now provides additional insurance for white South Africa finds its purest expression in a pamphlet handed to me on one of my last days in South Africa as I entered Afrikanerdom's most hallowed shrine, the Voortrekker Monument, which sits atop a hill overlooking Pretoria. It read:
>
> "This noble structure, visible from afar, serves to remind our people of a covenant made with God by our brave and pious forefathers at a time of crisis in our history. It tells of men, women and even children who braved dangers daily so that we may live in peace and safety; of people who were willing to risk their material possessions as also their very lives and frequently to lose both, for the sake of freedom and independence; of ancestors who respected the culture and material possessions of others but who were prepared to defend themselves bravely against unprovoked attack. Both in thought and action they at all times relied on the Guidance of Almighty God."
>
> As I gazed on the marble cenotaph forming the monument's central structure, with its inscription of Afrikanerdom's sacred pledge, ONS VIR JOU SUIDAFRIKA ("We for thee, South Africa"), it seemed to me that here was the ultimate confirmation, if any were still needed, that there is an *Afrikaner Bomb.*
>
> For South Africans, black and white, its existence imparts a terrible new dimension of death and destruction to a future that already holds the certain prospect of violence and bloodshed.
>
> For others—and for Americans especially—the *Afrikaner Bomb* is another sobering step in a global journey of death and destruction, a journey that we initiated, that we have hastened, that we have popularized, that we have made respectable for white South Africa, and that we—perhaps only we—have the power to reverse.

The appearance of "The Afrikaner Bomb" in the September 1982 issue of *The Progressive* evoked a predictable cry of outrage from the South African government. Consul-General Gert J. Grobler in Chicago, writing to the magazine, recorded his "strongest protest and exception, not only

167

to the superficial, twisted, and malevolent contents but also to the highly unethical and unprofessional conduct of your journalist, Mr. Day." His reference was to my failure to disclose the precise purpose of my trip—the search for the *Afrikaner Bomb*. However, he did not deny the principal conclusion of the article, that South Africa had built and tested an atomic bomb.

The article attracted the interest of western publications specializing in African affairs, notably *Africa News*, published in Durham, North Carolina, but it received its biggest play in South Africa itself, where censorship laws restrict local news coverage of atomic energy and national security. The newspapers there reported my conclusions, most of them skeptically, without going into specifics.

A similar reticence marked the reaction of South African friends—some old, some new—to whom I sent copies of the article. Their response was silence. I had broken a taboo. The passionate interest in South Africa's future I had found in young Afrikaners and blacks did not seem to be shared by the few friends from my childhood I had managed to locate after thirty-seven years. Most of my English-speaking boyhood chums had long ago abandoned South Africa for England, Canada, Australia, the United States. The few who remained led lives of lonely affluence, cynicism, fear, and escape. Most were planning to leave South Africa some day.

For me, the scenes of my childhood—the fortress-like homes along Pallinghurst Road, the white faces in the schoolyard at the Ridge, the deserted beach at Umkomas, the Dallas-like commercialism of downtown Johannesburg—were ashes from the past. I found life and hope instead in a sector of South Africa I had not known as a child.

I discovered a new and vibrant South Africa in two young black men—white-collar workers by day and African National Congress revolutionaries by night—with whom I spent one of my last evenings in Johannesburg.

Both had persuaded themselves that armed struggle is the only policy that makes sense for black South Africans—the only tactic that will force concessions from a central government bent on perpetuating its control, that will attract the sympathetic attention of the outside world, that will hasten the revolution that seemed inevitable to them.

They seemed undaunted by the massive firepower and the counterinsurgency system South Africa has erected to beat back just such an attempt, the militarized infrastructure that has turned the country into a virtual police state. They were convinced that numbers—and the utter dependency of the white social and economic system on black labor— were on their side. What amazed them was the inability of white South Africans to sense the mood of the blacks who surround them.

"They go by what their servants tell them," one of them told me. "They are anxious, but they do not perceive. There is a complete absence of communication in South Africa. The whites do not want to communicate. The blacks no longer see any point in it."

I also heard hopeful signs in the earnest voices of two young Afrikaner medical students with whom I spent an evening in the club car of a train from Cape Town to Johannesburg. The descendants of sturdy Boers who had made the Great Trek into the Transvaal, they were impatient with the intransigence of their elders and ready to work with the black majority for a peaceful and just South Africa. But would their generation come to power before it was too late?

In Johannesburg I visited Bishop Tutu, who was later to receive the Nobel Peace Prize for his nonviolent approach to the problems of that troubled land. Bishop Tutu had recently told a student audience at Stellenbosch:

"What the future holds for our country will, ultimately, be determined by how Afrikaners and blacks relate to one another, simply because the one group is dominant in white society which currently enjoys over- whelming political, economic, and social power, whereas the other has an unassailable ascendancy in population numbers which give it a tremen- dous potential for playing a decisive role in the unfolding history of our land."

I left South Africa feeling that the decisive struggle between over- whelming power and overwhelming numbers was about to be joined.

# 16

# The H-Bomb in Our Midst

One highway patrol car, then another, fell in behind the white Ford Torino as it sped eastward through the Texas panhandle and into Oklahoma late one August afternoon. A flashing red light came on, followed by a siren.

The pursuing squad cars pulled the Torino over. Two state troopers advanced, their hands poised on their holsters. From one of the squad cars, a voice barked through a loudspeaker.

"First, the driver. Get out slowly and put your hands on the hood of the patrol car." A woman in her mid-twenties emerged.

"Now, the passenger." A man of about the same age climbed from the other side of the front seat and spread out his arms. When he reached for something in his shirt pocket, he was ordered to keep his hands on the hood of the car.

Methodically, the troopers frisked the pair, took their driver's licenses and other identifying papers, searched their automobile, and examined a book they found on the car seat. Meanwhile, the diesel-powered tractor-trailer the woman and man had been following disappeared into the distance....

On that note I began a story for *The Progressive,* "H-Bombs on Our Highways," that launched a new peace campaign for Nukewatch and set our organization on a new path in the summer of 1984.

The driver of the Torino, Roddey Cohn of Norman, Oklahoma, and her passenger, Brian Flagg of Amarillo, Texas, were participants in a project to seek out, follow, and report on movements of the unmarked trucks that transport nuclear weapons to various destinations in the United States. For most of a week we had sat in our cars at the gates of the U.S. Department of Energy's nuclear warhead final assembly plant (called Pantex) on the flat, sun-scorched Texas panhandle, waiting for convoys to emerge.

From time to time we had given chase, only to be eluded by the fast-moving tractor-trailers or pulled over by squad cars from the local sheriff's office. But on this occasion Roddey and Brian had managed to hang on all the way to the Oklahoma border, some eighty-five miles from Pantex. Her telephone call to friends in Oklahoma City, 150 miles to the east, alerting them to the approach of the convoy, enabled peace activists to witness for the first time the passage of nuclear warheads through the streets of an American city.

Thus was born the H-Bomb Truck Watch, a campaign which, over the years, has tracked warhead convoys for tens of thousands of miles from coast to coast and from Texas to North Dakota, focused the energies of grass-roots peace organizations from California to South Carolina, and made connections with antinuclear activists in Britain and Western Europe.

Together with our missile silo campaign, which began the following year and has continued on a parallel track since 1985, the H-Bomb Truck Watch enabled Nukewatch to project itself as an organization helping people make psychological contact with the Bomb. For me, the truck watch and the silo campaign (in which we located and identified Air Force underground missile silos in the Midwest and Great Plains) satisfied an appetite for investigative reporting and political confrontation. Chasing trucks and finding silos harnessed my aptitudes for journalism and political action to a noble chariot—the cause of nuclear disarmament. The campaigns also suited my taste for adventure. I threw myself into them with enthusiasm.

The purpose was never to stop the trucks or disarm the missiles. Our aim was to lift the veil that hid the warheads, much as *The Progressive* had done in the H-bomb case. We believed that experiencing the reality of nuclear weapons at close hand would motivate at least some people to greater exertion in behalf of nuclear disarmament.

The Department of Energy's nuclear weapons transportation system had come to my attention for the first time in 1978, when, as managing editor of *The Progressive*, I toured the Government's nuclear weapons production complex in several Western states. In a control room at Albuquerque, New Mexico, I watched as radio operators monitored the comings and goings of "safe secure trailers" (SSTs) transporting nuclear warheads and their parts and ingredients all over the country.

There was nothing secret about the existence of these armor-plated tractor-semitrailers and the paramilitary couriers who drove and guarded them. But the routes and schedules were "classified" for reasons of security. The convoys blended inconspicuously into the stream of traffic on freeways and other major highways, stopping for food and fuel and mixing casually with other travelers at truck stops, restaurants, and hamburger stands. Inconspicuousness served as the first line of defense against surprise attack. It also served the political purpose of shielding from public view the extent of the country's involvement in nuclear weapons production, transportation, and deployment.

I took note of this exotic transportation system in my report for *The Progressive*, "The Nicest People Make the Bomb," but its implications for my work as an antinuclear investigator and activist did not dawn on me until later.

In December 1982 some members of a western Washington peace group, the Ground Zero Center for Nonviolent Action, happened to notice a strange-looking freight train, painted an eerie white, enter the Navy's Bangor submarine base on Puget Sound. They made inquiries and discovered that the cargo was a shipment of nuclear warheads for the Navy's new Trident submarine fleet.

Like the highway tractor-trailers specially designed for such sensitive cargo, the Government's custom-built trains had been crisscrossing the country for decades without attracting much notice. But to those who saw it for the first time in 1982, the ghostly glow of the bomb-laden railcars, painted white to help keep the interior temperature under control, evoked images of the hell of nuclear holocaust.

"The Nuclear Train is both symbol and reality," wrote Jim Douglass, a founder of the Ground Zero community, likening it to the trains that carried millions to the death camps of Nazi Germany. "Its passage on thousands of miles of track across the United States is a symbol of our overall complicity in holocaust. The Nuclear Train's reality is an unimaginably destructive cargo."

When Ground Zero began focusing on the White Train at Puget Sound, the campaign broadened almost overnight into a national network of peace groups determined to draw attention to the cross-country movement of the nuclear warheads.

Small groups of train watchers concerned about nuclear weapons began forming in towns along the tracks of the White Train, from Bangor to Amarillo, origin of the rail shipments. Together, they called themselves the "Agape Community," a name taken from a Greek word (pronounced *ah-GAH-pay*) signifying a spiritual force embodying "the love of God operating in the human heart."

Demonstrators sometimes blocked the tracks when the White Train was coming, and arrests were made. In February of 1984, some 200 demonstrators in Portland, Oregon, stopped the train for two and a half hours. By mid-1984, the Agape Community had 200 trackside peace groups from coast to coast.

Hoping that the spirit and fervor that propelled the White Train campaign could be harnessed against H-bomb trucks, which carry a far greater warhead tonnage, I set out in the summer of 1984 to stimulate public awareness of the nuclear highway traffic. My first step would be an article for *The Progressive* describing the unusual highway transportation system and linking it to the ghostly White Train that had attracted so much public attention. The Albuquerque Operations Office of the Department of Energy answered my questions about the general scope of the operation—forty to fifty semitrailers on the road; four and a half million miles logged annually—and also furnished a photograph of a typical SST. But the story also needed action and color, so I set about organizing a field project to find and follow an unmarked convoy.

As a setting for the project I thought first of the Rocky Flats nuclear warhead trigger factory in Colorado, maker of the plutonium fission bombs that ignite the thermonuclear blast in a typical warhead. For years Rocky Flats had been a focus for antinuclear activists in nearby Denver and Boulder. I drove out to Colorado in the early summer, taking the SST photograph with me, and met with members of Denver's Agape Community, close allies of Ground Zero. We decided to set up an H-bomb truck watch the next day at a traffic intersection in the town of Broomfield, astride an approach to the Rocky Flats plant.

In the early evening of July 4th, carrying binoculars, two folding chairs, a water bottle, and my briefcase, I took up a post on an embankment above a commuter parking lot affording a view of traffic coming east from the factory. I remained there for forty-eight hours, joined from time to time by Agape volunteers who would drive up from Denver to take turns at the vigil. At about six in the evening of July 6th we saw our first SST.

"There it is," cried Shirley Whiteside, a soup kitchen volunteer who had arrived a few minutes earlier with Pat Montgomery, a Catholic nun, bringing an iced martini to relieve my thirst. We watched in awe as the big semitrailer approached from the direction of the factory, paused at the intersection, then disappeared into the freeway traffic bound for Denver. We could tell it was an SST from the distinctive shape of the radio antenna, looking like a luggage rack, atop the truck cab; from letters painted on the sleek, silver trailer, and from the Department of Energy federal license plates.

From the parking lot in Colorado the trail led to the Pantex factory in Texas. There I huddled with Hedy Sawadsky, a Mennonite activist from Colorado who had gone to Texas months earlier to establish a watch on the White Train, and with nuns from the nearby convent of the Franciscan sisters of Mary Immaculate. With Les Breeding, a native Amarillan, Hedy had learned how to detect telltale signs of a build-up of the White Train in the loading area of the plant, visible by field glasses from a road skirting the northern fence. Hedy and the mother superior, Sister Bernice Noggler, in black and white habit, had become familiar figures to Pantex security guards in their frequent visits to the north fence. The two women readily accepted my suggestion that we join forces.

Despite its reputation as a hawkish place, Amarillo proved to be an effective base from which to mount the enlarged H-bomb truck watch we were to undertake a month later.

For one thing, the nearby Pantex plant guaranteed a heavy concentration of Bomb traffic. For another, the attitudes of local residents had begun to change.

Three years earlier, Amarillo's Catholic bishop, Leroy T. Matthiesen, shocked the community by establishing a fund to help Pantex employes quit their jobs if they were troubled about working on the Bomb. The plant, with 2,700 workers, was the largest employer in the Amarillo area.

175

Matthiesen and other local peace activists had established a visible presence at the heart of the Government's Bomb production system.

Our truck watch began in early August, following the annual Pantex rally of the Red River Peace Network, at which we recruited volunteers. Seated in automobiles and on folding chairs positioned a few yards outside the main gates of Pantex, a dozen of us working in relays maintained an unbroken watch on the Government's nuclear warhead assembly plant for 192 hours.

Swatting flies by day and mosquitoes by night, the truck watchers kept a lookout on the roads that border the factory, searching for signs of Bomb traffic.

Trucks leaving the Pantex plant could be carrying cargo of two kinds: finished warheads destined for a military station, or warhead components for recycling at Rocky Flats and other weapons factories. The United States at that time produced between five and eight bombs a day, most of them replacing aging and outmoded elements in the worldwide atomic stockpile.

We guessed that as many as three weapons truckloads—containing twenty to forty warheads—might leave Pantex in a typical workweek. But we witnessed a number of Bomb trucks that far exceeded our expectations.

In eight days, we sighted seven incoming and outgoing convoys, each ranging from two to six vehicles. A single tractor-trailer was capable of carrying twelve Trident submarine missile warheads with a combined explosive yield of 1.2 million tons of TNT—the equivalent of 1,000 Hiroshima bombs.

The highway vigil had found one thin thread of a vast, unseen web that cradles the Bomb in America.

When our vigil group at Pantex gathered for a closing ceremony, we decided to offer the guards a flashlight as a peace offering and memento. Gingerly, we approached the guard shack at the main gate.

I was the one elected to make the presentation of the gift. The three men at the guard post eyed us with suspicion, as if we might be preparing an assault on the plant.

"We have this flashlight," I began, "and we'd like to present it to you as a token of..."

The lieutenant in charge, H.A. Hudson, eyed me coldly.

"We already have enough flashlights," he replied.

"But you don't understand," I persisted. "This flashlight was presented to us as a gift. Now we want to pass it on to you."

The officer remained unmoved. "If it was given to you, then you ought to keep it."

We were getting nowhere. Then I heard the voice of a member of our group, Peter Sprunger-Froese, who had spent one night alone on a chair near the little-used north gate of the installation. He and the same officer had talked a bit through the fence that night.

"Say, Hudson," Sprunger-Froese chimed in, "I want to thank you again for warning me about the rattlesnakes the other night."

That broke the ice. The officer's scowl dissolved into a grin—and he and the other guards wisecracked with our group about the hazards of rattlesnakes in the Texas panhandle.

There was a pause in the small talk, then Lieutenant Hudson turned toward me.

"Hell, give me that thing," he said, taking the flashlight.

We all shook hands with the guards. Then the ten of us walked away.

Since the first Pantex stakeout the H-Bomb Truck Watch has become a frequent occurrence for Nukewatch and affiliated groups. The Benedictine Peace House in Oklahoma City, a crossroads for H-bomb highway traffic, became our communications center for week-long truck watches, plotting convoy movements phoned in from the field and spreading the word to news media and peace activists in the paths of the convoys. With our telephone directories, our pocket calculators, and our maps and charts pasted to the walls, we were a homespun counterpart to the multi-million-dollar, high tech bunker from which the Albuquerque Operations Office directed its far-flung nuclear weapons delivery system.

In December 1984, accompanied by Bonnie Urfer of Madison (later to become a Nukewatch staff member), I drove to Knoxville, Tennessee, to help organize a truck watch at the Y12 atomic weapons factory in nearby Oak Ridge. While we were paying a courtesy call on the Oak Ridge police chief, Bonnie drifted over to a far wall of the chief's office, studied an aerial map she found there, and identified the vantage points from which we could cover the various factory gates in that wooded, hilly country. Later that week we spotted a convoy leaving Y12 and tracked it all the way to Oklahoma City, where activists from the Benedictine Peace House met it and provided a "citizens' escort" through town.

Scores of volunteers from Tennessee in later years were to track the unmarked warhead convoys west from Oak Ridge through Nashville and Memphis to Pantex and southeast to the Savannah River tritium production plant in South Carolina. On one occasion, Steve Clements of Knoxville, driving alone, followed an SST and its escort from the outskirts of Oak Ridge to the beltline around Washington, D.C., where the truck delivered a load of highly enriched uranium to a research reactor at the National Bureau of Standards.

Anne Murray, a staff volunteer at the Benedictine Peace House, has followed convoys from Pantex northwest to the Idaho National Engineering Laboratory and from Oklahoma City north to Grand Forks Air Force Base in North Dakota—journeys that took days of constant driving, broken only by brief stops for food and fuel. From the "Peace Farm," established in the late 1980s on a plot of land across the highway from Pantex, Les Breeding has followed SSTs southeast to Fort Worth and west through New Mexico and Arizona into California.

In the summer of 1985 Nathaniel Batchelder, a Benedictine Peace House staff member, accompanied me to England, Scotland, and West Germany to compare notes with the trackers (and occasional blockaders) of nuclear weapons convoys in those countries. Finding convoys is an easier task there because the bomb trucks are invariably accompanied by military and police escort. In exchange, British and German peace activists sometimes have taken part in our exercises.

In the United States, the Department of Energy has reconciled itself to our occasional presence, taking what steps it can to thwart our efforts to bring the movements of the convoys to public attention. These measures have included the extensive rescheduling and rerouting of H-bomb convoys to avoid being seen by roadside demonstrators. In recent years during H-bomb truck watches the Department has rerouted convoys around the entire state of Oklahoma, a detour of hundreds of miles, enabling Benedictine Peace House activists to assert with pride that, for a few days at least, the Sooner State was kept nuclear-free.

Unable to match the Department of Energy in technical sophistication or budget outlays, the H-Bomb Truck Watch never was able to focus sustained national attention on the clandestine nuclear weapons highway traffic. The convoys, racing at speeds of eighty miles an hour or more, changing routes without warning, and sometimes holing up at Air Force bases to elude us, did not lend themselves to the kind of peaceful, contemplative confrontation that was possible in the case of the White

Train, until the Department of Energy suspended that mode of transportation in 1987. Despite our best efforts, we never succeeded in confronting the convoys with large numbers of people. Getting people into close proximity with nuclear warheads was an objective better accomplished by a different Nukewatch project, which had its genesis on a Montana prairie in the summer of 1983.

For what seemed like ages, I stared at the odd assortment of pipes and poles sticking up from the ground in the middle of a vast Montana barley field, my nose pressed against the wire fence, my mind trying to comprehend the enormity of what I saw.

The enclosure was about the size of a modest residential lot, and a wooden light pole stood near each corner, ready to illuminate nocturnal work. In the center of the area were four tuba-shaped devices standing guard over a large concrete slab mounted on rails. The pipes, I was told, were electronic sensors; the heavy slab was a lid.

Except for a faint hum that came from what appeared to be a ventilation outlet, I might have concluded that this strange installation had been abandoned years ago. Grass sprouted here and there in the gravel, and the concrete lid had a large crack. Locking the gate to the site was a chain not much sturdier than the one I use to secure my bicycle back home.

I exchanged glances with the two friends who had brought me there and shook my head in disbelief.

The lock and three strands of barbed wire atop the fence made it plain that we were not welcome. The signs prominently displayed along the perimeter made it even clearer:

**WARNING**
Restricted Area
It is unlawful to enter this
area without permission of the
installation commander.
While on this installation
all personnel and property
under their control
are subject to search.
**Use of deadly force
authorized.**

The warning was ominous enough, but nothing in those words or in anything else I saw fully prepared me for the realization that I was standing only a few yards above the tip of an eighty-foot missile with the destructive power of a half million tons of TNT....

That was the way I began a story, "The Restless Ranchers of Missile Country," in *The Progressive* of October 1983. It marked my first visit to an underground intercontinental ballistic missile silo. The encounter sparked a campaign to summon people in large numbers to the fences of these launch sites—one thousand of them scattered across seven states of the Midwest and Great Plains—each capable of raining nuclear death on cities on the other side of the world.

My visit to Romeo-29 was a brief encounter occasioned by a stopover at a nearby peace camp during a get-acquainted tour of nuclear resistance groups in the western United States. But it was not until the spring of 1985—a year and a half later—that our missile silo campaign began in earnest, inspired by a dramatic "disarmament action" at a missile launch site in western Missouri. Four peace activists—all of them my friends— had broken into the fenced enclosure with a ninety-pound pneumatic drill and hammered away at the 120-ton steel and concrete lid of the missile launch tube. One of their aims had been to call attention to the 150 Minuteman missiles and fifteen launch control centers that had stood on alert in the "Show Me" state for a quarter of a century, near churches, schools, and shopping malls, each armed with a warhead one hundred times more powerful than the bomb that destroyed Hiroshima. We decided to help further that purpose.

Working with fuzzy, faded, small-scale missile silo maps obtained some years earlier from Strategic Air Command headquarters, two Nukewatch staff members—Bill Mutranowski and Colleen Germain—labored for weeks transferring the faint dots of the missile silos onto a Missouri highway map. Then, over the summer of 1985, teams of volunteers took to the highways and country roads of Missouri, copies of our map in hand, attempting to locate each launch site and launch control center. The project was coordinated in Missouri by Roy Pell, a retired airline executive active in the Kansas City Interfaith Peace Alliance.

By the fall we had accumulated enough information to produce a large poster map called "'Show Me!'—A Citizens' Guide to the Missile Silos of Missouri." The red dots depicting the military installations, scattered across a sixth of the state, looked like sores left by a scourge. Next to the map were precise directions for finding each silo and launch control center. ("L2. *Harried missile*. From county roads Z, N, and F north of Garden City, go 4.5 miles east on State Route 7. Missile is on the left.") We let searchers assign nicknames—some humorous, some ironic—to the missiles and launch control centers they found. The maps made note of the fact that it is legal to approach a missile, using the Air Force access road, to within twenty-five feet of the silo fence.

The effect of the missile silo maps was stunning, especially among Missourians unaware of the full extent of the missile silo field. The maps sold like hotcakes at a Nukewatch rally in a public park in the heart of the missile field in November. Many stayed on after the rally to spend the night at the fences of missile silos, sometimes leading to earnest exchanges with local farmers, sheriff's deputies, and Air Force security guards who stopped to check on them. It was the start of a silo vigiling tradition that has taken root among peace activists in Missouri and other missile silo states.

The Missouri mapping project and missile silo rally served as the model for campaigns in the five remaining missile silo fields—in North Dakota, South Dakota, Montana, and the vast plateau where Wyoming, Colorado, and Nebraska come together. After the last missile silo field was mapped in the fall of 1987 we put the six maps together in a book, *Nuclear Heartland*, that has become a reference work in libraries around the world. (To double-check the accuracy of the earlier maps we sent a Minnesota couple, Barb Katt and John LaForge, on a four-month, 30,000-mile tour of all 1,000 launch sites and 100 launch control centers.)

Nukewatch also has sponsored missile silo peace schools that have drawn hundreds to the fences of missile launch sites—to Don Lee's wheat field surrounding E46 near Starkweather, North Dakota, in 1987, and to Ralph and Mary Fran Clary's cow pasture next to J2 near Montrose, Missouri, in July 1990.

The unique appeal of the missile silo campaign was that it provided Americans with an opportunity to approach almost within touching distance of unimaginably destructive weapons built in their name. The unattended launch sites are the closest most of us can ever come, uninvited, to the physical presence of the Bomb—and its potential for nuclear Armageddon.

# 17

# Resistance

On the evening of August 6, 1981, the thirty-sixth anniversary of the dropping of the first atomic bomb, I found myself with three companions in a cell of the Chicago city jail, charged with criminal trespass. We had been booked for refusing to leave the downtown corporate office of Union Carbide, a company heavily engaged in the manufacture of nuclear weapons. It was my first arrest.

I had not intended to break the law that day. A guest speaker at a "Hiroshima Day" rally in the Chicago Loop, I stayed on afterward to accompany a procession to the nearby company headquarters in a skyscraper overlooking the Chicago River. Along the way we chanted, "Union Carbide, you can't hide; we charge you with genocide."

My participation up to that point was meant mainly as moral support for my friends in the Chicago Mobilization for Survival who had organized the rally and march. I was on the first leg of a speaking tour that would take me the next day to Buffalo. But once the action began I went with the flow. I accompanied a dozen demonstrators from the street to the company's thirteenth floor office suite, and stood by as our delegation demanded to speak to the company president in New York about Union Carbide's role in nuclear arms production. When the office manager lost patience with us and called the building security manager, and after a Chicago police lieutenant had ordered us to vacate the company's wood-paneled board room, I found myself—to my astonishment—among the half-dozen protesters who elected to remain.

I wrote later in *The Progressive*:

> The world will little note nor long remember the "Union Carbide Six"... But for me it was an unforgettable introduction to civil disobedience as a political tactic—and to those who practice it against America's preparations for nuclear war.
>
> My cellmates were a professor of sociology, a bookstore clerk, and a Catholic priest. (The two others arrested with us, Sylvia Kushner and Mary Lyons, were taken to the women's prison.)
>
> I looked at the priest, Bob Bossie, curled up in a corner of one of the cell's two hardwood benches, sleeping fitfully despite the unremitting glare of the overhead lights and the din from dozens of voices echoing against the steel and concrete walls. This was his fourth time behind bars in a single year. For Bossie, a full-time foe of nuclear weapons, going to jail has become part of his job. He goes to jail with much the same spirit of resignation as a Union Carbide technician might accept an unwelcome tour of duty in Katanga or Saudi Arabia.
>
> And I listened to the professor, Dan Stern, and his much younger companion, Rich Hutchinson, volunteer executive director of the Chicago Mobilization for Survival, who had learned his politics in Stern's class at Northeastern Illinois University. Stern, veteran of many civil rights and antiwar protests, was filling in his protege on what to expect in the jail. I had the feeling that a baton was being passed....
>
> I felt ennobled to be among them....

It was not out of any eagerness to go to jail that I became involved in publicly breaking the law. It was the result of happenstance rather than premeditation. I had not prepared myself for jail. Once incarcerated, I took advantage of the first opportunity to get out by posting bail, which was later forfeited when the charges were dropped. Nevertheless, my brief stay in the Chicago city jail, in the company of friends, was a heady experience.

Until that night I had discounted civil disobedience as a means of achieving antinuclear objectives in the United States. In college I had read the writings of Mohandas Gandhi, leader of India's independence movement, and in the 1950s and '60s I followed and applauded the civil rights struggle of Gandhi's disciple, Dr. Martin Luther King, Jr. I admired both leaders and recognized the role nonviolent civil disobedience had played in mobilizing broad-based support for their movements. But it did not seem to me that many hearts and minds could be changed on nuclear issues in the United States through moral example or by going to jail. In fact, I believed the opposite was true.

When, earlier in 1981, six men and women from distant peace communities climbed over the fence "to bring light in the darkness" of the Pantex nuclear weapons assembly plant in Texas, I shared the consternation of the local peace group, the Panhandle Environmental Awareness Committee (PEAC). For months I had worked closely with PEAC as an organizer for the Nuclear Weapons Facilities Project, affiliated with the Fellowship of Reconciliation and the American Friends Service Committee.

The Amarillo-based PEAC, anxious to avoid alienating workers and others economically dependent on the bomb factory, had stressed environmental and public safety issues in raising questions about Pantex. With PEAC's leaders, with Pam Solo and Mike Jendrzejczyk of the Nuclear Weapons Facilities Project, and with the peace movement establishment, I believed it was counterproductive to be confrontational. To me the tactic smacked of fundamentalism, especially when employed in a religious context.

We groaned when, in the spring of 1981, while we were coordinating and orchestrating simultaneous antinuclear demonstrations around the country, the press played up a blockade, accompanied by blood-pouring, by a religious group at a nuclear submarine base in Groton, Connecticut.

At Groton, at Strategic Air Command headquarters in Nebraska, and elsewhere on the front lines of the struggle against the military-industrial complex, we distanced ourselves from the tactics and the rhetoric of civil disobedience. It was not our style. Nor was it in the interest of the tax-exempt status granted our organizations by the U.S. Internal Revenue Service—a necessary feature for attracting grants and large financial contributions. But my personal reservations about this form of political expression were soon to melt.

A cyclical swing was under way in the peace movement in the early 1980s as I began my work as an independent activist. It started in Britain and Western Europe in the late 1970s with the decision of the Carter Administration to deploy new forms of nuclear weaponry in that part of the world.

For almost two decades Europe had seemed indifferent to the steady build-up of thousands of nuclear warheads on its soil—warheads of every kind, to be dropped from planes, shot from ships, fired as artillery shells, used as landmines to send mountainsides cascading into valleys to block the approach of troops and tanks. Since the early 1960s the NATO powers had acquired and deployed, with little public protest, enough nuclear ammunition to lay waste every acre from Norway's North Cape to the southern tip of Italy.

But in the late '70s, in response to the insistent demands of the U.S. weapons labs and the Pentagon for "modernization" of the nuclear stockpile, two innovations finally roused the sleeping giant of public opinion. First, in 1977, came the concept of "enhanced radiation" warheads, in which neutron radiation would be enhanced and blast effects suppressed in order to make nuclear shells and bombs more effective against tank formations. The purpose of the new warhead was to incapacitate Soviet tank crews while minimizing collateral damage to buildings and other fixtures on friendly soil, thus lending credibility to NATO's policy of first use of nuclear arms in a European war with Soviet forces. But the sinister notion of a weapon specially designed to kill people while sparing property fanned the fires of nationalism and anti-Americanism in Britain and Western Europe. The "neutron bomb," as it was quickly dubbed, awakened Europe's "Ban the Bomb" movement from its long slumber, sending protesters into the streets of European capitals.

Then, in 1978, following intense pressure from the United States, came the decision of the NATO powers to add a new generation of intermediate range missiles capable of hitting targets in the Soviet Union from a thousand miles away. This would mark the first deployment of a new weapon known as the cruise missile, a pilotless, low-flying craft capable of evading defensive radar by hugging the ground and of reaching its target unerringly with the aid of a terrain map imprinted in a computer in its nose.

Nuclear-armed cruise missiles, now a mainstay of U.S. land, sea, and air-based nuclear forces (as are "enhanced radiation" warheads), had long been viewed as the ultimate threat to arms control agreements because of the difficulty of detecting their presence. In 1979 and 1980 they raised a new storm of protest, especially in Britain, where they also evoked memories of the dreaded German "buzz bombs" that had terrorized England in the closing months of World War II. As NATO pressed forward with its plans for deployment of the cruise missile in Britain, Holland,

Belgium, and Italy, and the "Pershing missile" in West Germany, the demonstrations reached massive proportions.

And then, in 1981, came the rhetoric of the Reagan Administration. While the new president blustered defiantly about rolling back the "evil empire," his secretary of state, Alexander Haig, a former NATO commander and supposedly a restraining influence on the cowboy-actor-turned-politician, spoke blithely about "firing a warning shot across the bow" of the nuclear-armed forces of the Soviet Union. Britain and Western Europe went wild in protest, much of it taking the form of physical disruption of the new weapons systems. Pictures of demonstrators blocking the gates and climbing the fences of Greenham Common, a cruise missile base in southern England, filled the newspapers and television screens on both sides of the Atlantic. In Britain and Western Europe the peace movement was moving from protest to resistance. In the United States it was soon to do the same.

In the fall of 1982, following my return from a trip to South Africa to report on that country's clandestine nuclear weapons program, I decided to look into the new spirit of resistance that seemed to have arisen in the peace movement in the United States. As had happened in the past and would occur again in undertaking new ventures, I began my search as an investigative reporter for *The Progressive* in Madison.

In a comparatively short time public attitudes toward nuclear weapons and the arms race had undergone an incredible transformation in this country, as in Britain and Western Europe. In 1974, when I stepped in as editor of the *Bulletin of the Atomic Scientists* in Chicago, the magazine founded by scientists who built the first atomic bomb had given up almost all hope of reawakening popular fears of nuclear Armageddon. Readers found the subject dull, passé, even quaint. The only nuclear threat that seemed to evoke much interest in those days was the environmental and public health impact of nuclear power.

At *The Progressive*, in 1979, readers who followed our battle against nuclear secrecy in the H-bomb case found much more to worry about in the nuclear secrecy issue raised by the reactor meltdown at Three Mile Island, which happened at the same time. In speeches and interviews dealing with the H-bomb case I found myself repeatedly referring to Three Mile Island in explaining and justifying our stand. To most, the threat from the civilian technology still seemed more real than the threat from the weapons culture that had spawned it.

But by the end of 1981, after the neutron bomb and the Euromissiles, and into the era of Greenham Common and the Reagan Administration, all that had changed. Freezing the nuclear arms race and stemming the threat of nuclear holocaust had moved to center stage in this country, as in Britain and Western Europe, propelled by physicians, teachers, and other professionals as well as by masses of ordinary citizens.

A rally to stop the nuclear arms race drew almost a million to New York's Central Park in June of 1982, drawing the attention even of the *Rand Daily Mail* in far-off Johannesburg, where I was conducting a different kind of peace work at the time. Even more remarkably, the New York rally was accompanied by the arrest of 1,691 demonstrators at the United Nations. A week later another 1,400 were arrested for blocking the gates of the Livermore nuclear weapons laboratory in California.

My investigations into nuclear resistance (opposition rooted in civil disobedience) began in the Tempe, Arizona, apartment of two friends, Jack and Felice Cohen-Joppa, who, as publishers of the *Nuclear Resister*, a newsletter, maintained what was then (and still is) the nation's most extensive and up-to-date archive on contemporary antinuclear civil disobedience.

Poring through the Cohen-Joppas' files for the better part of a week in January 1983, I was astonished by the range and scope of antinuclear resistance in the United States—more than 4,000 arrests the previous year—most of it ignored or trivialized by the mass media. It was an aspect of the peace movement I had almost totally overlooked. Later, summing up my impressions of the New Resistance, I wrote in *The Progressive*:

> Month by month, antinuclear civil disobedience moves forward in the United States along two parallel tracks.
>
> One path—the older of the two—is deeply rooted in Christian scripture, proceeds on faith, deals in religious symbolism, and speaks of love, martyrdom, and redemptive suffering. It draws heavily on the examples and teachings of Jesus, Mohandas Gandhi, Martin Luther King, Jr., and Dorothy Day, founder of the radical Catholic Worker movement. Its best known current practitioners are Daniel and Philip Berrigan, Catholic priests who have been going to jail for civil disobedience since the early days of the Vietnam war and who are currently appealing ten-year prison terms for hammering the nosecones of nuclear warheads at a General Electric plant in King of Prussia, Pennsylvania, an act of "beating swords into plowshares" for which the Berrigans and the six

other members of the Plowshares Eight now are widely celebrated in the civil disobedience community....

In that spirit, religious pacifists in recent years have acted out their opposition to nuclear armaments by far more forceful means than most Americans—even dedicated antinuclear activists—are yet prepared to undertake. They have not only blocked doors and sidewalks and committed other conventional trespasses, but they have also damaged military equipment, destroyed nuclear weapons blueprints, and splashed copious quantities of blood on the walls of factories, on the desks and leather sofas of nuclear weapons plant managers, on the marble thresholds of the Pentagon, even on the Great Seal of the President of the United States....

The other major branch of antinuclear civil disobedience is an amalgam of interests—pacifism, feminism, environmentalism, and others—which see nonviolent action less as a personal witness than as a political tactic. They want to stop and reverse the nuclear arms race, and, if possible, reform or transform the entire power structure that gives rise to the arms race and other societal ills.

The credo is summed up in a recent pamphlet written for the Livermore Action Group, which calls itself an "antinuclear and anti-militarist peace community," by Ken Nightingale, a former Mennonite divinity student who now serves as one of its four paid staff members:

"Nonviolent direct action is only one of a number of avenues of protest that is necessary if the arms race is to be stopped. Nonviolent direct action plays a special role in that it emphasizes the sincerity of our demands and the urgency of the nuclear predicament. It is a direct challenge to the system which has proved to be out of touch with its citizens. It illustrates the length that a few have to go to in order to force an entrenched system to respond to our desire for peace."

It was the personal stories that impressed me most. I read of the actions of James Richard Sauder, who carried a wooden cross over the fence of a nuclear missile silo in Missouri and conducted an Easter service there; of Peter DeMott, who jumped into an unattended truck on a naval dock in Connecticut and drove it repeatedly into the rudder of an attack submarine; of Jeff Dietrich, a former Catholic priest arrested and jailed for passing out pens with Christmas messages for workers at a military aircraft factory in southern California.

Later, I looked up Dietrich's wife, Catherine Morris, in the soup kitchen of the Los Angeles Catholic Worker House, where she was a staff member. I wrote in *The Progressive*: " 'We're feeding 800 a day, about 200 more than usual,' sighed Morris. 'Reaganomics are really getting to us here.' I had come to learn about civil disobedience, not about feeding the poor, but the more I talked with this former nun the clearer it seemed to me that the two went together."

In California I also interviewed a seventy-year-old, self-described "civil disobedience junkie," Eldred Schneider of Berkeley, whose proudest possession was a chart on his living room wall depicting his civil disobedience record of thirty-five arrests and 142 days in jail.

"I have given up going to political meetings," Schneider told me. "Peaceful demonstrations don't do it for me any more. I want to stop business as usual."

The growing national interest in civil disobedience was also felt in Madison, where activists were employing that tactic to call attention to the community's involvement in the nuclear arms race. Our attention centered at first on military research at the University of Wisconsin. In 1983 a Nukewatch staff member, Bill Mutranowski, organized a blockade of a university building housing a mathematics research project for the Army. One of our inspirations for this and later demonstrations was a group in Minneapolis called the Honeywell Project.

In the spring of 1983 I attended a preparatory meeting for a nonviolent blockade of the headquarters of the Honeywell Corporation, which manufactured a variety of nuclear weapons systems. I filed this report with *Nuclear Times*:

> There was much earnest talk of how to deal with the police, of how to submit to arrest, of what to do at the police station, of whether to accept an arrest citation (much like a traffic ticket) or to ask for a written complaint (setting forth full particulars of the crime). One reason for asking for a written complaint, commented one civil disobedience veteran in the crowd, to much laughter, is that it results in a document that can be framed and hung on a wall.
>
> What does one wear to a blockade? Several announced their intention to be arrested and be carried off in coat and tie in order to dispel what they called the "hippy-yippy stereotype" of civil disobedience. Others vigorously defended their right to dress down. One well-dressed woman suggested that the planners be mindful of the next day's "main door

look," by which she meant the impression created by demonstrators assigned to the door where the television crews were most likely to be.

But mostly the talk was of finding the best way to challenge the weapons work of Honeywell without alienating the employees, of raising the consciousness of Minneapolis, of connecting the next day's action to civil disobedience movements elsewhere in the country, and above all, of carrying off the action in a spirit of nonviolence.

In the summer of 1983, following my survey of the New Resistance for *The Progressive*, I was jailed a second time—this time for getting too close to a nuclear missile silo in Montana. Once again I had wandered into the clutches of the law without premeditation. Continuing my get-acquainted tour of U.S. nuclear resistance groups, I had stopped in Montana to visit "Silence One Silo," a Montana peace group then holding an encampment near Missile Launch Site R29.

The Air Force was concerned about the presence of a camp so close to one of its launch sites, so on one of our visits to the silo fence it asked the local sheriff to question us and write down our names. To our surprise, six of us were then charged with illegally entering the unmarked twenty-five-foot zone around the silo which delineates the Government's property line. Three of us pleaded innocent and went on trial a few weeks later before a federal magistrate in Great Falls.

Rehearsing our defense the night before the trial, we decided to attack the Government's case by arguing that it was impossible to read the small print on the No Trespass sign without approaching within twenty-five feet of the silo fence. Even though we had no lawyer, the case went well for us the next day, especially after a Government witness expressed doubt that he could identify the people at the silo. But then, to the astonishment of the prosecutor (an Air Force captain) and the judge himself, we put each other on the witness stand and freely admitted we had stood at the silo fence. We had done so, we said defiantly, in order to set an example for others.

"Next time, you get permission from the base commander," said the judge sternly. He sentenced me to a fine of $100, which I elected to serve in jail at the rate of $10 a day, with one day off for good behavior. My co-defendants, Karl Zanzig and Mark Anderlik, organizers of the peace camp, got thirty days.

Once again, I found jail a tolerable experience, knowing that I would be confined only a short time. Equally tolerable were my occasional visits in later years to the Dane County Jail in Madison for refusing to pay fines levied on me for civil disobedience actions in my hometown.

In Madison, Nukewatch in 1983 became the focal point for nonviolent civil disobedience as a way of calling public attention to the nuclear threat and related social issues. Over the next few years we blockaded university buildings to protest military research and CIA recruiting. We dug graves in the lawn outside the Reserve Officer Training Corps classrooms in a symbolic funeral for campus militarism. We unfurled our banners in bank lobbies to deplore the investment of trust funds in corporations making nuclear weapons. We occupied and sometimes chained ourselves to fixtures in the Federal courthouse lobby to vent our opposition to continued nuclear weapons testing by the Federal Government.

We sat in front of post office trucks delivering federal income tax returns to the Internal Revenue Service. We distributed leaflets and sang antiwar Christmas carols in the city's privately owned shopping malls—activities that prompted legal suits culminating in a state supreme court decision enjoining us from further entry into the malls for any purpose other than shopping.

We even conducted a school for civil disobedience in which uniformed officers of the Madison Police Department participated as guest lecturers. On graduation day twenty of us crossed the property line at a nearby National Guard airfield to protest U.S. intervention in Central America. We were arrested and found guilty of trespass. Most of us spent a few days in the county jail.

For me and other participants, civil disobedience in Madison served as a means of drawing attention to our community's adherence to objectionable federal policies of one kind or another—the nuclear weapons build-up, the invasion of Grenada, support for the Contra rebels in Nicaragua. I and others at Nukewatch looked upon this as a form of political action to supplement, if not supplant, mainstream electoral politics. Breaking the law nonviolently and for a good cause had more impact than writing a letter to the editor or telephoning a senator, we felt, because it reflected a deeper commitment. We wanted to demonstrate that political activists need not be intimidated by fear of arrest or jail.

Civil disobedience began for me as a tactic. But in time, moved by the example of others, I made it a personal calling. I was moved by Bob Bossie, the crumpled figure asleep on a hard bench in the Chicago jail, by Ronald Coleman, the officer who gave up a promising future in the

Strategic Air Command because he could no longer push the button, and by others acting more on religious faith than a sense of politics. Of all these, none moved me more profoundly than a friend, Helen Dery Woodson, who lived less than a mile and a half from my home in Madison.

Woodson, the mother of one child and custodian of seven others, most of them mentally retarded, had left her charges in the care of friends and gone to Washington to pour blood in the White House, for which she went to jail for two and a half months. In her newsletter, *Harvest of Justice*, she reprinted the letter in which she explained her actions to the judge:

"It is morally incumbent upon us to defend the children. I have done so at home for eighteen years. I did so on September 2 at the White House, pouring my blood to speak against the death of nuclear weapons and for the life we could build instead—a life of reconciliation and peace.

"The acts through which I serve life at home are considered to be exemplary and noble; my nonviolent witness at the White House is considered to be criminal. After the more than two years of prayer and thought which preceded my civil disobedience and after the seventy-six days I have spent in the D.C. jail, I cannot, in all good conscience, see any difference between the two."

In researching my story on the New Resistance I had read back copies of *Harvest of Justice* and gotten to know its editor, a Catholic activist whose clarity and determination had impressed me from the start. I became a friend not only to her but also to her children and to others in her religiously based peace-and-justice group, which called itself Gaudete (Latin for *Rejoice!*).

On a September afternoon in 1984, at Woodson's invitation, I took part with her in a ceremony on the steps of the county courthouse in Madison, symbolically joining the nonsectarian and religious sides of the Madison peace community. I wore a rented top hat, she a silk dress. Her friend Carl Kabat, a Catholic priest, led us in our vows. Afterwards we went with our friends to a shopping mall, distributed leaflets, and danced in defiance of the mall's policy forbidding free expression on private property.

Two months later, by prearrangement, I drove to Woodson's house and picked up two friends. Opening an envelope of instructions prepared by Helen, we drove 550 miles to a Catholic Worker House in Kansas City, Kansas, where two other supporters were waiting. The following evening we were joined in a simple eucharist service by Helen, Carl Kabat, his brother Paul (also a Catholic priest), and Larry Cloud-Morgan, a Native American activist from Minneapolis. Then the four bade us farewell.

On the next morning, November 12, 1984, after a long wait, we were greeted at the door by one of our fellow supporters, Elmer Maas, who had slipped away before dawn and now was returning with news from a nuclear missile launch site in western Missouri.

Woodson and her three companions, taking a ninety-pound jackhammer and other implements with them, had broken into the enclosure of Missile Silo N5, battered and poured blood on its concrete lid, and waited for Air Force guards to arrive.

Elmer Maas's face was radiant. "Praise be to God," he said.

The four activists called themselves the Silo Pruning Hooks in reference to the biblical mandate, in Isaiah, to "beat swords into plowshares and spears into pruning hooks." For their audacious action they were charged with multiple crimes and given stiff sentences—Helen and Carl eighteen years each (later reduced to twelve), Paul ten years, and Larry eight. I attended their trial and listened to the ironic sermon delivered by Federal Judge D. Brook Bartlett in pronouncing sentence.

"What a waste," the judge said. "What a monumental waste" of talent that might otherwise be employed in such vital peace work as opposition to the proposed MX missile system, which had just won another narrow victory in the U.S. House of Representatives.

Later I wrote in *Isthmus*, Madison's weekly newspaper:

> Don't be fooled by Judge Bartlett's crocodile tears for the peace movement. Unlike those who share Helen Woodson's desire for nuclear disarmament and now genuinely grieve for her, the judge is a willing protector of the nuclear arms race and was happy to put her away for a long time...
>
> Laboring for congressional votes against the MX missile and other nuclear weapons systems is an important part of the struggle for peace. But as a means of drawing public attention to the need for fundamental policy changes, it cannot compare with examples of ultimate personal sacrifice like that of the Silo Pruning Hooks. The magnitude of the sacrifice compels public attention.
>
> A few can and will follow Helen Woodson and her cohorts into the missile silo enclosures—and into the harsh retribution sure to follow. But for most of us the more feasible response to Judge Bartlett's sentence is to let the shock and anger strengthen our resolve to do something more than we have already done, raising the level of our resistance in some way commensurate with the way they raised theirs.

Weep not for Helen Woodson and her partners in crime; they knew what they were getting into, and they are sustained now by a faith that surpasses our meager ability to comfort and support. Weep instead for the world if you would help the Silo Pruning Hooks. Then get out and act.

Four years later I was to follow Woodson and the other Silo Pruning Hooks into a nuclear missile launch site, and into prison.

# 18

# Missouri Peace Planting

The steel padlock gave way like butter as the blades of my bolt-cutter sliced through its narrow neck, sending it clattering to the ground. I lifted a latch and gave a push. The gate swung open easily.

Before me, in a grainfield off a county road in western Missouri, stood a flat concrete slab enclosed by a chain-link fence topped with three strands of barbed wire. At my side was a companion who had come with me from Kansas City to perform a ritual at that site. I wore a clown's suit; she played a recorder.

As our driver sped away, Katie Willems and I, carrying balloons, walked the few yards to the concrete hatch of Launch Site K8, triggering an alarm in the underground bunker of a launch control center thirty-five miles away. We had entered the inner security zone of one of 150 Minuteman missile silos controlled by the 351st Strategic Missile Wing of Whiteman Air Force Base, far to the north.

Katie and I tied our balloons to a lightpole in a corner of the enclosure and to other instruments we found protruding from the depths of the launch site. We decorated the fence with banners and signs and ribbons. We scattered seeds on the barren ground and placed pictures of children on the concrete lid of the tube that cradled a weapon more destructive than a million tons of TNT. Then we waited for the Air Force to arrive.

Fourteen of us cut or climbed our way into ten nuclear missile launch sites in Missouri at precisely the same hour—7 a.m.—on Monday, August 15, 1988. We called our project the Missouri Peace Planting, a symbolic reclaiming of the land for peaceful purposes.

The peace planting was an outgrowth of a series of missile silo "disarmament actions" that began in 1984 with the entry of the four Silo Pruning Hooks into Launch Site N5 east of Kansas City. After the action of the Silo Pruning Hooks came a similar entry by a lone demonstrator, Martin Holladay, in the winter of 1985; then another, by five activists, on Good Friday in 1986; then another in the summer of 1987.

Each confrontation of the missile silos brought criminal charges, trial, conviction, and heavy sentences from Federal judges intent on deterring such behavior. But these repeated assaults on policies of nuclear and judicial deterrence also kindled interest and support in Kansas City, particularly among Catholics, many of them sensitized by the church's professed opposition to nuclear weapons.

Over the years, as one missile silo action followed another, a matrix of support began to crystallize in Kansas City, centering in the peace and justice committee of St. Peter's parish in a middle-class neighborhood on the city's south side. The group provided an increasingly effective local base for "disarmament actions" initiated by outsiders. The impetus for these actions came primarily from the Chicago area, much of it stemming from the work of a Catholic religious group called the 8th Day Center for Justice and Peace.

At the core of the organizing effort at St. Peter's in Kansas City were Mary Knebel, who had committed civil disobedience at the missile silo air base east of Kansas City, and Joan and Bill McGonigle, a retired couple who lived a few blocks away. The network spun by these activists grew to include others in nearby St. James parish and in the Kansas City Interfaith Peace Alliance. Much encouragement came from a priest on the staff of the 8th Day Center who also had a following at St. Thomas Church in Chicago's Uptown neighborhood. The priest was Bob Bossie, with whom I had shared a Chicago jail cell in 1981.

The example of a remarkable Chicago area couple—Jean and Joe Gump—helped cement this alliance of outside actors and local supporters. The Gumps were parents of a large Catholic family who became "plowshares activists" in their late fifties, after their twelve children were grown. Jean was one of five people who entered and damaged two Missouri launch sites in the spring of 1986, for which she received an eight-year term. Joe followed her into a launch site, and into prison, eighteen months later.

By the winter of 1988, soon after the sentencing of Joe Gump and his co-defendant, Jerry Ebner of Milwaukee, the 8th Day Center activists and their Kansas City supporters were ready to raise the ante. So, too, were friends in Milwaukee and Madison who had watched and applauded the missile silo disarmament campaign from the start. We wanted to escalate the challenge to nuclear deterrence—in the field and in the courts—by putting more people inside the fences of nuclear missile launch sites.

The plan that eventually evolved, after months of deliberation, balanced psychological impact against legal risk. We wanted an action that would carry more weight than a simple "line-crossing" at an Air Force base, resulting in nothing more hazardous than a warning letter from the military. At the same time, in order to maximize the number of participants, we felt it necessary to limit the potential risk. So we decided to refrain from damaging the weapons system in ways that would invite penalties as severe as those levied on "plowshares" activists. Our action would be purely symbolic—a seed planting inside the fences. We referred to it jokingly as "plowshares light."

Y ou, the individual on the superstructure, you must vacate the installation immediately!" The young man in the steel helmet and camouflage suit stood at the open gate of the launch site, motioning me toward him. He and a second Air Force security guard had driven up in an armored vehicle about an hour after our entry into K8.

The young airman's voice reflected rising annoyance as Katie Willems and I stood motionless on the lid of the underground nuclear missile, ignoring his insistent commands. Thereupon, the other soldier entered the launch site, automatic rifle in hand, alternately running and crouching, circling the inner perimeter until he had reached a point behind us, as if following an oft-rehearsed military maneuver. As the guard approached us Katie and I gave way, stepping slowly toward the gate to a tune she played on her recorder.

Once outside the gate, I was ordered to lean, spread-eagled, against the fence while a guard searched me for hidden weapons, unamused by the costume I had rented in Madison and worn to the silo for the purpose of providing a comic touch to the seriousness of our mission. (I had been inspired by the example of a friend, a Methodist minister in northeastern Colorado named Ed Bigler, who, calling himself a "fool for Christ," had donned a clown's costume and conducted a worship service at a missile silo near his church on the previous Good Friday, which also happened to be April Fool's Day.)

By now a pot-bellied, mustachioed police officer, the local sheriff, had arrived in his squad car, bringing a female deputy to search Katie Willems. The sheriff scowled at my bedraggled costume and the sweat-streaked paint on my nose and cheeks. "I know what I'd like to do to that character," he growled at one of the Air Force guards, gesturing toward me. "But I'd better not say."

My hands cuffed tightly behind my back, I was driven to the county courthouse in nearby Butler, Missouri, where already the sheriff's office had begun to fill with captured Missouri Peace Planters and their supporters. I was soon joined by Gail Beyer, a long-time protester from my hometown of Madison (the first mother ever to graduate from Yale University); by Ariel Glenn, who, like Katie Willems, was a staff volunteer at Casa Maria Catholic Worker House in Milwaukee; by Betty Lewis, sixty-one, of Chicago, whose picture was to appear the next day in the *Kansas City Star*, an airman's rifle pointed toward her snow-white head, and by others.

The mood grew more festive as our numbers swelled through the morning, swamping the work of the sheriff's office. We were moved to the more spacious quarters of an empty courtroom, from whence we were summoned one by one for interrogation by an Air Force investigator. At day's end, to our intense surprise, the Air Force gave each of us a "ban and bar" letter, warning us not to trespass again on Air Force land, and let us go.

Returning that evening to our base at a Catholic Worker house in Kansas City—elated by our tactical success but let down by the mildness of the Air Force response—the Peace Planters considered their next move. Some, myself included, were satisfied with the outcome and intended to return the next day to the lives we had left behind. Others, including some who had rearranged their lives to make time for six months or more behind bars, felt cheated of an opportunity to challenge the legal system which protected the missile launch sites.

The result was a division which for a while split the Peace Planter community. Some returned to their homes while others returned to the launch sites—time after time after time, burning their "ban and bar" letters on the lids of the silos, until the Air Force finally decided to take stronger measures.

On the day after the first silo entries, on my way home from Kansas City, I stopped to observe and support a group of six or seven Peace Planters who had assembled on the lid of Silo C11, near Booneville, Missouri. As an armed airman approached the intruders, imploring them to leave, I heard the golden tones of Kathy Kelly, a schoolteacher from Chicago, wafting across the prairie: "We shall not, we shall not be moved...."

As if to make amends for its previous leniency, the Air Force filed multiple charges—of criminal trespass and property damage—against all who had returned to the silos in defiance of "ban and bar" letters. Federal prosecutors in Kansas City began going to court in late August and within ten weeks had secured convictions against seven repeat offenders. My Nukewatch colleague Bonnie Urfer refused to take part in the judicial proceedings and received a term of nineteen months. Others got sentences of up to twenty-six months.

We expected that to be the end of it, but, to my surprise, I learned in December that I, too, would be prosecuted, along with three others who had entered launch sites only once. (The Federal government eventually charged and convicted all fourteen of the August 15 missile silo trespassers, along with a fifteenth person who took part in a later entry.) The charge against the four of us was a single count of criminal trespass, carrying a maximum penalty of six months in prison, a $500 fine, and $25 special assessment.

To me, the news that the charge had been filed brought an elation reminiscent of the euphoria I had felt years earlier upon receiving notice to report for Army induction, and later upon hearing that the Department of Energy would proceed against me in the H-bomb case. I welcomed the unexpected turn of events and looked forward to the challenge. The thrill outweighed the anxiety. My cohorts in the Missouri Peace Planting and other antinuclear resisters understood and appreciated my exhilaration because they shared in it. But for Kathleen and others in my family the news was devastating. Unable to fathom my lack of concern about trial, conviction, and probable incarceration, they were torn by feelings of commiseration and alienation. We tried, without notable success, to sort out our differing emotions.

For our three sons—Philip, Sam, and Josh—the shock of this new confrontation would soon pass. They had their own problems to worry about. But for Kathleen the pain and alienation continued. She bore it alone, unreachable either by me or by other spouses and loved ones whose lives also had been affected by the court action in Kansas City. I also sensed, for the first time, the active disapproval of the other members of her close-knit family, whose affection for me had always been important to both of us. I resented that. And I anguished over my inability—and the inability of others—to provide Kathleen with the support and counsel she needed and deserved. Still, I felt deeply that what I had done was right.

At Nukewatch my indictment, following hard on the heels of Bonnie Urfer's conviction, paved the way for a new lease on life for our ever-struggling organization. With one staff member a prisoner of conscience and the other about to become one, a ready-made role awaited us as peacemakers carrying on from behind prison bars. It was a role that appealed to me and Bonnie as well as to many of our supporters.

Over the next few weeks we made the most of our new opportunity. We moved the office to the attic of my home in Madison, turned bookkeeping and other functions over to Kathleen, and hired a long-time volunteer, Susan B. Nelson, to carry on as acting director.

On Tuesday, January 17, 1989, I went to trial in a Kansas City Federal courtroom with three Chicago activists all younger than my own sons—Katey Feit, a staff member of St. Francis Catholic Worker House; Sam Guardino, who worked at the time for a nonprofit organization providing affordable housing for low-income people, and Michael Stanek, the youngest of the Peace Planters, who worked with the poor and the homeless.

My attorney, serving without fee, was Delany Dean, daughter of an officer in the Strategic Air Command, who, moved by the example of Jean Gump, had become swept up in the silo resistance movement and was one of its principal supporters in Kansas City. In representing me and providing guidance to the other three defendants, she tried repeatedly but unsuccessfully to raise nuclear policy issues at our trial.

The judge, Joseph E. Stevens, Jr., outwardly imperturbable but inwardly angry, was a white-haired jurist of about my age who received his law degree from Yale the same year I graduated from Swarthmore.

Judge Stevens tapped his desk impatiently as Delany Dean put me on the witness stand and elicited my credentials as a writer, lecturer, and editor on the effects of nuclear war.

"I'd like nothing better than to sit down some evening with Mr. Day over a scotch-and-soda and chat with him about the effects of nuclear war," he said, urbanely, interrupting my testimony. "But this is neither the time nor the place for that." Hearing the case without a jury, he found us guilty in short order.

Six weeks after my conviction I received word that I would be the first to be sentenced—on March 27, the day after Easter.

On Thursday, March 9, our thirty-second wedding anniversary, I went with Kathleen and our son Philip for a periodic visit with his psychiatrist, who had diagnosed him as suffering from schizophrenia. Philip, then thirty-one and often out of touch with the real world, had been living with us for three-and-a-half years.

On Saturday, March 11, dressed in the same red and white clown suit I had worn into Launch Site K8, I entertained almost a hundred guests at a gala "going-in" party at my home. A friend, Bert Zipperer, later elected to the Madison City Council, donned a military uniform to portray the Air Force guard who had flushed me from the silo.

The following Saturday, March 18, I had a farewell dinner with the children of Helen Dery Woodson—Debbie and Suzie, preparing to move into an apartment of their own as handicapped but semi-independent young adults; Danny, a husky and rambunctious teenager; Michael and Sarah, rapidly growing out of their childhood, and Jeremy, youngest in the family, brain-damaged at birth but making miraculous strides toward near-normalcy. I had visited them often in their mother's absence and had come to know them well.

On Wednesday night, March 22, I said goodby to my uncomprehending mother, who, her mind scrambled by repeated strokes, had been brought from California three years earlier to live in a nearby nursing home, where she was my legal ward. Kathleen would be substituting for me as her frequent visitor.

The next morning a long-time friend, Cassandra Dixon, drove me to Kansas City. Along the way we bought a dozen white roses for Helen Woodson. As dark was gathering I laid them on the gravel inside the fence of a missile launch site overlooking the Missouri countryside, already lush with the approach of spring.

Over that long Easter weekend I joined my hosts, Bill and Joan McGonigle, and a roomful of their children and grandchildren in a sumptuous holiday dinner, attended services at nearby St. Peter's, and sat alone on a bench on their front porch, wondering what the morrow would bring.

At the appointed hour of 1 p.m. the next day, accompanied by the McGonigles and a dozen other Kansas City supporters, I reported to the

Federal court, only to learn that Judge Stevens had indefinitely suspended his calendar because of an automobile accident that had injured his daughter the day before. But I was unprepared to put my own life on hold at that point.

Knowing that a prison term was almost certain to be my sentence, I persuaded a Federal magistrate to accept my surrender so that the term could begin forthwith. By midafternoon I was on my way in a marshal's van to the Lafayette County Jail in nearby Lexington, Missouri.

Three weeks later, summoned from my jail cell to hear my sentence pronounced in Kansas City, I pondered the brief statement I had written out and tucked into my shirt pocket for delivery to Judge Stevens.

A few weeks earlier he had sentenced the oldest of our Peace Planters, Dorothy Eber of Chicago, a sixty-four-year-old grandmother, to twenty-six months in prison, only two months short of the term he had meted out the same day to a Kansas City man convicted of selling three pounds of cocaine. The difference in the two cases was that the drug dealer had expressed remorse.

I expected no leniency from this man and I wanted none.

Encouraged by the sight of friends and supporters in the courtroom, I took out my statement and read it slowly when the judge invited me to speak:

> ... I entered K8 in the full knowledge that the law upholds the Government's right to be free of interference while preparing to blow up the world. But I also know that such laws are subject to judicial review. It was my intention to give a court the opportunity to strip away legal protection from nuclear genocide in the same way courts in earlier times have struck down slavery, racial segregation, and similar practices once accepted but now repugnant to civilized people.
>
> In finding me guilty of trespass, Judge Stevens, you rejected such notions. So be it. I was prepared for that judgment. And I am prepared now for your sentence, whatever it may be. I shall wear your judgment and sentence like a badge of honor, accepting them as the price of conscience.
>
> This is not the first chapter in the story of nonviolent resistance to laws sanctioning nuclear annihilation. Nor will it be the last. Just as I have been moved by the example of others, so I hope and believe that I will serve as an example to others. Together, and in all humility, we hope to give you and your colleagues in the Western District of Missouri

many more opportunities to reconsider your responsibilities as judges and as citizens.

Flushing, Judge Stevens sentenced me to the maximum of six months in prison. "My responsibility," he said, "is to enforce the laws of the United States."

# 19

# Prison Witness

Like a child tossed into the water, I learned that incarceration is not so frightening once you get the hang of it. Even the noisy, bug-infested Missouri jail that harbored me for the first five weeks of my sentence offered moments of enrichment. Immersed in a potpourri of drug dealers, thieves, tavern-brawlers, and other unfortunates ensnared in the trammels of the law, I rediscovered a companionship-in-misery I had not known since my days as an Army draftee many years ago.

In Missouri I was befriended by some black Nigerian cellmates—Eddie, Tony, Winston—who had turned to white-collar crime, and got caught, after graduating from the University of Missouri and failing to find work in their field. They taught me how to hold my own in Spades, a popular card game in jail.

"Say yes to de mastah," Winston would yell triumphantly, slapping hands with his partner, after winning a round of Spades. With a handful of aces and kings, who cared about the fumes from the nearby toilet?

From Missouri, I wrote in the weekly *Isthmus*, where I've been a columnist since 1984:

> The place where I've taken up residence lately is a lot like the office in my home in Madison.

I get up at 7 a.m., eat a light breakfast and read for a while. When the morning mail arrives, I get to work.

Letters, memos and other writings keep me busy into the night. It's a routine interrupted only by meals, card games and visits with the neighbors.

Undisturbed by telephone calls, meetings, parties and other time-consuming social engagements, I've gotten as much work done here as in any other five weeks I can remember. And I've even managed to have some fun.

None of which is to suggest that the Lafayette County Jail in Lexington, Missouri, is a pleasant place to be.

My office is a small metal cage I share with six others. My desk is an iron bunk lined with envelopes and books stuffed between the mattress and the wall. It's also where I lay my head at night, the community toilet a few feet below my nose.

The neighbors all are prisoners, like me, except that none chose to be here. Some twenty of us are locked into three small cells, where we are kept 'round the clock except for brief forays into a nearby "bullpen" for meals and showers and an adjacent recreation room for pingpong and handball. We are permitted one outside visit (through a glass window) per week.

On the morning of May 3, the cellblock gate clanged open and the voice of Paula, our friendly jail matron, cut through the television din: "Mr. Day, get all your things together, you're goin' all the way."

It was the summons I had been expecting. Paula's cry—"you're goin' *all* the way"—was her special way of proclaiming an inmate's imminent departure from the Lafayette County Jail.

With mixed feelings I said good-by that day to the filthy, noisy, crowded jailhouse in Lexington, Missouri, that had been my home since March 27. I would miss the new friends—especially the Nigerians in Cell Three— with whom I had whiled away much of the spring in card games and earnest conversation. But I looked forward with curiosity and excitement to the new experiences awaiting me in the Federal prison system.

Three hours after leaving Lexington in the company of two Federal marshals, I found myself in handcuffs and leg chains climbing the long flight of marble steps leading to the front door of the United States Penitentiary at Leavenworth, Kansas. The scene was straight out of a Hollywood set: a domed, colonnaded building looming behind a high fence topped with razor wire rolled in menacing coils. I gaped in disbelief: Could this be me, a mere nuclear protester, walking into the maw of the biggest of the big joints?

My stay at Leavenworth lasted only a week. I was a "holdover," a prisoner in transit, locked into a dormitory that also served as the "hole" for the nearby Leavenworth prison camp.

My cellmates in the hole were camp residents placed in detention for such infractions as having money in their possession or flunking one of the surprise urine tests given randomly to check for the presence of drugs.

Compared with the bedlam of the Lafayette County Jail, the Leavenworth hole was a piece of heaven. I had a real mattress to sleep on, a good light to read by, fresh air to breathe. I could look out the window and see the sky. The food, brought to us by orderlies and eaten on our cots, was plentiful and tasty.

Security was tight at Leavenworth. Whenever I left the hole, which was seldom, I had to back up to the door and put my arms through a slot so the guard could apply handcuffs. We went everywhere—to the TV room, to sick call, to the exercise yard—with our hands locked behind our backs. On two occasions, I was taken with other prisoners to a small courtyard for an hour's exercise. And there, once again, I was in Hollywood—pacing to and fro under the watchful eye of guards in the towers atop the high stone walls, nodding to the other convicts, listening to the pigeons and swallows which freely come and go at Leavenworth.

My cellmates at Leavenworth were con-wise. Our leader and protector was a long-termer named Tom. He interpreted the intricacies of prison rules and customs for newcomers like me, and also made sure our room was adequately supplied with toilet paper, toothpaste, and other necessities. And he was the one who supervised the illicit still, hidden in a corner of the room, that made booze from our hoarded rations of sugar, oranges, and grapefruit.

On the afternoon of May 10 I was taken from the hole, led down to the bowels of Leavenworth, stripped, searched, reclothed, handcuffed and chained, then herded into a pen with about twenty others from all parts of the penitentiary. Accompanied by guards equipped with radios at their belts, we filed through the vast main lobby and down the marble stairs over which I had entered the prison a week earlier.

As I stepped blinking into the bright sun, careful not to trip over the chains that bound my ankles, I beheld an amazing sight: Fanning out from the prison bus that awaited us at the foot of the steps were half a dozen United States marshals at parade rest with shotguns on their hips, pointed skyward. Shotguns. Did they think that one of us would hobble off and disappear too quickly to be tackled by a burly guard? Or that commandos from the mafia or the PLO might arrive by helicopter to engineer a mass escape?

I was soon to learn that shotgun deployment is as inherent to prisoner transportation as handcuffs, ankle and waist chains, and strip-searching. A shotgun posse awaited us again when we drove into a remote corner of Kansas City International Airport to board the prison plane, and when we alighted later at Oklahoma City.

The prison plane, a Boeing 727 seating about 200, flew in from the east and disgorged a load that included two dozen young soldiers handcuffed forlornly in their dress uniforms. As a drill sergeant marched them away, we filed into the plane through the tail ramp. Our cabin attendants were marshals outfitted in blue jump suits. While we waited for the plane to take off, I noticed that no one was wearing seatbelts. I pointed this out to a marshal and remarked, half jokingly, that failing to fasten seatbelts is a violation of federal aviation regulations.

The marshal reddened and replied, "There's the strap. You can put it on yourself if you want." His tone implied that seatbelts were a frill for the faint-hearted. Like smelling salts. When I pointed helplessly to my handcuffs, he leaned over curtly and snapped the seatbelt for me. "The stupid old bastard," he seemed to be saying to himself.

My travels on the prison "airlift" resumed the next morning after an overnight stay at the Federal penitentiary in El Reno, Oklahoma, which serves as the hub of the Federal prison air transportation system. The same plane, one of two in constant service, was waiting for us at the Oklahoma City Airport. For the next seven hours the plane flew 2,000 miles back and forth across the Midwest region of the Bureau of Prisons, picking us up and dropping us off like so many mail sacks.

While marshals patrolled the aisles, we shifted uncomfortable in our seats, trying to ease the pressure of the cuffs on our sweating wrists and ankles. Accomplishing bodily toilet functions in these restraints was a task I found impossible, so I took no liquids on the long flight. Our plane flew first to Springfield, Missouri, site of a large prison hospital, then to Terre Haute, Indiana (Terre Haute Penitentiary), Detroit (Milan Penitentiary), and Chicago's Midway Airport (Chicago Metropolitan Correctional Center). The sack with my name on it was dropped off at Rochester, Minnesota.

It wasn't until the marshals sorted us out on the Rochester airstrip and herded me into one of several waiting vans that I learned my new prison home was to be Yankton, South Dakota, a town of 12,000 across the Missouri River from northeast Nebraska. After an overnight stay at the Minnehaha County Jail in Sioux Falls, South Dakota, I arrived there in the afternoon of Friday, May 12, with several others who soon became close companions.

Yankton Federal Prison Camp was one of the newest institutions in a penal system that was expanding at the rate of 800 inmates a month and was expected to double in population (from 50,000 to 100,000) by the mid-1990s. It opened in 1988 on the campus of Yankton College, established in 1881 as the first school of higher learning in South Dakota. The college reached a peak enrollment in the 1960s, faltered in the hard times of the 1970s, and was closed by its creditors in 1984. Some of the college buildings still looked brand new. Others had grown gracefully old, with Victorian cupolas, towers, and handsome brick facades. Walking through the grassy, tree-lined grounds in a quiet, residential neighborhood, I could close my eyes and see the students going to and from the tennis courts, the Nash gymnasium, the Forbes Hall of Science.

The previous summer the Federal government, as the new owner, had sent a small cadre of inmates to Yankton to begin converting the college into a prison camp. By the time I arrived, the population had risen to about 200. Our job was to help prepare the way for another 300.

"Essentially this is a work camp," we were told in an early briefing by Yankton's hard-driving superintendent, Stephen F. Pontesso. Yankton had no fences or guard towers. Located just across the street from middle-class homes, it was a "minimum security" facility, where every prisoner was a "trusty," free to come and go within the camp grounds.

To the typical incoming prisoner, Yankton represented the ultimate in freedom and comfort within the prison system. We slept four to a room in a nicely appointed unlocked dormitory with polished tile floors and handsome wooden closets and cabinets. We dressed in well-fitting khaki uniforms and sturdy work boots. We ate on tablecloths in a dining hall that served meals as varied and as tasty as I have enjoyed in any restaurant in Madison.

The camp had a library, tennis courts, gymnasium, pool tables, laundry room, TV rooms. Except for occasional head counts, our time was our own from midafternoon until after midnight. At Yankton I soon had to begin reminding myself that I was a prisoner. It felt more like being back in the Army, or at Phillips Exeter Academy.

Yankton offered the additional advantage of carefully screened inmates better educated and more mature than most. Virtually all of us were there for nonviolent white-collar crimes, mostly drug-dealing. I roomed with a paint contractor from Denver, a Sioux from Spearfish, South Dakota, a clerk who typed purchase orders and cared for potted flowers in the administration building. My table mates included Peter, a vegetarian who practiced yoga and read the Bhagavad Gita; Mark, a bartender who preferred cocaine to alcoholic beverages, and Bill, a gentle, grandfatherly man who had been the administrator of a mental health center. I made some good friends in my short time there.

Also, there was the attraction of useful work under congenial conditions. All of the inmates complained with good reason about the pay—a uniform 11 cents an hour for all work, some of it paying $15 a hour on the open market. Aside from that, the inmates at Yankton were so well treated and so highly motivated (in some cases) that some volunteered for extra work on weekends to make the time go faster.

Ten days after my arrival in Yankton, following an initial orientation, I was assigned quite by chance to one of the choicest jobs the camp had to offer—healthful, nontaxing outdoor work with the landscape crew. But by that time I had made up my mind to cease cooperating with the institution.

Even before my convictions for violating laws sanctioning nuclear anni-hilation, I had mused about noncooperation in prison, a concept that flows logically from noncooperation with nuclear policy. I had been moved by the writings of Richard Miller, a nuclear resister who spent much of his prison time in the hole for refusing to work, and by similar examples set by Joe and Jean Gump, also imprisoned for nuclear resistance. My thoughts on this began to crystallize in the Lafayette County Jail, but before thought could lead to action I was diverted by another matter.

On the morning of May 4, the day after leaving Missouri, I awoke at Leavenworth to discover I could no longer see out of my right eye. A dark grey disc had moved up from the bottom of my field of vision, like the moon eclipsing the sun, obscuring everything except a thin crescent at the top. The eye needed medical attention, but because I was in transit I was unable to get it looked at until a few days after my arrival at Yankton. The physician's assistants at the prison camp were most helpful and considerate. They arranged for me to be examined by two ophthalmologists in Yankton, who ordered a CAT scan because they were concerned about the possibility of a brain tumor causing pressure on the optic nerve.

Facing the possibility of immediate transfer to a prison hospital, I deferred further thought of noncooperation. My indecision was resolved on Monday, May 22, by the welcome news that there was no tumor. The blindness had been caused by a mild stroke, which damaged the optic nerve but had no other apparent ill effect.

With that, I drafted a letter to the superintendent declaring my noncooperation and announcing my intention to leave the prison camp the next day. (I had in mind a prison version of symbolically "crossing the line" as at an Air Force base.) Fortunately, I had the good sense to show the draft to inmate friends, who pointed out that such an act could precipitate a charge of attempted escape, which could lengthen my prison time. They urged me to stick to the idea of refusal to work. So I wrote a second draft and delivered it to the camp superintendent the next morning:

> Having thought the matter over since my arrival ten days ago, I have come to the conclusion that I cannot support the mission of the Yankton Federal Prison Camp. Accordingly, I will respectfully refuse work assignments after 8 a.m., Wednesday, May 24.
>
> I make this declaration as a matter of conscience and in full appreciation of the courtesies shown me by the staff and fellow inmates of this institution.
>
> Much as I applaud the conscientiousness of your staff, I find I cannot willingly participate, directly or indirectly, in the work of this camp, which is the enlargement of the Federal prison system. I look upon the growth of the prison system with the same repugnance in which I hold the Federal nuclear weapons policies that are the cause of my incarceration.
>
> I respect the differing needs and circumstances of other inmates, for whom any work can be a relief from the tedium of long prison confinement. But my own circumstances give me the luxury of a choice. I choose not to cooperate.

The reaction was swift. That afternoon I was called into a counselor's office and interrogated by three staff members. They wanted to know if this was some kind of antinuclear protest. When I told them my point had more to do with building prisons they argued briefly with me and then dismissed me. The showdown was postponed until noon the following day, which was my next scheduled appointment for work. Ten minutes before the hour I walked into the office of counselor William Lee and informed him I would not report for work.

For a second time, Lee warned me of the consequences. Then, seeing that I had made up my mind, he gave me some parting advice: "Keep this to yourself and you'll be okay. But if you start stirring up the others, you're going to be in big trouble." It was the confirmation I needed that I had made the right choice.

The decency of the staff people at Yankton made this a difficult decision for me. I did not wish to give the false impression that I was too good to work, or that I lacked appreciation for their efforts in behalf of prisoners, or that I was some kind of nut with a masochistic streak. It would have been easy for me to fade into the woodwork at Yankton and do my time without trouble, as many of my friends in and out of prison had counseled. But in the end I succumbed to the urge to confront the dishonesty of a prison masquerading as a prep school.

The Yankton Federal Prison Camp lost no time expelling me. Within two hours I was mustered out and on my way to the Yankton City Jail, where I found myself in the more congenial setting of iron bars, an iron bunk, and the ever-murmuring, inescapable TV set. It was a prison that looked and sounded and acted and felt like a prison—the proper place for an antinuclear activist to be. I felt good once again.

In the place where I took my meals during most of June and July, the massive profiles of the Presidents, chiseled from the granite bulk of Mount Rushmore, looked down on me from a mural that dominated the room. It was a typical South Dakota scene.

On the left, George Washington. On the right, Abraham Lincoln. Next to the Great Emancipator, a square set jaw and bristling mustache identified Teddy Roosevelt.

But it was the fourth figure that held my attention each time I shuffled with my fellow prisoners, plastic cup and spoon in hand, into the mess hall of the Minnehaha County Jail in Sioux Falls. The high cheek bones, flaring nostrils, and jutting lips where Tom Jefferson ought to be suggested instead a warrior of the Lakota Sioux.

I liked to think this substitution by some unknown, unsung muralist was revenge on the President whose purchase of their ancestral lands condemned the Lakota and other tribes to subjugation by the White Man. Perhaps it was also a subtle call to continue resistance.

A fifth to a fourth of the inmates of the jail were Native Americans, who also constitute the largest ethnic minority in South Dakota, which is the most Indian of American states. At mealtime they clustered at a table near the painting, as if drawn to the mutilated yet still sacred Black Hills.

One of the inmates was named Yellow Earring, a young man with laughing eyes and a black pony tail whom I came to know because I shared a cellblock with him and five others. Joining his group for lunch one day, I asked him out of curiosity how many of his twenty-eight years he had spent in captivity.

Yellow Earring made a quick mental calculation, adding up the years of reform school, jail, and prison. "Eleven," he said.

A friend from across the table volunteered that his total came to seven years. But he explained, as if in mitigation, that he was still only twenty-one.

The Minnehaha County Jail, largest local jail in South Dakota, served as my home for seven weeks en route from the Yankton Prison Camp to a higher level Federal prison in Minnesota.

Unlike the noisy, crowded, dirty Lafayette County Jail in Lexington, Missouri, Minnehaha was clean, spacious, and modern. I lived in one of seven single cells opening into a day room with shower, television set, and two metal tables with attached stools. My cell had an iron bunk, washbowl and toilet, bookshelf and writing table.

Through the bars of my cell window I could see cars and people coming and going in the parking lot of the Minnehaha County Courthouse, the neon lights of a Chinese restaurant, the bustle of traffic on tree-lined North Dakota Avenue, the approach and retreat of majestic summer thunder-clouds. The daily connectedness with the outside world made this a livable place.

My connectedness was reinforced daily by the arrival of cards and letters from friends and loved ones, and sometimes from strangers sending encouragement from all over the country and far parts of the world—from Canada, England, Scotland, Belgium, Australia. (From each letter a jail clerk had meticulously removed the postage stamp and envelope flap as a precaution in case the sticky stuff contained LSD.)

Also arriving almost daily were letters containing chapters for a "peacemakers' guide to jails and prisons" being written by friends and colleagues incarcerated for breaking laws sanctioning nuclear annihilation. I was the editor of a book, *Prisoners on Purpose*, that would emerge from our confinement.

From the Federal women's prison at Alderson, West Virginia, Bonnie Urfer (Nukewatch co-director) sent pen-and-ink sketches to illustrate her own and other stories about penal life.

From his skyscraper cell at the Metropolitan Correctional Center in downtown Chicago, Duane Bean wrote about the despair and bitterness of prisoners by the hundreds stacked like cordwood in an airless glass and concrete tower designed to hold half as many.

From the "hole" at the Federal prison in Oxford, Wisconsin, to which he was consigned for refusing to submit to the indignity of daily strip-searching, Jerry Zawada, a Franciscan priest, wrote how two guards grabbed him and pulled his shorts down.

As editor of the project I utilized my banishment from work camp as an opportunity for work of my own. Instead of a broom I pushed a stubby lead pencil. Instead of cigarette butts I picked up chapters for the book. I watched the clock not in longing that the time might pass more quickly, but in panic over the swift approach of each new deadline. Rather than ruing the boredom and isolation and spartan sterility of a county lockup way out in the middle of nowhere, I thanked Minnehaha for the chance to do my thing in peace and quiet.

One of my neighbors at the Minnehaha County Jail was an inmate in his thirties named Jeff, who made his living for a while as a rodeo clown.

Being funny is only part of a rodeo clown's job. The clown's most important duty is the deadly dangerous one of distracting an angry Brahma bull long enough to permit the downed bull rider to pick himself up off the ground and run to safety.

Jeff told me he had been hit, horned, trampled, and thrown so many times by so many bulls that every rib on his right side had been broken at least once by the time he decided to retire from the ring.

But taunting bulls is a habit not easily broken. Jeff exhibited it again on the afternoon of Monday, July 17, when he and I were ordered out of Cellblock C and told to get ready for the federal prison airlift.

"Gee, that's a good-looking suit," said Jeff, pleasantly, poking fun at the grim-faced marshal who approached him with handcuffs and waist chain. "Did they have one in your size?"

Herding us into a couple of vans, the marshals drove me and Jeff and a dozen other federal prisoners to the Sioux Falls airport, where, chained hand and foot, we hobbled aboard the Boeing 727 prison plane. An hour later, we were in Oklahoma City, hub of the prison air transportation system. Buses took us to El Reno Federal Prison, just west of Oklahoma City, where male airlift prisoners are housed.

As an inmate undergoing disciplinary transfer for refusing to accept work, I was one of the unfortunates kept under lock and key at El Reno, along with Jeff and a great many others. For the next ten days, my home was a two-man cell adjoining others facing a long corridor into which we were released for exercise a few hours each day.

We were like caged animals, fed from trays slid through slots in the cage door and let out to pace up and down the corridor. Twice they let us outside to a small exercise yard enclosed by a high fence topped with coiled razor wire, where armed guards kept an eye on us from nearby watchtowers.

My first cellmate at El Reno was Norman, a diabetic whose schedule of insulin shots had been interrupted by the trip. Catching the attention of a passing guard, Norman said, in a surprisingly matter-of-fact tone: "You should be aware that two hours from now I will be unconscious." Later that day, he was gone.

Next came Hakim, a Lebanese American who abandoned Beirut for Los Angeles in the 1970s, operated an international jewelry business, added cocaine and other illegal drugs as a sideline, salted away several million dollars, and now was serving a five-year prison term. Hakim was on his way back to his California prison camp after a New York City court appearance. He kept a battery of lawyers in Los Angeles and another in New York. To Hakim—cultured, cosmopolitan, at home in five languages—dope was strictly a business (he never touched the stuff) and jail a normal business risk.

Michael, my next El Reno cellmate, was a Tennessee auto salesman who sold cocaine as a sideline and made the mistake of using the stuff, which led to a $1,000-a-night addiction. Michael and his older brother both were serving long prison terms. He told me he agreed to a guilty plea after the federal prosecutor threatened to indict his mother.

With Hakim and Michael, and with other members of the ever-changing cellblock population, I waited night after night for my plane to come in. At about 2:30 each morning the lights would come on and guards would go from cell to cell, summoning the lucky few whose turn it was to leave El Reno.

My turn came on the morning of July 27th. With Jeff and Michael and at least a hundred other transients from El Reno, I boarded the prison plane at Oklahoma City. My destination was the Federal Correctional Institution at Sandstone, Minnesota, but first there was a stopover at the United States Penitentiary in Terre Haute, Indiana.

With about fifteen other hard-core offenders headed for Sandstone, I sweltered through four days and nights in what we called "the black hole of Terre Haute." Locked into two-man cells twenty-three hours a day, we had only two metal bunks, a toilet, and a washbowl. We stripped down to our shorts, trying to beat the heat. My cellmate, David, a Lakota Sioux from the Rosebud Reservation in South Dakota, slept on the concrete floor, trying to find a few wisps of cool air.

It was with infinite relief that we boarded a prison bus (the "federal express") on Monday, July 31, for the two-day trip to Minnesota. I slept that night at the prison in Oxford, Wisconsin, with Jerry, a con-wise old-timer on his way to Sandstone from the prison hospital at Springfield, Missouri. For Jerry, the brief stopover afforded an opportunity to pass along the news about old buddies in the penal system.

Hearing that Jerry was passing through, an Oxford old-timer had come to our cell to supply him with cigarettes, magazines, and other needs. For an hour or more they traded prison gossip through the slot in the cell door.

"Hey, remember Fat Tony?" said Jerry. "Saw him at a party in Spring-field. Tell everybody he's okay."

Arriving at Sandstone the next day, I found an attractive, spacious institution carved out of the Minnesota pine forests, with lawns and flowerbeds, benches for us to sit on, a fine running track, even a miniature golf course.

What made Sandstone special for me was the presence of three old friends serving time there for damaging missile silo launch sites in Missouri, the scene of my own crime. They quickly took me in tow.

Joe Gump introduced me to his friends in the Native American Club and served as my sponsor at the three-hour prayer service (at 150 degrees) in the club's sweat lodge. Jerry Ebner got me into the prison toastmasters. Carl Kabat let me sit beside him at Catholic mass in Sandstone's "Chapel of the Lakes."

The first three weeks slipped by almost as pleasantly as a Caribbean cruise. I met people from all over the world (Columbia, the Dominican Republic, England, Pakistan, the Middle East—almost all of them there for drug offenses); polished off a few books (Harper Lee: *To Kill a Mockingbird*, Richard Rhodes: *The Making of the Atomic Bomb*); worked on my push-ups; took ten turns a day around the track.

But the trip ended abruptly on August 22 with the posting of a notice advising me of my first institutional work assignment. I was to report the next morning to Food Service. By this time I had decided to forgo the relative ease and comfort of life in the general prison population in order to repeat the point I had made under similar circumstances three months earlier at Yankton Federal Prison Camp in South Dakota.

At Sandstone, as at Yankton, I felt compelled to make a statement of noncooperation with the prison system. I was there to do my time, not to help maintain the prisons. Refusing to do prison labor—any labor—presented a clear and emphatic way to make the point. And it was a relatively easy thing for me to do because I had only a short time to serve.

Gertrude Kolker, my caseworker, was ready for me when I knocked on her door the next morning to announce my refusal to report to work. "Go to your cubicle and wait," she said.

Soon two guards appeared. "Give him a direct order," one of them told the officer in charge of my unit. He complied. The answer was hardly out of my mouth before the handcuffs appeared and I felt myself being dragged across the prison compound.

I spent the final thirty days of my Federal prison term in a cage at Sandstone, locked up twenty-three hours a day and taken everywhere in handcuffs, even to the shower room a few paces down the hall. I wrote letters, read books from the prison library, put the finishing touches on *Prisoners on Purpose*, Nukewatch's 160-page prison-jail guide, and got my push-ups up to seventy-five.

In choosing to go to "the hole" at Yankton and at Sandstone, I managed to maneuver the Federal Bureau of Prisons into giving me the harshest treatment available to a short-term offender. Of my 178 days in confinement, all but thirty-four were spent under lock and key in cells at eight different jails, prisons, and penitentiaries.

I wanted to make myself clear to the Bureau of Prisons and to set an example for other inmates, bearing in mind that most have no real alternative to work because of the length of their terms and their need for income, even though prison pay is only a pittance.

I also wanted to experience the worst that the Federal prison system has to offer in order to confirm my belief that going to prison for the right reasons is thinkable and doable in the United States. My six months in the system provided abundant confirmation of that. This was the principle finding I took back home with me.

The other major conclusion I took home from prison seems outwardly in conflict: While prison is the proper place for those who break the law in the interests of peace and justice, it is no place at all for most of the inmates who find themselves incarcerated today.

Our jails and prisons nowadays are increasingly populated with men and women who traffic in dangerous and abusive substances. Not alcoholic beverages. Not tobacco. Not gunpowder or other explosives. Not harmful chemicals that pollute our air, water, and soil. Not even radioactive substances that can contaminate our planet for all time or even blow it to smithereens. They are locked up for dealing in substances that happen to be illegal: marijuana, cocaine, heroin, and the like. They now constitute an absolute majority in the Federal prison population.

Almost every inmate I met in jail or prison was there for dealing drugs. Some may have been big-time dealers, but by and large they were small fry scooped up by zealous prosecutors and slammed down by Federal judges reacting to community pressures. I met many who were paying with years out of their lives for selling a few grams to an informer. Over and over I heard bitter stories of a criminal justice system corrupted by convictions secured as a result of "snitches" turning against their former partners in order to secure more lenient treatment for themselves.

In Sandstone, as at other Federal prisons, whole cellblocks and buildings are set aside for "protective custody" of inmates who have informed on other prisoners in the Federal system.

I found that the hysteria of the "war on drugs" is giving rapid rise to a corrupt and bloated "criminal justice-correctional complex," akin to the military-industrial complex, its strength rooted in a constituency of investigators, lawyers, judges, psychologists, prison guards, and probation officers dependent on an ever-growing number of convictions.

I don't have a solution to the problem. But I think part of the answer lies in legalizing drug use just as we have legalized other sins, and treating drug dependency as a problem for doctors, not judges.

# 20

# Knowing the Bomb

In the iron and concrete cages that held me for six months, I had ample opportunity to reflect on the circumstances that had made me a prisoner of conscience. A psychoanalyst might say I had maneuvered myself into captivity to satisfy an unfulfilled childhood urge to attract the attention of my mother. Was this just the latest of many adult scrapes, a 1989 version of Sassie breaking his glasses and secretly savoring the resultant commotion? Could this have been just another attempt of the ninety-pound weakling (now grown to twice that weight) to prove his physical prowess to himself and others, to play out his private neuroses on the public stage? I am sure that some who have known me longest would accept such interpretations. I wouldn't dispute them entirely. Doubtless there is a psychological explanation for my long history of choosing the unconventional approach.

Still, looking back, I could identify some hard phenomena in the outside world that had helped put me where I was.

One of these was the existence of the atomic bomb. I had known about it since the first news of Hiroshima had crackled around the world on August 6, 1945. Like many people, I had always held misgivings about our government's unrestrained development of nuclear weapons. But I did not really begin to *know the Bomb* until later, when an accidental career change brought it more closely into focus. At the *Bulletin of the*

*Atomic Scientists*, I was moved by Albert Einstein and Eugene Rabinowitch and Robert J. Lifton, the Yale psychiatrist, who had comprehended the white heat of nuclear fission, recognized its revolutionary impact, and written passionately about the need for a new way of thinking.

I came to know the Bomb better at *The Progressive*, where, as a defendant in the H-bomb case, I felt the crushing weight of governmental power applied directly against me in defense of the Bomb's secrets. To be singled out in such a way is to know helplessness and vulnerability.

Later, I was to know the Bomb again when I sensed it in the ground just a few yards under the tips of my shoes at the fence of Romeo-29, the Minuteman missile launch site in David Hastings's barley field in Montana. And again when I followed just a few yards behind the unmarked trucks carrying nuclear warheads from the final assembly plant near Amarillo, Texas. And I knew it, finally, when I stood on the lid of launch site K8 in Missouri, with nothing but my body and 120 tons of concrete between the Bomb and its intended victims on the other side of the planet.

In coming to know the Bomb in this way, I came also to decide that nuclear weapons are evil. There is no better word for it. I have never thought this of the people who make the Bomb. We are all part of that process in one way or another. But the weapon itself is evil, and so too is the policy from which it springs.

The policy by which we justify the Bomb goes by the name of nuclear deterrence. It is an evil policy because it presupposes a national willingness to kill on a truly massive scale. The case against nuclear deterrence has been aptly put by the Jesuit priest Richard T. McSorley, whose words are framed on the guest-room wall of my friend Mary Knebel in Kansas City:

> The taproot of violence in our society today is our intent to use nuclear weapons. Once we have agreed to that, all other evil is minor in comparison. Until we squarely face the question of our consent to use nuclear weapons, any hope of large-scale improvement of public morality is doomed to failure.

At some point in my middle years the recognition of a unique evil and the urge to confront it crystallized into a religion. By fits and starts I crossed the line from observer to doer, from dispassion to passion, from agnostic to believer. You cannot do this work for long, I am convinced, without religion of some kind. But mine was not an ordinary conversion.

I tapped into a secondary source. I came to believe not in God but in those who believed in God—people of deep religious faith who had been moved to action by the call of the Holy Spirit.

Call them God's creation or just a speck whirling around a spark in the infinity of space, I looked upon the world and the Earth as uniquely threatened by two evils to which I, as an American, had given my consent. One was the evil of nuclear violence. The other: The public acceptance of that violence.

Whatever the origins of or reasons for our policy of threatening to destroy the world in order to save it, I resolved on a personal level, to the extent possible, to withdraw my consent to the policy. Not in my name, I would say, nor in the name of others who cared to join me in that stand. On the nuclear weapons truck routes, in the missile silo fields, wherever the policy was in evidence, we worked together to help each other know the Bomb, and, having come to know it, to withdraw our consent in ways that might prompt others to do the same.

Our work brought a sense of solidarity and purpose. It also brought pain.

On a Saturday afternoon in January 1990, four months after my release from Sandstone prison, I sat in Kathy Kelly's livingroom in Chicago in a circle of people who had taken part in the Missouri Peace Planting of 1988. About twenty of us, some recently freed from jail, had gathered to talk about what we called the "post-prison blues."

We went around the circle. Kathy led off, telling how she missed the friends she had made in almost a year of incarceration with other women in Missouri, West Virginia, and Kentucky. Others told of the difficulty of getting back in touch with the lives of friends and loved ones at home. Then it was the turn of Michael J. Bremmer.

We all knew that this would be a difficult moment for Mike. Sentenced in June to six months, he had been placed in the Yankton prison camp and assigned to the grounds crew. In the camp visiting room that fall he had proposed marriage to his long-time companion, Mary Jude, and they had set the wedding for late January. Hundreds of invitations had been mailed out by Christmas when Mike, home from prison, decided he could not go through with the ceremony.

Now, with Mary Jude at his side, on the eve of what would have been their wedding day, Mike had come to tell his friends about his personal crisis.

Slowly, painfully, choking back tears, Mike Bremmer told us how the euphoria of his engagement and impending release from prison had dissolved into confusion and despair after his return home. Day by day he sank more deeply into a black hole. The glitter of the Christmas season only made matters worse. Even the most casual social contact was beyond his capability. The wedding was just too much to contemplate. So he and Mary called it off.

Holding Mary's hand and looking around the circle, Mike told us, "You know, this is the first time I've been able to say these things. I'm beginning to feel better already."

Although I had not experienced the feelings so keenly, I knew the pain and disorientation Mike Bremmer and the others spoke of that day. Emerging from the isolation of prison, I found it difficult to convey the trauma of that experience, much less to explain, without seeming to trivialize the hardships of those left behind, how being a "prisoner on purpose" can be uplifting. The insistent needs of Nukewatch and its continuing resistance projects quickly restored a routine to my life. But I know of many activists for whom going to prison and coming out proved to be crushing experiences.

Mike Bremmer, long active in Central America support work before becoming a Missouri Peace Planter, was not one who succumbed to post-prison depression. He and Mary Jude have picked up their lives and remained together in peace and justice work since his release from Yankton. But many who took up the banner of civil disobedience for nuclear disarmament have fallen by the wayside, and all of us have felt the loneliness and isolation of the struggle.

I have often had to deal with self-doubts in discerning my own role in civil disobedience actions.

Would I be playing the part of a fool, a masochist, a Don Quixote? Was I responding to some overwhelming inner need for attention? Or was this an action that seemed right for the time and place?

What would my professional colleagues, my friends and family, and my detractors say? What impact would the action have on Nukewatch's tax-exempt status under the Internal Revenue Code, its precious "501(c)(3)," which was its ticket to grants and large donations? And did those things matter?

What would be the effectiveness of this action? How would "rotting in jail" advance the cause? Or did it matter whether an action was "effective," so long as it was right?

Such questions were not easily answered. Nor was it easy to assuage the guilt I often felt for indulging a passion at the neglect of those closest to me. My wife, Kathleen, always troubled by the risks, had been drawn closer to the world of Nukewatch by the workload that engulfed her when I left for prison, but these new ties fell well short of converting her to the cause of nonviolent resistance. My son Philip continued to wander in a mental world of his own, perhaps in some measure a victim of his father's preoccupation with other things at a crucial time of need. No other reality in my life had been more difficult for me to accept than the slow, painful realization of Philip's disability. He was physically whole but psychologically handicapped by his mental condition and the medications needed to stabilize it. My daily work with bright young men and women of his generation, their lives enriched by a sense of purpose, reminded me painfully of the misfortune of my oldest son. Should I have left him then?

No doubt I also paid a price for my cause in the psychological remoteness of my other two sons, Sam and Josh, now married and pursuing careers far different from my own. My six months away deprived me of the company not only of Sam and his wife, Bernadette, struggling in a difficult marriage, but also of my only grandchildren, Kathleen and Emmanuelle, then four and three. Josh, newly married, was in the process of changing careers. Neither son came to see me in prison. But from them, as from Philip, I sensed filial support.

And my mother, Margery Day—had I done right by her? In our nightly encounters at the nursing home I had become not only the guardian and protector of my mother but in a sense her mother as well. She looked to me for the closeness and emotional sustenance that in her long life she had provided easily to others but only with great difficulty to me. I longed to convey to her in her final years that I understood and that I also forgave. And that I appreciated all she had given. Should I have left before the message was fully transmitted, perhaps never to see her again?

In the end I made my peace with those doubts and guilty feelings. I did my best to help and comfort those close to me who bore the brunt of actions I felt called upon to take. I tried where possible to ease the pain of others. I shared their pain as the cost of crossing the line.

One of my close companions at Sandstone prison, in the three weeks before they sent me to "the hole" for refusing to work, was Joe Gump, a retired engineer in his early sixties. Joe had led an unremarkable life as a businessman and father of ten until Good Friday, 1986, when his wife,

Jean, long active in liberal causes, turned to radical activism by taking a hammer to a nuclear missile silo in Missouri. Eighteen months later, on the forty-second anniversary of the bombing of Hiroshima, Joe and a friend followed Jean's example by damaging another missile silo in Missouri.

Making our rounds each afternoon on Sandstone's running track, Gump and I decided nuclear resistance was a calling especially well suited to people of our age and circumstances. We had raised our children and discharged our familial obligations, advanced our conventional careers as far as they were likely to go, and achieved at least the modicum of financial independence made possible by a social security check.

For others so inclined, we asked, why not take the opportunity to pursue a second (and perhaps more meaningful) career, much as a business executive might turn to gardening or a public school teacher to volunteer work at a literacy training center?

Not only are women and men our age better situated in many instances to bear the burdens of nuclear resistance, including long prison terms, they also bear a heavier responsibility to do so because it was their generation that got the world into its present fix. We gave a name to our embryonic organization—Old Codgers for Peace—and we vowed to begin recruitment after our release from prison.

Even as Joe Gump and I and other resisters—young and old—were leaving prison at the end of the 1980s, the world was undergoing profound changes suggesting the end of the Cold War and the nuclear threat that had prompted our resistance and incarceration. The Berlin Wall came tumbling down and the nuclear superpowers, well into a new era of good feeling, began scaling back their arsenals—nuclear as well as conventional.

Following the 1988 Intermediate-range Nuclear Forces (INF) agreement pulling NATO ground-launched cruise and Pershing missiles and their Warsaw Pact counterparts from Europe, the United States and the Soviet Union made plans to cut the numbers of their long-range strategic nuclear forces. In prospect for the 1990s was a substantial reduction—perhaps even elimination—of the underground missile system that for more than thirty years had covered a large part of the United States.

Many in the United States, including some in the peace movement, declared the nuclear threat to be over and turned their attention to other concerns. My old magazine, the *Bulletin of the Atomic Scientists*, pulled back the minute hand of its Doomsday Clock and redesigned the face of the clock to encompass a range of environmental dangers broader than the nuclear threat. Once again, after a decade and a half, it was getting harder to sell nuclear Armageddon. "Beyond War," a peace discussion group which had talked its way into millions of American living rooms in the 1980s to promote "a new way of thinking," declared victory and withered away.

But had the world really changed that much? Had "a new way of thinking" really arrived in this country? Had the nuclear threat really receded?

True, the ground-launched cruise missiles were on their way out of England, their departure acclaimed by hilltop bonfires set by British peace activists happy to celebrate their victory and turn to other causes. But for each departing weapon the Pentagon enhanced its European inventory of air-launched and sea-launched cruise missiles.

True, Minuteman rockets would soon be coming out of their underground launch tubes in the American Midwest and Great Plains, their metal bodies to be chopped into pieces and their nuclear payloads disarmed. But by 1990 Minuteman was obsolete, decrepit, vulnerable to attack, beyond the end of its projected lifetime. The Air Force was on the way to replacing it with superior nuclear war-fighting systems—the mobile missile, Star Wars—more deadly in their effects and also less accessible to the public.

Despite the fundamental changes that have now come to pass in East-West relations, the evidence suggests that we are lopping twigs and branches off the organism of nuclear violence—merely pruning it—rather than getting to the roots. Here and there a weapons system is cut away, but the trunk continues to grow. The fins and nosecones and sleek metal bodies of the delivery vehicles are reduced to junk to achieve the numerical quotas set forth in "arms control" agreements. But the organs that really matter—the nuclear warheads—are returned to the assembly pits at Pantex to be taken apart and recycled into newer and more efficient weapons of mass destruction.

Tellingly, the United States Department of Energy in 1990 beat back a public effort to close its aging nuclear weapons production complex because of potentially catastrophic health and safety problems and signs of environmental contamination that could take hundreds of billions of dollars to clean up. After ceasing production for a year, the Department completed emergency repairs and began turning out warheads again.

Meanwhile, it has put together a "modernization" program to keep the factory system going through the year 2015.

The end of the Cold War will not by itself bring an end to nuclear weapons production and the threat this poses to humanity. That is because the Cold War was never the reason for nuclear weapons production—it was the rationale. The supposed threat from the Soviet Union, our putative enemy in the Cold War, was a fiction which took on greater credibility with each new Soviet response to U.S. strategic initiatives, beginning with the dropping of the first atomic bomb at the end of World War II.

As "enemy," the Soviet Union and the world-wide Communist conspiracy, of which it was the supposed architect, filled the vacuum left by the defeat of our enemies, Germany and Japan, in World War II. The military and industrial elements that had come to power in the United States during the war needed new enemies to justify continuation and consolidation of their franchise. The Soviets and the Communists lent themselves readily to the mythologizing of a national threat, justifying the continuation of extravagant claims on public resources in the name of national security. In time, the huge amounts of public spending required for nuclear and conventional armaments and other props of empire acquired a vast constituency extending beyond the Pentagon and the nuclear establishment into much of industry, organized labor, academia, and whole sections of the country. An enemy always was needed to justify the nation's costly and ever-risky participation in the "arms race," which was not so much a race between us and the Soviet Union as it was a competition among sectors of our own society for power, prestige, and money.

With the decline of the Soviet Union and the international Communist conspiracy as viable enemies, a search is under way for new villains—in the Middle East, in the Third World, in our very midst—whose presence will ensure continuation of the play. One way or another they will be found or fabricated.

As that search goes on, and as the nuclear organism continues to flourish in the rich soil of American militarism, I remain an Old Codger for Peace, ready to continue my resistance and to recruit others to the cause. There is more work for me to do, whatever the risk and whatever the pain. I want to continue to speak truth to power—as an editor, activist, and inmate— and to help others undertake that high calling. The truth is that the nuclear threat continues. It is a threat not just to our skins but to our integrity.

Now, more than ever, there is good reason to cross the line. In crossing over, I want to help build a society of peace and justice on the good ground beyond.

# Readings

Over the years I have written about war and violence, terrorism, drugs, prisons, the media, capitalism, the struggles of ordinary people, and related topics. Here are some of the columns I have liked best.

## Why Shield the Press?

The scene is an Idaho courtroom. The defense has just lost a key motion that the witness, a news reporter, be excused from testifying on the grounds that he should not be forced to reveal his confidential sources. The judge and jury lean forward in anticipation. The witness slumps dejectedly in his chair. The prosecutor, leafing excitedly through the reporter's notebook, begins to read aloud:

"For immediate release. Boise, Idaho—The J.R. Simplot Co. today announced that..."

Frowning, the prosecutor flips to another page:

"For immediate release. Burley, Idaho—The Idaho Potato Growers Association, meeting at the Ponderosa Inn, voted today to..."

Turning to another page, then another, the prosecutor drones on:

"For immediate release. McCall, Idaho—Wayne York, executive secretary of the Idaho Education Association, today charged that..."

Perhaps the dread of such revelations is what has launched so much of the Idaho press on its current crusade for a shield law to provide immunity from disclosure of unidentified news sources. It isn't, as you might suspect, the mafia, government tipsters, political revolutionaries or other cloak-and-dagger types whom the news people desire to shield. It's the legions of public relations agents whose names seldom appear in new stories and on whom the press depends for much of its information.

A shield law might protect the press from the embarrassment of having to acknowledge the debt and of having it become known that with some notable exceptions, there is really very little in their notebooks worth going to court over. Beyond that, not much can be said in its defense.

To be sure, more and more reporters around the country are spending their time in jail these days for refusing to divulge to the courts the sources of their news stories, and more and more newspapers—from the *New York Times* to the *Idaho State Journal*—are being brow-beaten by prosecutors for one reason or another. Such incidents are cited by those who seek special protection for the press. They say the press must be free of harassment and intimidation if it is to do its job of informing the public.

To some extent, these cases arise out of a conflict between two constitutional guarantees—a free press and a fair trial. What a reporter writes or testifies to can have a direct bearing on the fairness of the trial. The reporter is in essentially the same position here as any other citizen. He must do what he can to assist the cause of justice or be prepared to pay the consequences. Unless one equates the relationship of a reporter to his news source with that of a physician to patient, clergyman to confessor or spouse to spouse, there is nothing in the principle of a free press which dictates that a judge should value a reporter's interest in his confidential news sources over the public's interest in a fair trial. A shield law would shift the balance.

Well, why not give the press the same immunity which physicians and clergymen enjoy in court? The answer is that there is no way to delineate or credential the press for such immunities without some form of licensing, which in turn threatens the very concept of a free press.

Who is to be granted the immunity? The editor of the *Washington Post*? A correspondent for CBS? A city hall reporter for the *Twin Falls Times-News*? There would be no question about their qualifications. But what about the reporter for an underground newspaper, or for the college and high school press? What about the lobbyist who writes a newsletter? They, too, are exercising freedom of the press. License some, and you automatically exclude the rest.

The essence of freedom of the press is that, like freedom of speech, it applies to everyone. Professional members of the press are prone to the misconception that they alone are the custodians of that freedom. Since shield laws are meant to apply not to everyone but to the custodians, they serve by their very nature to fortify that misconception and thus erode freedom of the press.

In addition to jeopardizing the right to a fair trial and eroding freedom of the press, shield laws also shield the press from its job. The intimidation of the press these days—from the White House all the way down to the courthouse—is real enough. But it is not occurring in a vacuum. It is part of a broad assault on a wide range of freedoms in this country—against free speech, against dissent, against diversity. Its victims by and large have been the powerless—the poor, the ethnic minorities, the politically and culturally unorthodox.

Now that the heat is beginning to be felt by the press itself and in particular some of its more established elements, perhaps the press will begin to acquire a better understanding of the nature and scope of the threat to the liberties of the American people. The press needs more exposure to the threat, not less. The shield law would be just another press cop-out. Fill the nation's jails with enough reporters and their notebooks are likely to become interesting.

—*Intermountain Observer*, February 3, 1973

## Some Questions About Entebbe

The world would react with justifiable disapproval if the Soviet Union, angered by what it believes to be illegal actions against the interests of its allies, should send a military strike force to the Middle East to close Israeli settlements which have recently been established in the occupied West Bank.

Given the military superiority of the Russians, there is nothing Israeli alone could do to prevent, repel or avenge such a strike. But Russia would pay a price in world opinion. Even many of her friends would look upon it as a return to gunboat diplomacy, a setback for peace in the Middle East, a defeat for the cause of peaceful settlement of disputes.

It is for such reasons that even some of Israeli's best friends do not share the general elation in that country over her July 3d strike against Entebbe Airport in Uganda to rescue the hostages from the sky-jacking of a French airliner.

There are some obvious differences between the two cases. For one thing, the Russians do not have the same kind of flesh-and-blood stake in the West Bank that the presence of hostages gave Israel at Entebbe. For another, the provocation at Entebbe was more sudden and more flagrant.

For all its humanitarian aspects, though, this was the imposition of a military solution by a government which could act that way toward a weaker neighbor only because it was strong enough to get away with it.

One can admire the great valor and skill of the Israeli commandos who executed this bold action. And one can share in the gratitude over the safe return of hostages who had faced an uncertain fate.

But, even looking at the action in its most favorable light, one wonders whether the raid accomplished anything more than to inflate the egos and boost the political stock of those who ordered it, and to please the galleries in Israel and the United States.

Did the raid really save lives? That cannot be known because negotiations for release of the hostages were interrupted by the raid. What is known is that the raid brought death to at least 30 persons—hostages, hijackers and Ugandan soldiers—to say nothing of the many innocent people whom the humiliated President Idi Amin of Uganda has evidently killed in reprisal. It was not planned that way, of course, but as far as bloodshed is concerned, the raid has turned out essentially to be the insuring of white lives at the expense of black lives.

Could the bloodshed have been avoided? Yes, presumably, by acceding to the demands of the hijackers for the release of Palestinian guerrillas from jails in Israel and elsewhere. But Israel was not willing to pay that political price.

The rescue raid has been widely acclaimed as evidence of the success of a get-tough policy, as a good example for other governments to follow, and as a message to guerrillas that they can no longer get away with terroristic acts like hijacking airplanes.

But does it really deter terrorism? Or does it merely increase the ante? If there is any lesson at all for terrorists to learn from this episode, perhaps it is only that, in dealing with Israel, at least, they must go for higher stakes. The next prize must be more than a mere hundred or so hostages. It must be something which Israel, or any other government, cannot afford to lose.

Rather than deter terrorism, the Entebbe raid is more likely to facilitate it in the long run. It does this by deluding the public into believing that unilateral, national, pre-emptive force is the most effective answer to the problem, rather than a cooperative, international approach based on peaceful, nonviolent solutions.

The world will be safe from sky-jackers only when there is no longer a safe place for them to go. This can come about only through an international convention in which all parties agree that a crime against one is a crime against all. In such a situation, where sky-jackers are denied the ordinary protection of civil laws wherever they may land, no government need shrink from acceding to any demand because there would be no practical way for the sky-jackers to enjoy the fruits of their blackmail. Shunned and hunted down by every government, they would lose the leverage which makes them such a menace today.

The Entebbe raid has hampered what little progress the world was making toward solution of the sky-jacking problem through international agreement. Such an agreement would be immensely valuable not only for its own sake but also as a model for a peaceful, nonviolent world order in which no nation has a greater stake than Israel itself.

*—Bulletin of the Atomic Scientists*, September 1976

# Behind Candied Bars

For sheer down-home hospitality in a place you'd least expect it, you could hardly beat the county jail in Bozeman, Montana, where I was a guest for a week last summer.

Here are some of the rules I found in a SPECIAL NOTICE TO ALL RESIDENTS posted on a wall near my cell:

Rule 7 - "The officers will try and serve your meals at 7:30 a.m., 12:00 noon and at 4:45 p.m."

Rule 13 - "If there is no recreation at your scheduled time it is due to the workload of the staff. The officers will do their best to get you out at your scheduled times."

Rule 15 - "If you are in the day room and you have to use the toilet, call on the intercom and your room will be unlocked so you may use the toilet."

The sign-off by head jailer Dave Dunn sounded almost jolly: "If you follow our rules and regulations, we'll all get along real good while you are here."

This was a jail? It seemed more like a retirement home.

A cheery wake-up call, piped into each cell, aroused us in the morning. "Good morning," a voice would say. "It's a lovely Saturday outside."

We were served three regular meals, and then the "staff" would bring us coffee three times a day; answer our calls at the press of a button located in each cell; take us to the library, the exercise yard, and the game room, and fetch cigarettes, candy bars, fruit juice, and assorted sundries from the commissary.

Four other "residents" and I shared a "day room" equipped with stools and tables, shower stalls, and television set. Thick glass replaced the customary steel bars. My cell window looked out on a magnificent mountain range just north of the city.

I was one of three inmates who had chosen time in jail rather than pay a fine for trespassing at an Air Force missile launch site. For us, the solicitous treatment lightened what was already an easy burden—I had been sentenced to only nine days and they to thirty each. The hospitality helped the short time pass even faster.

For other prisoners, too, the Gallatin County Detention Center, a model penal facility, was, as jails go, a piece of cake. "You should see the puke I've run into in other places," said one of my neighbors, who had been in many an older Montana jail.

Still, I wonder whether, in some subtle way, we weren't defrauded by the very niceness of the place. As the days went by, it seemed to me we were paying a price for this ostentatiously enlightened treatment.

I arrived at Bozeman in chains and handcuffs, determined to withhold any untoward cooperation from a system that would be depriving me of my liberty. But it's not easy to resist in an institution that is plainly and sincerely trying to cater to your every need. It hardly seems fair.

By the end of the week, meal times found me lined up meekly with the others, cup in hand, patiently waiting beside the slot in the door through which the food would be delivered. The reliability of our keepers had made trained animals of us.

Equally bemusing was the way I found myself adjusting to the remote-controlled electronic lock system that the staff used to regulate our movements between day room and private cell.

A *click* in the door locked me into my cell for the night; a *click* let me out in the morning; other *clicks* during the day locked me in or let me out, according to the requirements and dictates of the institution.

At first it struck me as a chilling practice. But by week's end I found myself subconsciously anticipating the metallic commands. It was as if I had become a laboratory rat. How does a rat resist?

Realize it or not, like it or not, I had readily become a collaborator in my imprisonment. My docility was the price the institution exacted, most successfully, for its consideration.

Call it a prison or some grander name, the Gallatin County Detention Center is just as much a jail as any other place designed to deprive people of their liberty. Call them inmates or residents, its inhabitants are no less prisoners for all the folksiness of its chief officer, for all the friendliness of his staff.

Like other jails, it manipulates. It isolates. It controls. It erodes the independence and self-respect of those in its charge. It suppresses their sense of solidarity with other prisoners, their connectedness with the outside world. Like all jails everywhere, it institutionalizes hatred.

What makes this place different is that it pretends to be something else. And the disguise, I found, is effective. It sapped this prisoner of the balm of despising the system that jailed him.

*—The Progressive*, November 1983

## The Office Baby

In the place where I work there is a new clerk whose specialty is de-filing. He takes things off the shelf, examines them for taste and feel, then strews them on the office floor.

He is impatient with long telephone conversations, interrupting them with insistent and occasionally piercing wails.

He often drinks on the job—to the discomfort of office visitors who aren't used to that sort of thing. And those of us who come in frequent contact with him have learned what it's like to be dumped on.

All of which might lead you to conclude that I regard Carl—the boss's baby— as a pain in the neck. Well, nothing could be further from the case.

Little Carl is the best argument I can think of that every workplace ought to have a baby.

To be sure, some of our precious floor space had to go when the nursery came in. But it's hard to remember now what important function was displaced by the playpen and the stuffed dogs and cats that have taken over a corner of the office. True, Carl has cut into many a telephone conversation. But this has taught us how readily interruptible and compressible such conversations can be.

It's also true that Carl sometimes distracts us from our tasks of typing, stuffing envelopes, opening the mail, and conferring with important people. It's strange, though, how these routines seem to hang more heavily when the baby is away.

You won't believe this, but one of my co-workers (not Carl's mother) actually admits to getting restless on weekends and coming to work a little early on Mondays because she misses the baby.

Equally incredible but true is the case of another co-worker who delayed his planned departure from the office by several days just to have a little extra time with Carl.

Carl's hold extends well beyond the confines of our small office. Workers from another establishment across the hall have taken to dropping in just to check up on the baby. This is especially true after long holiday weekends.

We are not above using Carl's influence to our own advantage. On busy days, when he starts fussing from lack of attention, one of us is apt to pick him up and carry him across the hall for a "baby break." The people over there get to pass him around for fifteen or twenty minutes while we get our work done. Everyone wins.

The boss in charge of the workers across the hall has never complained, even privately, about this unsolicited impingement on his domain. I suspect he knows better than to provoke a mutiny.

Carl is exceptionally personable, no doubt about it. But the success of his office relationships is due to more than his pleasing personality. It stems mainly from the simple fact that he is a baby.

A baby in the office is like a fire in the hearth or a cat on the living room couch. It takes the chill out of the air. A child's presence can warm and simplify the interrelationships of people in the vicinity; it can give new meaning to their work.

The pieces of paper we push around in our office deal mainly with political strategies for coping with and countering the terrible imminence of nuclear war. It shouldn't be hard to imagine how this little newcomer gives added point to these endeavors. But his presence would be equally suitable in other types of places where people gather to do their work.

Why not a baby in the courtroom if its mother or father were the judge, the clerk, the stenotypist, the bailiff, the defendant, or any other party who had to be there? If it caused lawyers to look up even for a moment from their sterile books and papers, a dirty diaper might well enrich the quality of mercy and justice.

Likewise, young children underfoot might be useful reality therapy for policy makers in City Hall, the governor's office, and the Board of Education—to say nothing of those who make the wheels turn at General Dynamics, General Electric, and General Motors.

What's good for General Motors might also be good for the children—as well as for their parents and other adults with whom they would share the workplace.

If Carl's experience is any indication, young children seem to benefit from an assortment of nearby parental figures. While his mother is still clearly his favorite, especially at feeding time, he seems to thrive on the variety of attention he gets. I can't help but think he'll be better off in later life for having learned to make rapid adjustments from fat people to thin people, smokers to nonsmokers, management to labor, liberals to conservatives.

Adults, too, have something to gain from a baby in the workplace. The most obvious beneficiaries are mothers, for whom maternity often exacts a stiff price in child-care payments and in professional advancement. Why should women have to choose, if they don't want to, between motherhood and a career?

Working fathers also deserve a break. They too have a stake in the emotional growth and development of their offspring, in the nurturing of parental ties. Employers are used to providing comfortable offices, lunch hours and coffee breaks, health benefits, pensions and parking space for their valued workers. Why not also accommodate working fathers who would appreciate the company of their young children?

Lastly, and perhaps most important, babies in the workplace are for everyone. They are a way of breaking through the barriers that separate most adults from the young. Their presence enriches all of us—not just the biological parents—by introducing a human ingredient into our everyday working lives.

For all of you who, like me, are fortunate enough to have a baby in the office, that's something to think about as you grope through the muck on the floor for that file folder last seen on the second shelf.

—*Isthmus*, June 14, 1985

*(Carl Dixon is the son of Cassandra Dixon, who served as Nukewatch director from 1984 to mid-1986.)*


# Journey of Hope

"All together now, 'One, two, three...Hi, Mommy!'"

We must have been quite a sight. There we were, hand in hand, yelling our heads off, walking through the front gate of the Federal Correctional Institution for Women at Alderson, West Virginia, acting as if we meant to take the place over.

Indeed, the officers who guard the visiting room were hardly a match for the six youngsters who came bounding through the door on that long-awaited morning a few weeks ago.

One of the visitors, barely eleven, introduced himself to a guard with a hug and a hearty, "Hello there." Another darted through a gate that led into the room, ignoring the insistent beeping of a metal detector. Two others made straight for a hobby-horse on the grass outside.

By the time the kids had checked out the television set, the candy vending machines and the two dozen other visitors already on the scene, Mom's arrival seemed almost an afterthought.

While the children played, one of us spotted her coming across the prison yard in faded green jeans and a yellow blouse. She appeared at the visiting room door, was whisked away to be strip-searched, then reappeared and gathered up the youngsters one by one in her embrace.

That was the scene when Helen Dery Woodson, the forty-two-year-old Madison peace activist, was reunited with six of her mentally handicapped adopted children—ages six through twenty-six—for the first time since she "kicked the bomb" ten months ago.

"Kicking the bomb" is the name of a bedtime game the Woodson children play, with much gusto, using the drawing of a bomb stuck to the living room wall. It's also the phrase the family uses to describe what people like Helen do to nuclear weapons. The last bomb Mother kicked (with a jackhammer, acting with three others) was a nuclear missile underground silo near Kansas City, Missouri—an offense for which she was sentenced to eighteen years in prison.

The Woodson children have grown up with positive thoughts about such acts of civil disobedience. "Kicking the bomb" is important work that grown-ups do, and enforced absence sometimes goes with the job. They don't think of their mother as undergoing punishment or being out of circulation. She's kicking the bomb in West Virginia.

While Mom is at work, the children are being cared for round the clock by a team of resident child-care workers and outside supporters pulled together by an old and close friend, Mary Beth Schlagheck of Middleton. For her, the family's well-being has become a full-time concern. It was at Mary Beth's invitation that I accompanied her, her husband, Jim (a Madison school psychologist), and Mary Rasmussen, one of the child-care workers, to West Virginia as an extra hand to help with the driving and the dishwashing.

Anyone who has taken even one child on a family outing can imagine the hazards of transporting two carloads of them 800 miles across Wisconsin, Illinois, Indiana, Ohio, Kentucky and West Virginia. But the Woodson children, products of a disciplined and devout upbringing, were a snap.

At our lunch stop in a highway rest area this side of Indianapolis, I couldn't help noticing the approving glances of passers-by who looked and listened as the children recited grace, their heads bowed and their hands clasped.

As the miles and hours dragged on and our nerves grew understandably frayed, I came to appreciate the value of a softly but firmly spoken word on the lips of a knowledgeable child-care worker. The magic phrase our experts used was "time-out!" - which is the modern, nonjudgemental way of getting young people to pipe down.

At the end of that long first day we took our passengers to a Big Boy restaurant as a reward for good behavior. Our order of ten ice cream cones attracted so much attention at the dairy counter that the manager of the establishment came around to introduce himself—and to visit.

You'd expect a closely knit family brought up in faith and love to make these kinds of good impressions. This fragile little group has an extraordinary ability to get through to other people.

Since last November the Woodson house on Spruce Street on Madison's south side has become the focus of a growing community of concern. A local business-man helps manage the family budget. A friend with an infant of her own comes in once a week to fix supper. Each day's mail brings donations (sometimes only a dollar or two; sometimes more) to help pay the bills.

This power to engage others proved equally potent on the road.

In Cincinnati, a religious group, the New Jerusalem Community, made room for all ten of us when our motel reservations fell through on the first night. Our hosts had not heard of Helen Woodson and her children before we showed up on their doorstep. When we left the next morning it was with their pledge of hospitality on the return trip and on future journeys to and from the prison.

And in West Virginia, the Woodson kids helped brighten the mood at Alderson Hospitality House, which is the only overnight lodging place in the small town that contains the only all-women's federal prison in the United States. It is a nonprofit institution that caters to more than a thousand friends and relatives of inmates in the course of a year, including as many as thirty at a time on peak weekends like Mother's Day.

Ordinarily the lodging house is quiet and almost sorrowful, said Vita Shively, a lay Franciscan worker who runs the place with her husband, Bob. Sitting on the porch of the hospitality house, she told me the story of a little girl who came running down the stairs one day, crying for her father.

"He had just gone out to put some things in the car, but she thought he was leaving without her. All I could do was hold her and tell her that he would be right back, but I could see fear in her eyes that he was going to leave her as her mom had."

At the hospitality house, as at the prison itself, our rambunctious little troupe brought a different kind of message that the rest of us might well heed. It said that some of the folks in jail these days haven't left us at all. They're just temporarily away, doing their jobs.

—*Isthmus*, September 13, 1985

## The Price of Satisfaction

Let us begin by agreeing that the murder of Leon Klinghoffer, a helpless American tourist, on the Italian cruise ship Achille Lauro off the coast of Egypt was a despicable act that ought not to go unpunished.

The United States is right to demand that the perpetrators of this crime be brought to justice.

It seems clear, too, that Egypt acted hastily in granting safe passage to the four hijackers of the Achille Lauro before making certain that no blood had been shed aboard the vessel. And Italy may have blundered in not detaining the man accused of masterminding the hijack plot.

But none of these considerations justifies the conduct of our government in taking matters into its own hands in the eastern Mediterranean skies three weeks ago.

The U.S. Navy's interception of the Egyptian airliner carrying the hijackers and their diplomatic escort out of Egypt caused immense satisfaction at home. It was also an act of folly that complicates the already vexing problem of maintaining peace in the world.

In the name of combating terrorism, we committed an act of air piracy. In the name of law and order, we violated international law.

The action was, in the first instance, an unwarranted repudiation of Egypt's role in protecting hundreds of lives aboard the ship by negotiating the surrender of the hijackers to the Palestine Liberation Organization. Our guns overruled the judgement of Egyptian President Hosni Mubarak, thereby humiliating a good friend acting in good faith.

We may also have damaged our relationship with Italy, especially as it becomes clearer that the interception of the Egyptian airliner was just the first step in a larger, unfulfilled plot to spirit the hijackers by military means out of the Mediterranean and on to the United States.

The action has undermined the Middle East peace process by undercutting moderate elements in the PLO who were working in good faith with Egypt and Italy toward a solution to the hijack crisis and whose encouragement is essential to peace with Israel.

Paradoxically, our gun-barrel diplomacy may also have short-circuited swift and painful justice for the hijackers, whose bungling ways had plainly angered higher-ups in the PLO. Whatever the ultimate fate of the hijackers might have been had they returned home to face the music, it seems clear that the PLO would have been under heavy pressure from Egypt, Italy and the world community to see that justice was done. Will an Italian court feel the same pressure?

By its intemperate action, the United States took the PLO off the moral hook. In doing so, we once again turned Palestinian nationalism in the very direction we deplore.

Worst of all, our unilateral act over the eastern Mediterranean set aside the rule of law and exalted force and violence as the final arbiter of human differences in the international world. It was a highly publicized, loudly championed triumph of "might makes right" and "the devil take the hindmost." That is a sure formula for more murders and more war.

"We won one," as the domestic headlines proclaimed, because we happened to have an aircraft carrier handy and because Egypt—in her innocence—had not felt it necessary to guard against U.S. violation of international law.

Our Navy pilots did not have to pull the trigger, but the political mentality that sent them aloft was not unlike that of the hijackers themselves, who, possessing the firepower to take unchallenged control of a ship, could pump a bullet into the brain of an unoffending old man and dump his body into the sea.

We have learned to expect such things from the Reagan administration. This latest demonstration of "might makes right" is not much different, after all, from what has been happening in Grenada, Nicaragua and other regions where pushing people out of the way has come to be the touchstone of American foreign policy. Our president makes no bones about his vision of an imperial America "standing tall" in the world.

But what really hurts is the way so many others—most notably the U.S. mass media, including the liberal press—fan the flames of frustration, jingoism and xenophobia that are ravaging our society. What also hurts is the silence from those who ought to know better.

Our State Department has a conniption over Palestinian "terrorism" aboard the Achille Lauro but looks the other way when Israeli warplanes bomb homes and offices in Tunis—and no one points to the double standard.

Our government wrings its hands over the death of one American in a wheelchair but is indifferent to the suffering of millions, Americans and others, at its own hands—and no one notes the hypocrisy.

Our president invokes God's blessing on a distraught widow for spitting in the faces of the men accused of murdering her husband—and no one rebukes him.

America's actions of the last three weeks have revealed our weakness as a nation, not our strength. Rather than strutting and bragging and pounding our chests we should be hanging our heads in shame.

—*Isthmus*, October 25, 1987

# Eleanor and I

A gray-haired woman approached me one evening last April in the front hall of the nursing home in Middleton where a day or two earlier I had placed my eighty-eight-year-old mother as a patient.

"Excuse me, sir," the woman said. "Could I bother you for a lift into Madison?"

I was suspicious. My first thought was that this might be a patient looking for an opportunity to flee. So I brushed past her, mumbling that I was headed in a different direction.

But then something told me I had made a mistake. Retracing my steps, I apologized, offered the stranger a ride home and discovered (to our mutual surprise) that we lived only a block from each other.

That was my first encounter with Eleanor Wilson, a retired Latin teacher at West High School. From then on, Eleanor and I traveled the ten miles to and from Middleton Village together two or three times a week. Our lives became entwined by the fact that each of us had a loved one in the nursing home.

Eleanor's older sister, Minnie Whipple, moved into Middleton Village from the family home on Keyes Avenue about three years ago after suffering a stroke. My mother, Margery, who came to Wisconsin because she could no longer live by herself in California, was assigned to a bed across the hall from Minnie's. Thus, by a double coincidence, the frequent journeys which Eleanor and I came to share began on adjacent blocks in Madison and ended in adjacent rooms in Middleton.

Nursing home visits can be discouraging for the friends and relatives of the patients, even in well-run places like Middleton Village. They remind us all too graphically of how our own lives may someday end—in helpless loneliness, deprived of our mobility, our senses, our faculties. There is also the pain of witnessing the decline of people near and dear to us.

Minnie, a former purchasing agent for the University of Wisconsin System, once was a leader among Madison's business and professional women and an avid gardener of local renown; now she sat half-paralyzed in her wheelchair, unable to speak or feed herself or recognize anyone except her surviving sister. Margery once thrived on Henry James and the theater and elegant dinner parties; now she roamed the corridors of Middleton Village in mindless agitation, cards and letters accumulating unread in her darkened bedroom.

Our journeys to the nursing home helped Eleanor and me come to terms with our pain by drawing us into the lives of others. "Well, Margery seemed to be full of beans tonight," Eleanor might remark on the way home, drawing some solace from what may have been a particularly dispiriting visit with Minnie.

In time, we came to discover Betsy, the ex-schoolteacher whose booming voice would roll through the nursing home corridors, lecturing rows of imaginary students; and Ruth, rouged and bejeweled like a queen holding court in the hall outside her bedroom; and Scott, the laid-back nurse's aid from California, and many more.

Indeed, through Minnie and Margery, Eleanor and I discovered a community of people behind the sterile facade of waxed floors and white uniforms and endless television sit-coms. It was also the kind of community that cannot last for long. We got an inkling of that last August when Margery fell and broke her arm. After surgery and weeks of treatment, the limb still hung limp and useless from her shoulder.

Worried though we were about Margery's crisis, we both knew that Minnie's medical prospects were more ominous. All through the summer and into the fall Minnie's weight had been dropping. By the time her ninety-sixth birthday arrived, in November, she was a shadow of her former self.

As the year ended, Minnie grew weaker by the day. She had virtually ceased eating. She barely stirred in her wheelchair, and sometimes it was difficult even for Eleanor to tell if she was asleep or awake. Then Minnie contracted pneumonia.

One evening early last week, after I had said goodnight to Margery and it was time to go, I went into Minnie's room and found her cradled in her younger sister's arms.

The next day Eleanor spent the afternoon and early evening at Minnie's bedside. "Let me take you home," I told her. "She's asleep, and there's nothing more you can do."

We drove home together in silence that night along Old Middleton Road. An hour later a call from the nursing home advised Eleanor that Minnie was dead.

The trips to Middleton will be a little longer and lonelier for me now. But Eleanor still lives just a block away, and she has promised to keep me company from time to time. I'm grateful that ten months ago I refused to let my suspicion get the better of me.

—*Isthmus,* February 13, 1987

## Corporate Generosity

In the pile of unanswered mail on my desk is a letter from John B. Fery, chairman of the board and chief executive officer of Boise Cascade Corp., inviting me to attend the company's annual shareholders meeting on April 28.

"Regardless of the number of shares you own, your vote is important," the letter says.

The number of shares I own is one. Some time ago I bought it jointly with one of my sons. The investment has not made either of us rich (our dividend checks range from 57 cents to $1.34), but it has helped open my eyes to the world of capitalism.

One thing I've learned: Capitalism has been good to John B. Fery.

It seems to be a legal requirement of the state of Delaware, where Boise Cascade and many other companies are incorporated, that shareholders be kept posted on the compensation of principal corporate officers. Thus, along with the letter were some interesting details on the earnings and other emoluments of Fery and his colleagues. Life at the top of this mid-sized American corporation, apparently, is not without its perks.

Take, for example, the compensation of John B. Fery. The chairman's salary for 1986 was $480,000. A cash bonus of $111,250 raised his base pay to $591,250. Then came the add-ons:

During the past three years, Boise Cascade's contributions to the well-being of its chief executive officer included $65,394 in life insurance premiums, $59,751 in payments to a deferred compensation plan and $22,144 in health-care premiums for the Fery family. Add those up and divide by three for an average yearly total of $49,099, and Fery's 1986 compensation stands at $650,349. That's still not all.

Like many corporate executives, Fery serves on the board of directors of other corporations. The annual meeting notice I received identifies these as Albertson's Inc., Hewlett-Packard Co., Moore Financial Group Inc. and Union Pacific Corp.

Not being a shareholder of any of these corporations, I don't have ready access to their fee policies. But let's assume the payment rates are the same as Boise Cascade's—an annual fee of $20,000 for board membership plus various amounts for additional services.

At $20,000 per year for sitting on the boards of four other corporations, tack on another $80,000 to Fery's earnings for 1986. In addition, Boise Cascade pays its outside board members $1,500 for attending each meeting. Last year the directors met eight times. Assuming the meeting rates and frequencies are the same for Fery's four other corporations, this comes to $48,000.

Boise Cascade pays another $5,000 just for being a committee chairman. Let's say Fery chaired at least one committee on one of his other boards. Add $5,000.

The company's directors also get $600 for each committee meeting they attend. Directors frequently serve on several committees of the same board. Let's assume that Fery answered the roll call at fourteen such meetings last year. (True, that's a lot of meetings, but you don't exactly have to be there to get paid. At Boise Cascade you can earn this $600 just by picking up the telephone for a conference-call meeting or by being part of what the company calls "an action by consent in lieu of meeting.") Add $7,200.

Adding it all up, Fery's corporate directorships could have been worth as much as $145,000, bringing his compensation for the year to $785,349.

This is perhaps an adequate sum to get by on for now, but what about the future? At fifty-seven, Fery's retirement years can't be too long in coming.

Not to worry. To begin with, the board chairman's thirty years as a corporate officer will entitle him to a pension of at least $37,500 a year. In addition, he has a nest egg of 50,125 shares of Boise Cascade stock. They're worth about $3.5 million.

And, in case the company should hire some other chief executive officer before he's ready, Fery holds a severance-pay contract for $1,695,540.

With all that going for him, I don't know why John B. Fery cares whether I attend the annual meeting. If he wants my vote the least he could do is send me a bus ticket to Boise.

*—Isthmus,* March 27, 1987

# A Letter to the Judge

Dear Judge Shabaz:

On Friday, May 29, my friend Gillam Kerley of Madison will appear before you for sentencing upon his conviction for refusing to register for the draft. He is the last of twenty young men from all over the country who were indicted five years ago for violating the registration law. Fifteen were convicted and the other five changed their minds.

I have known Gillam Kerley almost since he arrived in Madison a decade ago as a precocious sixteen-year-old with a college degree. Filled with youthful convictions, he wrote for and became the last editor of *Free for All*, a relic of the city's turbulent '60s. I watched and helped him put in long hours as a volunteer for the *Press Connection*, the Madison strike newspaper that bit the dust at the end of 1979.

I have been impressed by Kerley's contributions, as an unpaid researcher, to the University of Wisconsin community—especially his documentation of bio-logical warfare research in university laboratories and his exposure of the Math Research Center's role in helping the U.S. Army develop weapons of mass destruction. And I have admired the skill and doggedness with which this young man, now a self-taught lawyer, has held the United States government at bay for four-and-a-half years in his determination not to be a part of its preparation for war.

Now, having pleaded "not guilty by virtue of sanity" to violation of the registration law, having argued the case for freedom of conscience in courtrooms and in meeting halls across the country, and having tried and failed to persuade a jury of his innocence, Gillam Kerley comes before you for sentencing.

I have been asked by a support group, the National Resistance Committee, to join in a letter campaign in behalf of Gillam Kerley: "The letters should point out to Judge Shabaz that, since an act of conscience is not a crime, Gillam should not be punished for resisting registration—and that if Shabaz must impose a sentence, it should be as lenient as possible. The letters might also point out that, since Gillam has been dragged through the court system for the past four-and-a-half years, he has already received a stiff penalty."

Judge Shabaz, I beg to differ. While expressions of sympathy and compassion are understandable, I do not believe they serve either Gillam Kerley or the cause for which he stands.

Violation of the law on grounds of conscience is indeed a crime in the eyes of the state and ought to be treated as such. To deal leniently with Gillam Kerley would be to minimize the importance of his action. Kerley deserves a prison sentence of appropriate duration—and I ask you to give it to him in recognition of the significance of his courageous act of resistance.

There are other compelling practical reasons why a prison sentence, following the appeals that are yet to come, would be the most appropriate conclusion to Kerley's long and lonely struggle:

*His point will have been made more forcefully and lastingly. As in the case of Madison's Helen Dery Woodson and Carl Kabat, now serving long terms for damaging a nuclear missile silo, Kerley's "prison witness" would focus continuing public attention on the issues he raised.

*A prison sentence, contrasted with probation, community service or some other leniency, would underscore the importance of Kerley's action and help secure his place in history.

*The nation needs prisoners of conscience more than it needs lawyers. Prison would enable Gillam Kerley to inspire others to deeper and more lasting forms of resistance.

*For all its vicissitudes, prison could make Gillam Kerley a better citizen and lawyer by exposing him to the dreary treadmill of the nation's criminal justice and correctional systems. Too few potential leaders of his capabilities have opportunities for that kind of education.

Judge Shabaz, please don't trivialize Gillam Kerley with a slap on the wrist. Throw the book at him. It will do us all some good.

*—Isthmus,* May 29, 1987

*(Gillam Kerley was sentenced to three years in Federal prison but was released after four months when the sentence was overturned on appeal. Later, he changed his plea to guilty in a plea bargaining agreement.)*

## Resisting Day to Day

I have been invited to a gala graduation party next week by a friend in Brodhead, Wisconsin, who bids me to "eat, drink and be merry, for tomorrow there is no botany."

The happy graduate, Susan B. Nelson, has good reason to be exultant. Not only did she complete four tough years at Beloit College, but she accomplished it with academic distinction while rearing five daughters and doing her share of the dishwashing, vacuuming, shopping and other activities that go with maintaining a large household.

A full load in school and a full load at home ought to be enough for one person. But the most remarkable thing about Sue Nelson is that while doing all this she has also been carrying a full load as an active resister to the status quo.

On May 20, with final exams and graduation out of the way, she will begin serving a four-day sentence in the Dane County jail—rather than pay a fine—for sitting in at the Federal Center in Madison as a protest against U.S. aid to the Nicaraguan contras.

It will be her tenth jailing, following her twelfth arrest, in a career of nonviolent civil disobedience that goes back to the WARF building demonstration of June 20, 1983, when hundreds of protesters blockaded the Math Research Center on the UW-Madison campus to call attention to the university's research contracts with the Pentagon.

Since then, Nelson has taken part in innumerable demonstrations designed to spotlight what she rightly regards as abhorrent national policies. She has been arrested for trespassing in the lobby of the Federal Courthouse in Madison to protest continued U.S. testing of nuclear weapons and for trespassing at Truax Field in opposition to U.S. intervention in Central America.

She has been thrown out of East Towne Mall for distributing leaflets on peace-and-justice issues. She has chained herself to the door of U.S. Rep. Les Aspin's district office in Janesville, and was once bodily removed from that office after participating in a day-long "occupation" of the premises by peace activists.

Nelson's bent for "direct action"—as distinguished from electioneering, letter-writing, lobbying and other forms of mainstream political activism—stems in some measure from her experiences as a worker in Aspin's office. Initially attracted to the congressman by his liberal record and rhetoric, she soon came to the conclusion that his principle interest was in perpetuating and enlarging his own influence and power.

Her politics also stem from her faith. A member of the Beloit Meeting of the Society of Friends, she is a firm believer in the Quaker principle of "speaking truth to power," which means confronting evil whenever and wherever she finds it.

When friends from the more traditional political world question her confrontational tactics, Nelson likes to bring up the case of Rosa Parks, whose refusal to go to the back of the bus kicked off the civil rights revolution.

"What should she have done instead? Write a letter to her congressman?"

Not all of Sue Nelson's arrests have resulted in conviction. Charged with disorderly conduct for digging a mock grave in the well-manicured lawn outside the University of Wisconsin ROTC building, she and other defendants pleaded not guilty, argued in court that the digging had been done in an orderly manner, and won.

And not all of her jail time has been meekly served. When asked on one occasion by a jail admittance clerk to give details of her medical history, she looked him in the eye and replied politely but firmly, "None of your business." The jailers put her in solitary confinement to teach her a lesson, not realizing that they had done her a favor by keeping her away from the cigarette smoke and television noise that permeate the regular jail cells.

Lumped together as they are here, these confrontations make Sue Nelson seem like an extraordinary person. And indeed she is. But equally important is the ordinary way she has worked them into her everyday life.

Neither a martyr in some distant prison nor a knight embarked on some holy crusade, Nelson is the embodiment of day-to-day resistance to oppression and injustice by people whose lives are normal. She fits demonstrations in between trips to the library and the grocery store, arrests into her class schedule, jail time into her semester breaks. At the same time, she makes a point of going to her children's school programs and showing up at her husband's annual bowling league banquet.

Sue Nelson's lifestyle tells us that standing up for the right thing—even going to jail for it, if necessary—can be as normal and as possible as cleaning the attic or spending a weekend with your family or getting a B in botany. It's a good example for all of us.

—*Isthmus*, May 6, 1988

## Preying on the Poor

Every other Wednesday night for the last ten years it has been my custom to put aside worldly cares for a brief time by escaping to the poker table.

I do it partly for the company. Our group is a compatible mix of old friends with roughly comparable card skills. Some were playing together before I joined the group.

I also play for the education. Poker has taught me some valuable lessons in how to count, when to quit and how to control my emotions.

And let's face it, poker is also my contribution to the Madison economy.

I mention all this as a way of prefacing a point about the Wisconsin state lottery, which will be upon us next fall because of a bill passed by the state legislature and signed into law by Gov. Tommy Thompson.

As a gambler myself, paying good money in the hope of being dealt good cards, I am in no position to criticize gambling per se. But indulging a habit is not the same as foisting it on others. And it breaks my heart to see the state of Wisconsin about to become a pusher.

There's a little of the gambler in most of us. The risking of a few bucks by consenting adults in private card games or office betting pools ought to be no more the public's business than what goes on in the privacy of the bedroom.

Public gambling, whether sponsored by a church or tribal council or racetrack, deserves a much closer look because of its impact on large numbers of people. For most, perhaps, it is affordable entertainment. But large-scale public gambling also carries a high social cost. States like Wisconsin should closely regulate the sponsors to ensure that those who profit from it are held accountable for the costs.

But should the state itself be the profiter? Should Wisconsin be following the example of other states and other countries in promoting gambling as a source of revenue? Better to ask: Should a state prey on its own people?

The Wisconsin lottery was sold to the legislature on the grounds that other states (notably Illinois) were doing it. It was argued that this would be a way of recovering Wisconsin gambling dollars now going elsewhere and generating additional gambling revenue at home.

The arguments are true. Additional revenue will be generated for Wisconsin from those who now buy lottery tickets outside the state and by additional Wisconsin residents newly drawn to the habit. Most of the lottery ticket buyers (which is to say, most of the lottery losers) will be Wisconsin residents induced by their own state government to risk their money on games of chance.

From whom in Wisconsin will this new money come? Mostly the poor. Studies show that, taken together, the heaviest purchasers of lottery tickets are poor people, prevailed on through gullibility and despair to buy into the fantasy of get-rich-quick. By-and-large it is money that would otherwise have gone for rent, food and clothing for the kids.

Few poor souls, scrimping to pay for a ticket here and a ticket there in hopes of a million-dollar jackpot, will ever win a dime in the Wisconsin lottery. Only a tiny fraction of the big spenders will ever strike it rich.

Should the state of Wisconsin be promoting false hopes and dreams? Should it be gulling its own people?

Should it be putting money into one pocket now—only to be taking out more money later to pay for additional state services for poor and desperate people made even more so by the state itself? Should Wisconsin—the birthplace of progressivism—be stooping to the most regressive of revenue-raising measures, a come-on aimed at the poor?

And to what end? About half the take from the lottery ticket sales will be returned to a few lucky buyers in the form of cash prizes and spent on promotion to attract more gamblers. Current estimates put the state's share of the lottery revenue at $54 million the first year. For less than 2% of our general fund budget we should sell our souls?

I say no. Not even for double the money.

A tip of the hat to Madison's Fred Risser and other anti-lottery legislators who have fought hard, but so far unsuccessfully, to protect Wisconsin's good name.

—*Isthmus*, May 27, 1988

# Reflections on a Bad War

I was a boy of twelve when Hitler marched into Poland in 1939, precipitating the start of World War II. For six years I read the newspapers every day, studied every battle, anguished over every Allied defeat at the hands of the hated Axis powers and rejoiced at the ultimate victory for our side.

For me, as for many others in my generation, World War II was more than *The Good War*, as Studs Terkel entitled his excellent book on that conflict. It was the ultimate life experience. I thought it was the best thing that ever happened to this country.

Now I believe it was an unmitigated disaster. We should never have entered the war. No, not even to stop Hitler.

That does not mean we should have ignored the war or been indifferent to its impact. But rather than gearing up for armed conflict, the United States should have pursued a policy of moral suasion.

We should have opened our borders to the victims of Nazi oppression, applied economic and diplomatic sanctions against the fascist powers, given humanitarian aid to Britain, China, the Soviet Union and other victims of aggression.

But we should not have sent a single weapon overseas. We should have kept our armed forces away from Europe, Asia and other scenes of conflict. We should not have maneuvered the Japanese into striking the first blow. We should have heeded Robert La Follette and others who in the prewar years were derided as "isolationists."

Consider: If the United States had eschewed military involvement in World War II, what is the worst that could have happened?

Germany and Britain would probably have reached a negotiated peace following the Luftwaffe's decisive defeat in the Battle of Britain in 1940-41. With Britain out of the picture and the United States not militarily involved, Hitler would probably have conquered the Soviet Union by the end of 1942 and set up a Vichy-style puppet regime in Moscow.

Germany would have become the dominant power in Europe, the Mediterranean and the Middle East, replacing Britain and France.

Japan, unchallenged militarily by the United States, would have held economic sway if not military control over East Asia and the Western Pacific, from Burma through Indonesia to the Philippines, replacing colonial Britain, France, Holland and the United States.

And the United States, protected by the vastness of two oceans, would have remained the dominant power in the Western Hemisphere, as it is today.

Rather than the bipolar world that emerged from World War II—two superpowers confronting each other amid the wreckage of the prewar world order—we would have found a balance of three major powers amid a host of lesser nations relatively unscathed by the conflict.

True, Hitler would not have been defeated. Nor Mussolini nor Tojo.

An unappealing prospect, to be sure. But how long would Hitler have remained a factor in postwar Germany and how long would the Third Reich have endured as a monolithic oppressor in Europe? Joseph Stalin, no less a dictator, was in his grave eight years after V-E Day, and within a few more years huge cracks were opening up in the Soviet Union's eastern European empire.

Had America stayed out of World War II there would have been tens of millions fewer deaths by virtue of shortening the conflict. Tens of thousands of homes, factories, churches, schools and hospitals would have been spared.

There would have been no atomic bomb and probably no intercontinental ballistic missiles because neither side would have had the time or the motivation to develop them. There would have been no nuclear arms race as we know it today.

And there would have been no Holocaust. Remember that most of the slaughter occurred in the latter years of the war. The United States could have done more to save Europe's Jews if it had stayed out of the war and bent its efforts toward that end.

While the war pulled us out of the Great Depression, a recovery based on the New Deal's peaceful public works and other social legislation would have been much longer lasting. And the United States would not thereby have enslaved itself to what economist Seymour Melman aptly calls a "permanent war economy."

Nor would our politics, our diplomacy, our sense of national security and global purpose be enchained as they are today by an infantilism driven by unexamined notions of "peace through strength," paranoid fears of military sneak attacks and infiltration by unseen enemies, and the hubris that comes with total victory. These chains are the legacies of World War II.

We should have stayed home.

—*Isthmus*, September 22, 1989

## Symptoms of a New Madness

Visitors to Milwaukee should be aware that Wisconsin's largest city no longer permits the sale or purchase of "drug paraphernalia"—i.e., any device, appurtenance or trapping necessary for the consumption of a harmful or mood-altering substance.

No need to worry, though, in case you should arrive without your beer mug, martini glass or cigarette lighter. The new ordinance applies only to paraphernalia for *illegal* drugs—the kind the city's elected officials (or most of them, at least) aren't in the habit of getting high on.

Milwaukee's contribution to the war on drugs resulted from a flurry of activity initiated by Dick Gregory, the nationally known comedian and political activist, who came to the city recently to campaign for an anti-paraphernalia law. He and others sat in at a "head shop," were arrested and jailed, and threatened a hunger strike until the Common Council took action against the devices.

The council passed a tough measure banning the things you need for using marijuana, cocaine and other illegal drugs. Mayor John Norquist made haste to sign the bill into law before Gov. Tommy Thompson could come to town for the ceremonial signing of a tough new Wisconsin law on illegal drugs.

It was great politics. But to my mind the participant who made the most sense was Milwaukee Ald. Michael McGee, who proposed an amendment banning billboards promoting alcohol and tobacco use. (Lots of luck with that, McGee.)

Locally, regionally and nationally—not just in Milwaukee but everywhere—the war on drugs has become the new madness. It is right up there with the nuclear arms race as a form of hysteria that threatens to consume our society.

Like the war on communism, to which it bears a striking resemblance, the war on drugs erects fictitious enemies (the drug dealer, the paraphernalia pusher) and diverts our attention from the deep-rooted social problems that are the real causes of our concern.

In the process, the war on drugs has developed a bloated constituency of investigators, enforcers, judges, prosecutors, psychologists, social workers, jail and prison guards and administrators, and other job holders who constitute a driving force not unlike the military-industrial complex that drives the arms race.

And, like the war on communism and the nuclear arms race, our national crusade to stamp out illegal drugs is an exercise in hypocrisy and futility.

Like it or not, marijuana, cocaine and other mood-altering drugs are here to stay, consumed regularly by tens of millions of Americans—enough to create a real and substantial demand that will be satisfied one way or another.

In addition, a fatal double standard undermines and compromises the war on drugs. The problem is epitomized by federal drug czar William Bennett's addiction to cigarettes, a legal (and federally subsidized) product that annually kills almost 200 times more Americans than cocaine. The human toll from alcohol consumption (also legal almost everywhere) may be even higher.

Rather than outlawing pipes, roach clips and the like, we should be moving in the opposite direction by decriminalizing all drugs so that the trade could be brought under control. But decriminalization, along with more intensive education and treatment, is no more than a start in the right direction.

An effective war on drugs must also come to grips with the underlying roots of cynicism and despair that give rise to widespread public resort to drugs, including the ones now banned by law. Several essential elements of such a campaign come to mind:

1. A guarantee, imbedded in national policy, of equal opportunity for every child born in the United States, including, where necessary, full medical and educational support from the womb through graduate school.

2. Guaranteed employment at a decent wage in an interesting and worthwhile public service job for any who are willing to work.

3. Adequate housing and health care for all.

4. Recognition that booze and pot and other escapes from life's vicissitudes also serve as safety valves and social lubricants; that their use is part of the human condition; and that enlightened treatment programs always will be needed to deal with their ill effects.

Any chance of signing up the John Norquists, the Tommy Thompsons, the George Bushes for such a war? Don't hold your breath.

*—Isthmus*, February 2, 1990

## Learning from the 'Enemy'

As a journalist visiting Cuba for the first time last winter, and as a traveler long accustomed to paying forty cents every few miles on the highway that links my hometown with Chicago, I was puzzled to find that the toll booths were empty when our tour bus emerged from the tunnel under Havana harbor. So I asked our guide about it.

"This is a socialist state," he explained.

"I know," I replied, "but surely you need money to keep the tunnel open." I pointed to the dilapidated condition of the roadway, built by a French firm for the Fulgencio Batista dictatorship shortly before Fidel Castro came to power in 1959.

"The tunnel seems to need repair," I continued. "Wouldn't it be only fair that the people who benefit from the tunnel help pay for its upkeep?"

The guide smiled patiently. "But that would be a tax," he said. "Under socialism we have no taxes."

Like health care, like education, like hot meals and fresh milk for children in schools and day-care centers, like most of the real cost of housing, like many basic services North Americans take for granted if they have the money to pay for them, the ride under Havana harbor is free. It's as free to the wealthy tourist from abroad as it is to the 200-peso-a-month commuter riding home on a jam-packed bus.

In many ways the Havana tunnel is a metaphor for present-day Cuba, an island of economic and political experimentation in a perilous hemispheric sea.

In replacing private capital (especially foreign capital) as the driving force of the economy, the government has channeled Cuba's resources and human energy toward improvements in basic living standards. Although Cuba is still a poor Third World country of barely ten million people not overly endowed with natural resources, it has become a First World power by such measurements as literacy, human longevity, and infant morality. In a week of roaming through Havana and the nearby countryside, I sought but failed to find a single beggar, a single bloated belly, a single cardboard shack.

But the Cuban people have paid a price for their government's extraordinary commitment to raising the economic floor for all. Just as the tunnel shows signs of neglect, so too do other aspects of the country's material, political, and spiritual infrastructure.

The marketplace is overmanaged by the central government. In a grocery store, I found shelves of Nicaraguan coffee and canned Bulgarian meat patties, but not an egg, a loaf of bread, or a piece of meat. At a crowded government-run pavilion in downtown Havana, I stood in line almost an hour to buy an ice cream cone from the lone attendant authorized to do the scooping.

Young people and intellectuals chafe, justifiably, over the government's reflexive hostility to market innovations that might introduce a few luxuries, to its stifling of even the mildest political unorthodoxy (the Communist Party's *Granma* was the only newspaper I could find in Havana), to its continuing repression of those few religious evangelicals (notably Jehovah's Witnesses) who still openly buck the official line.

There's an understandable reason for paranoia in Cuba. For thirty-one years this tiny country has been under siege by a colossus twenty-five times its size and just ninety miles off its shore.

Evidence of the siege was placed in my hand by a U.S. customs officer at the Miami airport in the form of a pamphlet warning against "trading with the enemy." For spending more than a few hundred dollars in Cuba, I could go to prison for twelve years or pay a fine of $250,000.

Arriving an hour later in Havana, a city of one million, I found a terminal that could fit into a corner of the county airport building that serves my hometown (population 176,000). I stepped outside into a parking lot jammed with carefully preserved Chevrolets from the late 1950s, the last models available before the start of the U.S. economic embargo.

257

This is the enemy? If Cuba represents a threat to the United States, I found little evidence of it along Havana's handsome stone waterfront embarcadero, built by U.S. occupation forces ninety years ago. The most menacing weapons in sight were a couple of weatherbeaten billboards warning the Yanquis to keep their distance.

The official enmity hurled at Cuba by the United States does not appear to be reciprocated, except in occasional denunciations by Castro, who seemed tired but defiant when I heard him at a rally commemorating the 2,000 Cubans who died defending the independence of far-off Angola—a number proportionately equivalent to the U.S. death toll in Vietnam.

In Havana's Ebenezer Baptist Church, named for the home church of Dr. Martin Luther King Jr., I visited a display celebrating the American civil rights revolution. A wall poster showed a procession of black and white children behind two U.S. flags. Next to it were some lines from the slain civil rights leader's "I have a dream" speech: "...that my four little children will one day live in a nation where they will not be judged by the color of their skin but by the content of their character."

Our "enemy," I thought, has something to teach us about ourselves.

—*The Progressive*, June 1990